# Pennsylvania Dutch

## FOLK SPIRITUALITY

Edited by Richard E. Wentz

PAULIST PRESS
New York ◊ Mahwah

**Acknowledgments**

Selections by Rachel Bahn are taken from *Pennsylvania German Folk Tales,* edited by Brendle and Troxell, reprinted by permission of The Pennsylvania German Society. Material from John Joseph Stoudt's *Pennsylvania German Folk Art,* copyrighted by the Pennsylvania German Folklore Society, is reprinted by permission of the Pennsylvania German Society. The excerpts from Alfred J. Shoemaker's *Christmas in Pennsylvania* is reprinted by permission of *Pennsylvania Folklife.* Selections from the diary of Ezechiel Sangmeister, translated by Barbara Schindler, are reprinted by permission of The Historical Society of the Cocalico Valley, Ephrata, PA. Selections from *The Ephrata Cloister: An Introduction* by Eugene E. Doll are reprinted by permission of the Ephrata Cloister. Selections from *The Red Hills* by Cornelius Weygandt are published by The University of Pennsylvania Press. Selections of Pennsylvania folk art are taken from Frances Lichten's *Folk Art of Rural Pennsylvania* published by Charles Scribner's Sons.

*Cover:* The anonymous fractur drawing (c. 1797) is taken from the Cassell Collection of the Historical Society of Pennsylvania and reproduced by permission.

Library of Congress Cataloging-in-Publication Data

Wentz, Richard E.
    Pennsylvania Dutch/by Richard E. Wentz.
      p.  cm.—(Sources of American spirituality)
    Includes bibliographical references and index.
    ISBN 0-8091-0439-3 (cloth)
    1. Pennsylvania  Dutch—Religion—Sources.  2. Folklore—Pennsylvania—History —Sources.  3. Folk art—Pennsylvania—History—Sources.  4. Pennsylvania—Religious life and customs—Sources.  I. Title.  II. Series.
    BR555.P4W46  1993
    305.6′870748—dc20                          92-33184
                                                   CIP

Published by Paulist Press
997 Macarthur Boulevard
Mahwah, N.J. 07430

Printed and bound in the United States of America

# CONTENTS

*To all the Wentz, Zeller,*
*Snyder, and Berger Freindschaft*
*who*
*have shared with me*
*the spirit of the Pennsylvania Dutch*

\* \* \*

"Un doch treibt mich des Heemgefiehl
So schtark wie alle Welt"
—HENRY HARBAUGH

# GENERAL EDITOR'S INTRODUCTION

In this volume of the *Sources of American Spirituality* series, we are confronted with two terms that share a certain lack of definition. "Folk" is a term that has come to us via the relatively young field of folklife studies. Some, like Don Yoder, have attempted to lay out clearly the perimeters of meaning for "folklife" by linking it with its European predecessor, regional ethnology. Following the pioneering work of Swiss ethnologist Richard Weiss in 1946, Yoder spoke of folklife studies as an eclectic methodology that combines the theories of regional ethnologists with a concern for historical data. Thus folklife studies share data with the ethnologist who studies the interrelationship between the folk and folk culture, insofar as it is determined by community and tradition, and with the social historian who attempts to uncover the story of how common people lived and interacted with broader historical forces. Thus the student of folklife is by definition a borrower of tools of inquiry from many different disciplines: history, anthropology, geography, sociology, and economics, to name some.

Likewise, "spirituality" is a protean term that is often criticized for its vagueness. Yet like folklife studies it represents an attempt to look at data through new eyes. It borrows from disciplines like comparative religion, psychology, and anthropology. Most frequently it utilizes theological analysis. Yet, the degree to which it moves away from a strictly theological interpretation of the data is the degree to which it may be said to offer original interpretation. Obviously, the theological component will always play a key role, but unless "spirituality" represents a creative utilization of new methodologies in the study of the human experience of God, there can be no real justification for using the term "spirituality" at all. We might just as well speak of "ascetical theology."

In grappling with those issues, Richard Wentz looks at the religious

1

expression of the Pennsylvania Dutch, *die Pennsylfawnish deitsch*. Those people, whom some prefer to call the Pennsylvania Germans, are in fact a diverse stock, tracing their various roots back to Swiss, High Germans, and French Huguenots. Several generations of life in Pennsylvania and parts of New York produced a distinctive culture, one that, because of its use of the German tongue, has often been ignored by the Anglophile culture of mainstream America.

These people, like all peoples, have an ecclesiastical and what Richard Wentz describes as an "extra-ecclesial" religious expression. It is that latter dimension which this volume explores. Its concern is not merely with what some have called the disciplinary spirituality of the religious institutions, but with the actual religious expressions of the people that in fact take on many forms not defined by the rituals of any church. Study is made not only of what a given religious expression is supposed to mean in the eyes of the institutional cult, but what it actually means to the people involved.

The array of religious expressions surveyed here makes the presuppositions of the method obvious. We are presented with a motley blend of sources, from humorous stories, to sermons, to superstitions. Admittedly, not all of this material fits nicely into any one interpretive scheme. Granted, all people—some far more than others—need to have those analytical frameworks to deal with the world. If this book offends in its reticence to provide those, it shall not be an offense without purpose.

The study of spirituality should, if it does nothing else, remind us that this thing we call spirit is in the end far more effusive, far more ineffable than any single analytical framework can convey. To see its diverse traces on one fascinating folk is a lesson in perception that is the first, and perhaps the most important, that any student of spirituality should learn.

*John Farina*

# PREFACE

The resources for this book have been a long time in the gathering and will likely continue their manifestation long after the publisher's work is done. I am a Pennsylvania Dutchman, born and raised among the "church" Dutch in Carbon County, Pennsylvania. I grew up knowing that there were some among us whose heavy accents and inflections were an embarrassment to the rest. There were fellow pupils in grade school who could barely manage the parity of English discourse. They were considered "dumb," because that was the way the "outside" world thought of them. Not that the Dutch are some kind of deprived and ghettoized minority. In eastern Pennsylvania they have been a dominant cultural influence since the opening of Penn's Colony.

It was not until I went away to college (only 60–70 miles away) that I realized how much of a Dutchman I was. Students from Philadelphia, New York, and New Jersey didn't sound at all like me. I began to be conscious of the fact that I had a Dutch accent. I worked hard at getting rid of it; yet even today, decades removed from undergraduate times, I will occasionally be greeted by a student who asks me after a lecture: "What country are you from?"

The Dutch are, of course, primarily Deutsch in extraction. It was the English-speaking Pennsylvanians who rearranged the pronunciation because of their own failure of ear. The Dutch speak a dialect German, interspersed with English words which have been "Dutchified." But even those who do not know the dialect speak their English with an unmistakable accent that bears little resemblance to the German accents one hears in television and film. These people are a distinctively American breed.

I am pleased that I have been able to share an appreciation of this heritage through Paulist Press' series, Sources of American Spirituality. This opportunity permits me to communicate my own spirit along with the many things I have learned in years of study of the ways of my people. I have been a professor of religious studies, concerned primarily with the critical understanding of the nature of human religiousness and its relation to the fashioning of society and culture. But I have long been interested in spirituality, a word that has suffered from bad press. To me the word is a recognition of the indeterminacy of humankind. Even the historian is a being who transcends, chooses, and manipulates the events he seeks to interpret. An interpreter is by nature a transcendent being. He takes matter and fashions it into spirit.

As I studied American religion it became apparent to me that human religiousness, with its need to fashion spirit out of matter, is not exhausted by its participation in formal religious traditions. A person who is called a Christian very likely expresses himself religiously in many ways additional to those prescribed by the official doctrine and practice of the church. Therefore, if I wish to understand the religiousness of Americans, I must be open to those expressions of the spirit not mandated by the synods and confessions of church history. I must seek to comprehend the spirituality of the folk.

This conviction has led me to explore the ways of the folk to whom I owe a considerable measure of my own spirit. I am indebted to my own family, Pennsylvania Dutch in patrilineal and matrilineal descent. From my grandparents, Chester and Cora Snyder, Elmer and Susanna Wentz, and my uncles and aunts I learned the cadences of the dialect and spied on their secret lives when they assumed I didn't understand their language. My uncle Evan, a professor of physics at Ursinus College, has inspired much of my latter-day appreciation of my spiritual heritage. This is unknown to him. However, he has mastered the dialect to the point of being able to teach others how to use it, while I continue to struggle with a rather slovenly vocabulary and syntax. His dedication has convinced me of the worth of my own interest.

I acknowledge the assistance of librarians and collections at Muhlenberg College, Millersville University, Ursinus College, and the Pennsylvania State University. Without the assistance of faculty grants-in-aid from Arizona State University, this project would have remained mere *Sehnsucht*. The staff of the word processing center at my university have been of immense help to this member of an endangered species who does everything in longhand. And, of course, the secretaries of our Department of Religious Studies have contributed to the management of details. But most of all, I acknowledge the love, patience, and critical understanding of my wife, Cynthia, whose patient appreciation of my work makes this Dutchman one humble servant.

This book is offered in the hope that it will contribute to the understanding of an important element in American culture. May it deepen our spirituality and make us deeply aware of the wisdom of the people in their ordinary religiousness.

Richard E. Wentz
Professor of Religious Studies
Arizona State University

# INTRODUCTION

## I.
### THE NATURE OF FOLK SPIRITUALITY

Not long ago the annals of religious and theological scholarship would have made short shrift of the word "spirituality" before condemning it to certain destruction. It was a term plagued by guilt by association with rational anemia. To speak of spirit, spiritual, or spirituality was to deal with the obscure, the vague, and the insubstantial. Spirituality was a term without intellectual rigor. It was embarrassing to theologians and church historians, amusingly pious to the other intellectual and academic mentors of our society.

Then something happened. First, a respectable theologian began talking about "spirit":

> We have dared to use the almost forbidden word "spirit" (with a small "s") for two purposes: first, in order to give an adequate name to that function of life which characterizes man as man and which is actualized in morality, culture, and religion; second, in order to provide the symbolic material which is used in the symbols "divine Spirit" or "Spiritual Presence" . . . spirit as a dimension of life unites the power of being with the meaning of being. Spirit can be defined as the actualization of power and meaning in unity.[1]

Evidently there was no way to comment upon the indeterminate character of human existence without recourse to a time-honored word. Systematic discussion of the symbol material at the heart of Christianity began to acknowledge "spirit" as an unavoidable referent for the transcendent dimension of existence. The use of the noun made the adjective acceptable. And soon we were talking about something called spirituality.

But the return of spirituality had another harbinger. It was the increased attention to oriental thought and praxis that became quite evident by the late 1960s in America. Pundits like Jacob Needleman called attention to the fact that western religions had lost the "instrumental" character of their traditions. He attributed the rise and fall of psychiatry as evidence of the fact that religion no longer provided the disciplines and methods (the "instruments") necessary for the attainment of personal transformation. He advocated the rediscovery of traditional paths that lay in the depths of Christian and Jewish history. The way was open for the recovery of western spirituality.[2]

Still, the term lacks definition. Therefore, before we turn to a description of folk spirituality, it may be well to call attention to the several ways in which the term is used. Frequently we see reference to the spirituality of a particular person, even sometimes of a people or nation. So, for example, we may refer to the spirituality of the American poet Wallace Stevens, or to the spirituality of Japan. In either case, what is implicit is that each example represents a unique (at least particular) expression of the human capacity to transcend biological existence—to be free, to be culture-producing. In the work of an artist or the ways of a people we may discern a distinct spirituality, since it designates a disposition of human spirit, and so may speak of "dispositional spirituality."

It becomes readily apparent that there are other uses of the term spirituality. Sometimes we discover in the writings or teachings of a particular author or thinker the evidence of a concerted effort to reflect upon the mystery and meaning of existence. Thus, for example, I have written elsewhere of the spirituality of Loren Eiseley. In so doing, I am referring to a literary manner of religious exploration that is intelligent and probing, but avoids the mannerisms of systematic and analytical styles. Eiseley uses a form of personal essay to discourse upon natural history and the character of human "otherness" in the passage of evolution. We might also in this way refer to the spirituality of Reinhold Niebuhr and look to certain essays and sermons for a measure of that spirituality. In this fashion it is a disquisitional spirituality which interests us, a form of discourse upon the welfare of the human spirit.

What tends to interest us more and more, of course, is disciplinary spirituality. This refers to the tools and methods of discipleship, what Needleman calls the instrumental knowledge of tradition. This is the knowledge used by one who discovers that ordinary knowledge and understanding are insufficient fare for the human spirit. This is the knowledge discovered by those who are ready to learn, to become disciples, to turn to teachings and disciplines that open the way for superordinary knowledge. Disciplinary spirituality helps us to do justice to the transcending dimension of the human spirit, to gain the perspective for perceiving reality in a new and transformed manner. Now, the problem is that the human spirit in its transcending quest does not always wish to see things as they really are. Sometimes the human spirit wishes instead to give free expression to its desires and its drive toward ego-satisfaction. So it devises methods to attain self-esteem and success. Is this also a form of spirituality, of disciplinary spirituality? In some sense, yes; inasmuch as in the history of religions we usually observe people whose major interest is for healing, for miracles, often for self-identity that reaches ethnic dimensions. However, from the perspective of the great traditions of spirituality that are at the heart of the major religions, we may say that a spirituality that merely feeds ordinary human desire does not truly assist in the transcending mandate that the human spirit requires. This is what St. Augustine meant when he said in his prayer: "Our hearts are restless until they find their rest in thee."

The human spirit engages in all sorts of exercises to serve its egocentric assumptions. It must be driven to the wall with all of those exercises, in order to confront the fact that nothing will satisfy this restless transcending spirit other than an encounter with a reality that is always more than our present understanding of it, yet sufficient to transform our ordinary perceptions and to *control* the very desires that drive us toward ego-satisfaction.

Disciplinary spirituality includes all the methods and special knowledge that people use to nourish the transcending restlessness of the human spirit. Therefore, any study of disciplinary spirituality will be alert to both levels of activity. That is to say, it will deal with the level of satisfaction for the ordinary self and its desires, as well as the level on which that ordinary self is transformed. It will remember that there are spiritual exercises designed to help people to affirm order over chaos and meaning over meaninglessness. These ways or methods help people to know who they are and why they are living. They help to affirm the need for healing in the very ordinary circumstances of existence. But there is another level of spirituality, reserved for those who are aware of the need for ultimate transformation, for a transcendence of the ordinary ways of perceiving the need for order, for meaning and healing.

## The Spirituality of the "Folk"

As we study the religion and culture of America, it becomes apparent that there are strains of spirituality that tend to go unstudied. It is interesting that the late William A. Clebsch, in his work on *American Religious Thought,* had recognized the need to move beyond normative understandings of religious thought, derived mostly from the precincts of church history. "Religious thought," he wrote, "means something far broader than the denominational doctrines that theologians have certified, whether by appeal to traditional or to novel revelations, and also something more definite than personal opinions about things unexplained by accepted natural laws. Here religious thought means the reasoned, the cogent, and the evocative consideration of ways in which the human spirit of Americans seriously and strenuously relates itself to nature, to society, and to deity."[3] Clebsch's attempt to redirect the study of American religious thought was an important one. It led him to assert that a prominent characteristic of this way of thinking is the ability to deal with *one's own religiousness* in such a way that it described the spiritual hopes and attainments of other Americans. The denominational standing of a thinker has often been irrelevant, according to Clebsch.

In the course of his discussion, Professor Clebsch soon began to refer to this unity of thought and personal religiousness as spirituality. There was no definition of this latter term. It simply stood for the integration of religious impulse and intellection. The word spirituality occurs frequently throughout the text. Disquisitional spirituality and dispositional spirituality are readily conjoined so that the author is able to entitle a chapter "The Sensible Spirituality of Jonathan Edwards." Clebsch's analysis of the significance of Horace Bushnell concerns itself with the mode of his "spirituality."[4] Of Emerson, Clebsch writes that he "heard nature's summons to a spirituality of self-reliance that mitigated grief for his dead son."[5]

It is evident that Clebsch's search for a means of understanding the uniqueness of American religious thought led him outside the churches and into the use of a term that must make many academicians squirm. What is this "spirituality" to which Clebsch refers? I would reply that it is a word that acknowledges the interrelationship of logical reason, aesthetic evocation, and imaginal thought—all in the service of the transcendent character of the human spirit in its quest for order, meaning, and transformation. But Clebsch's foray outside the ecclesiastical jurisdictions does not go far enough. Just as there are forms of spirituality which beckon to us from outside the ranks of the duly certified theologians, so there are forms of spirituality that do not necessarily conform to the canons of the intellectual elite. There is also folk spirituality, the modes of spiritual integration that are not registered in the annals of ecclesiastical synods or recognized in the standard works of literature and philosophy.

Personal religiousness and reasonable thought are limited neither to the official doctrine of churches nor to the ruminations of the literati. Folk spirituality has to do with those ideas, beliefs, and practices which are part of the everyday life of the people. An interest in folk spirituality emerges from the realization that all of us are involved in what seems to be extra-ecclesial religion. We discover that there are spiritual resources which do not always conform to what synods, councils, and systematic theologians define and prescribe as normative. There are things that we think, do, and believe that are not officially religious, yet may in many instances have been hundreds, even thousands, of years in the making. Then too, one interested in folk spirituality is concerned with asking: what does a particular religion actually *mean* to the people—not what is it officially *supposed* to mean? Church history records the manner in which Christian orthodoxies came to be defined and defended. But the historian of religion wants to ask: what do people whom it is possible to identify as Christians actually think, believe, and practice? He also wants to know what people who have little or no connection with ecclesial or denominational Christianity think, believe, and practice.

These questions are important for several reasons. First, we may discover that Christianity requires a definition and an understanding that is quite different from what is recorded in the annals of the churches and the treatises of their theologians. Second, we learn something about the scope of religious needs and expressions. From our positions as academicians or as ecclesiastical spokespersons we may be inclined to arrive at theoretical distinctions about religion or Christianity that tend to overlook what people need religiously. Many years ago, before I became a professor, I was serving in a parish in south-central Pennsylvania. I had just recently begun to gain a kind of theological sophistication which I had not learned in seminary, but which resulted from my companionship with a religion professor at a small church-related college not far from my parish. I had begun to learn what was good and bad theology and become somewhat intolerant of the latter. I had also been nurtured in a catechetical tradition of the Evangelical and Reformed church, with powerful influence from the old "Mercersburg Movement" with its high doctrine of the church and of liturgy. This tradition I wished to defend and preserve with my intensified theological awareness.

There came a time for a visit home to see my mother. Imagine my chagrin to find some pamphlets lying on the end table with her Bible. The literature was from the Unity School of Christianity and dealt with various aspects of mental healing. I asked my mother what she was doing with that "stuff"; I told her that it had no place in the life of a good Reformed Christian. She was surprised at my arguments. To her there was no contradiction, no conflict, between her traditional Protestant church-manship and her need for resources to cope with the routine of existence. I was disappointed, irritated, at the time. But now I understand that religious needs are often more profound and extensive than the abilities of religious leadership to meet them or to tap the latent resources of a tradition. If the church does not provide modes and techniques for healing, then the people will find it in extra-ecclesial repositories. Sometimes they will turn to new religions or to ancient and occult practices.

All of us have recourse to folk spirituality. We are bound to find some means to assure our personal and social identity, to provide us a sense of wholeness and well-being, and sometimes to take a road less travelled into transformed existence. How is it that we call these extra-ecclesial religious expressions "folk" spirituality? First, because they are part of a tradition that is often unwritten. A colleague of mine at another university is a specialist in Native American, and what he refers to as nonliterate, religious traditions. On one occasion he visited a class that had been studying some of his books and essays. A student asked: "Have you ever been around any nonliterate peoples?" "Of course," was the reply "—my family." No matter how literate and sophisticated we become, we are also nonliterate creatures who rely, for a sense of ultimate worth, upon ideas, practices, and relationships that are often neither written nor read. We are all nonliterate as well as literate. We are all to some extent "folks."

Folklorists have set the tone for an understanding of who the folks are and what it is they do. As scholars they have argued over the nature of their studies. Professor Richard Dorson has made much of a lifetime career distinguishing between what he calls folklore and fakelore. "Fakelore falsifies the raw data of folklore by invention, selection, fabrication, and similar refining processes . . . for capitalistic gain. . . ." For Dorson, fakelore is often coarse and obscene, even "meaningless and dull to the casual reader."[6] True folklore is the voice of the folk, he tells us, not of mass culture using the medium of print. The folklorist may record and publish his findings, but he makes no attempt to refashion it as "froth and fun" for the commercial market. It must be recorded as it is told, reflective of the oral nature of its origins. So say the folklorists. They have compiled a rich oral tradition nurtured by ethnic groups, occupational classes (lumberjacks, cowboys, farmers, and oil drillers), and regional distinctions. But in American history, the people who nurture these traditions have seldom been removed from contact with the literate world. The oral development and transmission of these tales and ways have always interacted with literary forms. Therefore, any study of American spirituality cannot be confined to oral collections. It becomes the study of people's spirituality.

Perhaps the folklorists are justified in their vocation, collecting oral tales and other lore, recording the details of what is observed, with little commentary and no embellishment. They distinguish folk culture from popular culture, and preserve a valuable heritage. However, when we raise the question of folk spirituality, we are not so much concerned with preservation as with understanding those spiritual dispositions and disciplines that are not part of the normative character of carefully differentiated religious traditions like Christianity. Therefore, folk spirituality is the set of ideas, beliefs, and practices that are close to the ordinary lives of people, yet not usually considered to be part of the normative traditions, of which the people may or may not be members. Whether they are members or not, it is likely to be significant that a certain normative tradition is highly visible in the culture. Thus, for example, a study of Japanese folk spirituality would be alert to the historical presences of Shinto and Buddhism, even religious Taoism and Confucianism, as well as the ancient, continuing, and less definitive folk traditions of Japan. No tradition or practice is unaffected by the course of history and the interaction of other ways and paths.

Folk spirituality is not necessarily entirely oral or ritualistic. It includes tales, proverbs, sayings, healing techniques, divinations, fortune-telling, shamanism and spiritism, and ritual activity. However, it also includes a special literature. We discover almanacs, handbooks, esoteric manuals, and devotional literature that is not part of the prescribed life of the normative tradition. Sometimes this devotional material emerges out of the underside of normative traditions. Thus, for example, the writings of Jacob Boehme are part of a Christian and Lutheran context, but they are suspect by the normative tradition and become part of the nurturing and sustaining spirituality of the literate among the folk. It is difficult to deal with the phenomenon of devotional literature. In our own day much of this literature tends to be part of the programmed life of the churches. Of course, it is often produced without much theological judgment or supervision, thereby resulting in ideas that are overly sentimental or even heretical. The folk spirituality of contemporary America is constantly reinforced by devotional literature published by the denominations. In addition, such literature is issued by numerous religious groups which are unconventional or are outside the mainstream of the prevailing religious order. The result is that the folk read devotional material that comes to the public from various schools of New Thought, Jehovah's Witnesses, and the Latter-day Saints. Such materials become part of the disciplinary spirituality of the folk, regardless of their degree of literacy or allegiance to certain denominational bodies. But there is another form of devotional literature which is an important element in contemporary folk spirituality. This is the writing of celebrities, psychologists, and others who address us usually from outside the normative traditions. Some are influenced by

Asian, theosophical, and occult traditions; but their work is their own, directed toward self-help, self-assertion, and self-realization (in this respect at variance with the fundamental teachings of most of the world's great traditions). We have only to mention the writings of Shirley Mac-Laine and Leo Buscaglia in order to realize the pervasiveness and power of this form of folk spirituality.

Some may wish to argue that devotional literature is more properly understood as part of *popular* religion and spirituality. However, in a complex society it becomes increasingly difficult to confine the ideas and practices of the "folk" to nonliterate elements. Since the invention of the printing press the folk have used the written word as a means of preserving and disseminating what is important to them. In many instances the "books" themselves become objects of veneration and handbooks for practices that are not part of normative tradition. The Bible itself is something different for the folk than what it is for theologians and ecclesiastical leaders. What is popular today is readily adapted by the folk to their purposes.

Folk spirituality belongs to the everyday life of people who may be differentiated by regionality, ethnicity, race, circumstances, or some combination thereof. Southern Appalachia, perhaps much of the South, manifests a spirituality which shapes the more normative Christian churches of the region, but which is also differentiated *from* the ecclesial ways themselves. There is an Afro-American spirituality that is not limited to the black churches, but manifests itself in the streets of the ghetto as well as in the hollows and homes of rural blacks. Historians of religion may call attention to the African and West Indian roots of this spirituality; they may argue over the degree of influence—the presence of these "roots" in the black ecclesial traditions of North America. It is somewhat peculiar that many of them do not apply the same logic to the discovery that Christian people have always expressed their religiousness in ways that are somewhat deviant of official dogma and prescribed praxis.

Folk spirituality is apparent everywhere and has always been so. When the women in a Rumanian village begin the systematic preparation and decoration of Easter eggs, their lives are being given spiritual direction that is differentiated from, but complementary to, the richness of the normative tradition of Eastern Orthodoxy. When the people tell tales of the miracles of a saint and of the spiritual power of a sacred place, they are engaged in ritual expression which provides continuing order and meaning to an otherwise meaningless and sorrowful existence. In the classical Russian tale *The Way of a Pilgrim,* the pilgrim encounters a wolf who tears the precious woolen rosary given him by his *starets.* When the wolf attacks him, he strikes at the animal with the only thing he has in his hand, the rosary. The rosary becomes twisted around the beast's neck as he leaps away and gets caught in a thorn bush. The pilgrim moves to free him, to prevent him from running away with the rosary. The wolf lunges to escape and the rosary lays torn in his hands. A miracle! When he comes to an inn for night's lodging, he asks for needle and thread to mend his rosary. He sits working in the presence of an old teacher at an elementary school and a clerk at the County Court. "I suppose you have been praying so hard," says the clerk, "that your rosary broke?" "It was not I who broke it," answers the pilgrim, "it was a wolf." "What? A wolf? Do wolves say their prayers, too?" says the clerk jokingly. The pilgrim explains what happened and how precious the rosary was to him. "Miracles are always happening with you sham saints!" laughs the clerk. "What was there sacred about a thing like that? The simple fact was that you brandished something at the wolf and he was frightened and went off. Of course, dogs and wolves take fright at the gesture of throwing and getting caught on to a tree is common enough. That sort of thing very often happens. Where is the miracle?"

The old teacher comes to the defense of the pilgrim. "You remember when our father Adam was still in a state of holy innocence all the animals were obedient to him, they approached him in fear and received from him their names. The old man to whom this rosary belonged was a saint. Now what is the meaning of sanctity? For the sinner it means nothing else than a return through effort and discipline to the state of innocence of the first man. When the soul is made holy the body becomes holy also. The rosary had always been in the hands of a sanctified person; the effect of the contact of his hands and the exhalation of his body was to inoculate it with holy power—the power of the first man's innocence. That is the mystery of spiritual nature!"[7]

Now, a story such as this one may not be antithetic to the official teaching of the church in a particular period of its history. However, to read the story of the pilgrim and his many experiences is to live with the folk in their struggles to perceive the whole of existence as ultimately meaningful and intimately ordered and permeated with spiritual power. The way of the pilgrim is nurtured by the liturgy and the teachings of the church, but it uses those resources in its own way and complements them with a cluster of beliefs and practices that are outside the pale of synods and councils.

Since the emergence of Protestantism and the Enlightenment of the eighteenth century, there has arisen in Christendom a puritanizing and rationalizing process that seeks to eliminate or ignore folk spirituality. The religiosity of the folk is disdained as magic and superstition and assumed to be meaningless or regressive. Only in Roman Catholicism and

Eastern Orthodoxy does there seem to be a willingness to remain open to the spiritual needs of the folk, providing a genuine Catholic umbrella for all sorts and conditions of humanity rather than forcing them out into the storm, to exist on their own. Any alert observer of American life is aware of the fact that in the ethnic neighborhoods of cities like Buffalo and New York, even in small towns like Northampton and Womelsdorf, Pennsylvania, there are beliefs and practices that are not central to church life, but very important to the people who belong to those churches. The folklorist, if he makes any judgments at all about the material he collects, will reveal his Enlightenment beliefs by saying things like: "We are lured into believing in supernatural forces because we insist upon having explanations for events which have no explanation. If we do not know the cause of something, we will make one up. . . . Religion is one way people explain the unknowable. Superstition is another way. The world of our grandfathers was a religious world, but it was also full of very un-Christian and un-Jewish supernatural beliefs."[8] By whose standards un-Christian and un-Jewish? Why, by the standards of the elite, the defining elite. But to people who happened to be Christians and Jews, part of their spiritual existence.

The historian of religion would say that many people who are Christian or Jewish have ways of disciplining and ordering their lives in a manner that acknowledges the truth that life is "more than" it seems to be, "more than" it is possible to know, or "more than" the best explanation to satisfy. That "more than" quality is an encounterable reality. It is necessary to ritualize its presence and to remember its ways. These ritualizings and rememberings are themselves epistemologies—ways of knowing. They form the traditions of folk spirituality which might well be considered *part* of Christianity, Judaism, or any other normative tradition. Folk spirituality *is* and *does.* It is seldom normative, except as it is necessary to transmit the variety of ideas, beliefs, and practices to another generation. In that respect it becomes more like the apprenticeship of the shamaness, the training of catechists and acolytes, than of the preparation of clergy or theologians.

James York Glimm, in the work cited above, writes of a certain diffidence on the part of the people of north-central Pennsylvania to tell tales of the supernatural. "No doubt their reluctance was . . . the result of decades of Methodist and Baptist preaching which by the late twentieth century has driven the ghosts and witches underground. For years, the religion of these mountain people has taught that superstition—like fiddling, folksinging, and dancing—were the devil's own handiwork."[9] My grandmother was a devout and practicing Lutheran. Her Lutheran Book of Worship, in the German language, lies on a shelf in my study. But grandmother was also what the Pennsylvania Dutch call a "pow-wow" doctor. She was a practitioner of folk medicine. I can decide that she was a superstitious person who was a heretical Lutheran, or I can observe that her folk medicine and her Lutheranism were both part of her religious-ness, perhaps even part of her Christianity. "What the common man looks for in religion," writes Winston Davis, "is not metaphysics, but a kind of spiritual, or thaumaturgical, pragmatism."[10]

America has been a levelling culture. There is a spirit among us that resists constituted authority. We have been the nation raised on the grains of autonomy, sown in the fields that were cleared by the excesses of the Reformation, the meditations of Descartes, and the speculations of the Enlightenment. Some of us may now be convinced of the destructive force of autonomous thinking. Yet it is a force that continues to drive most of us, rejecting any heteronomous pretender to power. Not that we really escape heteronomy—a technological and corporate society is heter-onomous, but it placates the autonomous piety of the people by appealing to their meanest quality in the sanctification of greed. "The double fight against an empty autonomy and a destructive heteronomy," wrote Paul Tillich, "makes the quest for a new theonomy as urgent today as it was at the end of the ancient world. The catastrophe of autonomous reason is complete. Neither autonomy nor heteronomy, isolated and in conflict, can give the answer."[11]

Be all that as it may, American spirituality continues to display a very autonomous strain. The American people seek something that *works,* that gives them what they think they need. We were a people who had thrown off the hierarchical structures of politics, society, and *ecclesia.* We came to the North American continent often without benefit of clergy or tradition, and, like Emerson, we are convinced that we are each his own pope, that the past has nothing to give us. Americans love the simple, the down-to-earth, and, until recently at any rate, have been fundamentally anti-intellectual—especially when it comes to religion. If we wish to un-derstand America and its spiritual character, we cannot ignore the folk spirituality that is an expression of the democratic spirit. "Wer den Dichter will verstehen muss in Dichters Lande gehen." So wrote Goethe. It is to the land of the Pennsylvania Dutch that we turn for an examina-tion of American folk spirituality.

II.

WHO ARE THE PENNSYLVANIA DUTCH?

Many scholars would prefer to call them Pennsylvania Germans, but the English world has called them Dutchmen for so long and so indiscriminately, that it is a commonplace to refer to them as the Dutch—*die Penn-sylfawnisch deitsch. Deitsch* was the way they referred to themselves. We must remember that the original settlers came to Penn's Woods before there was any political and social unity among the many peoples of Europe who shared a variety of German language and dialects. They were all Deutsch, but there was more than one way to pronounce the word. To the English-speaking people of the British Isles and the American colonies they were all Dutch, even though they were not all the lowland Dutch, the Hollanders. After several generations of Germanic presence in Pennsylvania and parts of New York state, they had become an altogether differentiated culture, with their own dialect. They had become the Pennsylvania Dutch. And their forebears were a mixture of Swiss, High Germans, and French Huguenots.

The Pennsylvania Dutch are one form of a diverse stock of Germanic peoples. But they are their own people, their own culture. It would be incorrect to think of them merely as a transplanting of established Germanic culture in the New World. There are numerous settlements of Germans in places like Minnesota that still reflect the ethnic character of nineteenth century Germany. The Pennsylvania Dutch are something else. Some years ago I took a German friend of mine to visit my mother in Pennsylvania. In the course of polite conversation, the friend began to ask her about her "German" background. "Oh," she replied, "but we are not Germans; we are Pennsylvania Dutch." There is a difference, even though the Germanic ethos is part of the history and heritage of both the Pennsylvania Dutchman and the modern German.

I can detect the accent and inflections in the speech of a Pennsylvania Dutchperson wherever I may meet him. His use of the English language is distinctive and readily distinguishable from that of other English-speaking Germans. If one listens only to the German accents that are part of the movie world, one has no idea what to expect in encountering a Pennsylvanian.

A glimpse of the spirituality that was to assert itself in the forests west of the Delaware River, beginning in the late seventeenth century, may be seen in the works of the Englishman who was to make possible the Pennsylvania Dutch culture. William Penn wrote from Frankfurt in 1677:

> I dearly embrace and salute you all, in this day of the glorious fulfilling of His promise to His church in the wilderness. For He had reached unto us, and brought salvation near us! For, He hath found us out, and hath heard solitary cries, the deep mournful supplications of our bound spirits when we were as the dove without its mate, the lonely pelican in the wilderness, when

we were ready to cry out, Is there none to save, is there none to help?[12]

Penn had gone to Frankfurt to recruit settlers for his North American experiment. He was the scion of Admiral William Penn, who had served England under the Crown as well as the Commonwealth. The restored royal family had borrowed money from the Admiral, who bestowed fortune and legal rights to his son, William, even though the latter had earlier incurred his father's indignation because of his espousal of Quaker principles. The King's debt was cancelled when he agreed to grant young William a parcel of land in America. It was there that Penn hoped to realize a dream of providing a home for Europeans whose religious convictions placed them in an unfriendly and hostile world—living with the despair and loneliness of the dove in the Song of Songs and the pelican of the Psalms.

William Penn knew of the many sects and religious conventicles of the continent, spawned in the oppressive climate of religious wars and nurtured on the insights of the Reformation and the resurgence of mystical, hermetic, and cabbalistic religiosity. It was an apocalyptic era in modern history, a fact often ignored by secular historians. The thoughts and motivations of scientists and philosophers were drawn to a multitude of mysterious teachings and images. Even though the struggle for an autonomous reasoning power was strong among them, their minds had not yet demanded the tidiness of later Enlightenment assumptions. They were people for whom various modes of the rational and nonrational functioned side by side. The oppressed people of the Rhineland in Germany dreamed of *Lilienzeit*—the time of the lily—the time of the visitation of God's own peace. They were often organized into societies that looked to the dawn of the new age, and celebrated its presence with spiritual disciplines nurtured by a certain use of the Bible, along with the ancient wisdom that runs like an underground stream beneath the surface of our thoughts. The people called their societies by names like Rose-Tree, Rosebud, Lily, Wheat-Sheaf, Violet.

It was to these Palatines that William Penn turned for settlers. He wanted no drifters, no gold seekers. His visit to Frankfurt in the Rhineland Palatinate led to the formation of the Frankfurt Land Company, an organization designed to promote settlement in Penn's Woods and to finance the purchase of land. Although Penn's Quakerism was a bit too colorless for the mystical Christian pietists of the Palatinate, they responded to his welcome. They were in sympathy with his prophetic judgment that spelled doom for the Old World and apocalyptic fulfillment in the New.

The first Pennsylvania Dutchmen were Dutch and German Mennonites who came under the encouragement of Francis Daniel Schäffer, whose last name was Latinized to read Pastorius. He was the son of a prominent Roman Catholic family that had become Lutheran. Pastorius' own spiritual journey took him from the eastern German realms of Silesia, where mystical vision seemed to rise like mist from the earth, to the Pietist conventicles of Frankfurt. However, he was of a somewhat independent spirit, a pilgrim whose inner life was nurtured on the writings of Johann Tauler, Martin Luther, and Johann Arndt. Pastorius induced the Anabaptists from Krefeld and Kriegsheim to follow him to North America. We must understand, of course, that these Mennonites were not merely seventeenth century followers of Menno Simons and the traditions of the sixteenth century. In many ways they bore little resemblance to their stern and puritanized descendants who continue the Anabaptist tradition in the lush green valleys of twentieth century Pennsylvania. Their lives were deeply touched by the mysticism and theosophy of their times. They were an apocalyptic people; chiliastic imagery and symbolism were prominent in their spirituality.

"Almost half the Frankfurt Company of Mennonites in early Germantown were Lowland Dutch," writes Professor William T. Parsons. "But the Germans who arrived in Pennsylvania spoke their provincial dialects, though most commonly the dialect of the Rhineland—Palatinate."[13] Eventually the dialect became a common dialect with regional variations, under the influence of English and depending upon whether the region was mostly "church" Dutch or "plain" Dutch. Although Germantown was the first official settlement, the Dutch moved in ever increasing numbers into the hills and along the creeks and rivers of eastern Pennsylvania. The first ones came with the opening of the colony in 1683. By the early decades of the eighteenth century the farmers and craftsmen of the German lands had become a major factor in the developing culture of Penn's "holy experiment." The history books generally tell us that the Quakers of Germantown were the first to express serious objection to black slavery. However, it was the German pietists under the leadership of persons such as Pastorius who deserve most of that honor.[14]

In general, we may say that the prospective Pennsylvania Dutch culture was to be made up of Swiss Mennonites, Dutch Quakers, Frankfurt pietists, Silesian Schwenkfelders, Saxon Herrnhuters, Danish Doompelaars, Palatine Reformed, Wurttemberg Lutherans, Wittgenstein pietists, and Alsatian Huguenots. It has been the common heritage of European religious oppression and the vast storehouse of imagery and symbolism that has produced this curious American society. For two centuries the Dutch were sustained by the curious dialect that emerged. Although the use of this dialect is dying out, it is still possible to hear it on the streets of Lancaster, Reading, and Allentown, and in the crossroads inns that are part of the village and small-town life of the eastern Pennsylvania countryside.

Most of the colorful lore and crafts of the Pennsylvania Dutch have been preserved by the "church" Dutch. The American tourist who frequents the quaint shops and restored inns of Lancaster County maintains the erroneous assumption that all Pennsylvania Dutchmen wear black broad-brimmed hats and drive quaint horses and buggies. He does not realize that tourism has created its own world of commerce and artifacts. The Amish and Mennonite peoples have little to do with the vivid designs and quaint customs that are popularly associated with the Pennsylvania Dutch. The "church" Dutch are the people of Reformed and Lutheran heritage. "By and large," writes Frederic Klees, "they have made the Pennsylvania Dutchman what he is today. They gave him his ways of celebrating Christmas and Easter; they gave him his folk art, whether dower chest, taufschein, or barn sign; to a large degree they gave him his ardent patriotism, and to nine out of every ten they gave religion."[15] Although William Penn was more interested in the Anabaptists and pietists, members of Reformed and Lutheran churches were early settlers of eastern Pennsylvania. By the middle of the eighteenth century the laity and clergy of these two branches of the magisterial Reformation had established congregations and preaching spots throughout the lands beyond the Delaware and were pushing their way beyond the Alleghenies and southward into Maryland and the Shenandoah Valley of Virginia.

There is no doubt that the "plain" people add their color to the panorama of Dutch culture. These are the folk of Anabaptist and spiritualist extraction. They are the many orders of Mennonites and Amish, the Schwenkfelders, the Dunkards (Church of the Brethren) and a variety of small groups like the River Brethren. Their contribution to the culture lies in the quaint customs and traditions which have long been a part of their way of life. They have been separatist peoples, rejecting the ways of the world, maintaining styles of dress and domestic life that are simple and a throwback to the days in Europe before the impact of modernization. And, of course, they are a puritan people as well, dedicated to the ideal of a church unspotted by the world and devoid of externals in worship and demeanors which they would consider an impediment to the faith. Nevertheless, they, too, have spoken the dialect. And no people are able to live an entirely insular existence in a larger society as pluralistic and mobile as Pennsylvania. The plain people and church people often exchange stories as they gather at livestock auctions. There are certain other business transactions that bring them together. Storytelling, especially, is an art in which all the Dutch participate. It frequently reflects the spirituality of a people who share the land, its seasons, and its ways of fertility and earthiness. Then, too, the plain people have had a rich devotional life that has found its way into print, some of it continuing a tradition begun in the sixteenth century. The reader may wish to translate his or her own understanding of such Anabaptist classics as the Amish hymnal, *Ausbund.*

There is a third group of people among the Dutch, the Moravians. They are the heirs of the Unitas Fratrum, tracing their heritage back to the followers of John Hus in the early fifteenth century. Much of their early existence was centered in Bohemia. However, they endured persecution after persecution until 1722 when Nicholas Louis, Count von Zinzendorf, gave refuge to a Moravian remnant on his estate in Saxony. There they built the village of Herrnhut. Nicholas himself was attracted to the spirituality of the Brethren, and when he was banished from Saxony for practices at variance with established Lutheranism, he turned his attention to America. By 1742, Zinzendorf and the Moravians were establishing their communities in Nazareth and Bethlehem, Pennsylvania. The Moravian tradition has been piquant, with imagery and customs that were in contrast to the practices of church Dutch and plain Dutch alike. Early on they practiced a modified communitarianism and elevated music to a status unequalled in eighteenth century America. In their hearts, the Moravians were sufferers who shared the love of Christ in a language of love that reflected the Song of Songs and seemed incredible and shocking to their contemporaries.

It is easy to ignore the role of numerous sectaries and cultic movements that were part of the early history of the Pennsylvania Dutch. They have been so marginal to the proprieties of history. Toward the end of the nineteenth century, Professor Julius Sachse devoted considerable effort to the study of "The Woman of the Wilderness," a community that established itself along the Wissahickon Creek near Philadelphia as early as 1694. Under the leadership of Johannes Kelpius, Heinrich Bernhard Köster, and Daniel Falckner, the community practiced a curious blend of ancient Germanic religion, theosophy, and cabbalism. Yet persons such as Koster and Falckner maintained liturgical and theological ties to Lutheranism. The monastic and eremitic character of "The Woman . . ." eventually earned them the accusations of fanaticism.

However, Kelpius and his associates were the forerunners of several similar monastic experiments. There was to be the Ephrata Community under the charismatic leadership of Conrad Beiseel, certainly the most prominent of the movements. There were others, like Snow Hill and Rose Hill in central Pennsylvania. What is important for our consideration is the fact that these ascetic communities were both receptacle and breeding ground for a Pennsylvania Dutch spirituality that blends the religious expressions of common folk with the imagery of an ancient wisdom and the ecclesiastical traditions of Christianity. This folk spirituality extends far beyond the ruins of Ephrata and Snow Hill. It lingers in the rural haunts of contemporary Pennsylvania and has found a home in the minds and hearts of generations of Lutheran, Reformed, and Moravian church people. Even the Anabaptists have not avoided it. America has always been a pluralistic and denominational society. It has always been difficult for isolation and ascetic separatism to remain unsullied by contact with other ways and paths. In such a religious milieu the influences are often apt to be subtle. Neighborhood and marketplace form a marginal matrix in which boundaries are ignored and people are subjected to images, symbols, and ideas that become complementary to the traditions and world-views that form their primary identity. The influence may not be conscious. An Amishman or a Mennonite may not always be aware of the fact that his stories and the aphorisms which guide his work have come from outside the doctrinal precincts of proper Anabaptist heritage.

These then are the Pennsylvania Dutch. To Benjamin Franklin they were the "dumb Dutch" because they could not speak English. Yet he recognized their significance in the cultural climate of America. His printing presses sprang into action to supply their needs for Bibles and devotional literature, and to satisfy the entrepreneurial whims of Poor Richard. According to historians like Joseph Stoudt: "The full-blown rose of mystical transcendentalism blossomed in Pennsylvania a full century before New England's scrawny plant began to bud."[16] Stoudt waged the battle of a lifelong career of scholarship, hoping to gain due recognition for the cultural significance of the Pennsylvania Dutch. To Stoudt the Dutch produced more and better poetry than the English during America's colonial period. It was only their use of the German language that has permitted scholars to ignore the thought and artistry of the Dutch. They existed in subordinate relation to the aristocratic hegemony of British culture.

The dialect that served to unite the people and preserve a unique culture was a long time in formation. While it has a close affinity with South German dialects, it has been fashioned by intercourse and commerce within an English-speaking world. As the dialect developed, it remained for some time the everyday language of the people. "High" German continued to be the language of formal communication. Services of worship for plain as well as church Dutch were conducted in German. Even the small sects and cults that gave color to the Pennsylvania landscape used the German language and its mystical, theosophical, and cabbalistic literature. It was not until the middle of the nineteenth century that the dialect came to be accepted as a proper mode of literary and formal expression. The German Reformed pastoral theologian, Henry Harbaugh, is often credited with being among the first to write in the dialect rather than in High German. Harbaugh's writings are an important ingredient in the folk spirituality we are examining. He was encouraged by the eminent church historian, Philip Schaff, to preserve his verse in the everyday language of the people.

Whether the literary efforts were in High German or dialect, they are part of the spiritual heritage of a distinctive people. Generations of the lives of people of Pennsylvania Dutch extraction have been nurtured by the sayings, poetry, stories, proverbs, and devotional literature that give evidence of a disciplinary, dispositional, and disquisitional spirituality that is important to the understanding of America. Perchance there are also insights and resources that may enhance our own spiritual journeys.

### The Characteristics of Pennsylvania Dutch Spirituality

What are the characteristics of this spirituality? Although we have already alluded to them, it may be well to call attention to them by way of summary. First of all, the spirituality is expressed in material forms as well as in oral and ideational forms. The evidence of the spirituality is broadly phenomenological. For example, the arts and crafts of the Pennsylvania Dutch are fundamental media for the preservation and transmission of meaning and order. They are a means of religious and cultural identification. In a certain sense, they are often a mode of prayer. Sam D. Gill has shown how the nonliterate modality which is part of *all* human existence gives rise to ritual communications and expressions which have intrinsic significance. Gill's work has focussed primarily on Native Americans. He has demonstrated the manner in which the Navajo prayer stick is itself a prayer. We do not have to ask what the stick *means,* what prayer it *says* or *stands for.* It exists on its own right *as* a prayer.

The use of actions and objects as prayers is not only the prerogative of Native Americans. All folk *perform* prayers. All of us are engaged in nonliterate actions that are meant to express the need to provide ultimate order and meaning to our existence. Perhaps it is not too remiss to suggest that we respond to forces and energies that seem to influence our lives. A work of art exists as a lingering form of adoration, of petition or gratitude, even when its creator or its benefactors are unaware of the spirituality involved. Frederick Franck once wrote: "I . . . catch myself, at moments of unbearable joy, awe or sadness, making a little sign of the cross over my heart. It is an old, inexplicable gesture from childhood: I did not grow up as a Catholic. I cannot help it, and it is perhaps the only true prayer I have ever known."[17] Of course, Franck's confession speaks of a ritual action, yet it supports the notion of spontaneous action or deliberate creation as spirituality.

There are always those of us who rely less heavily on rationalizing intelligence, abstract reasoning, and literary activity than others. We express the holiness of existence by what we create, through objects and symbols that serve like visible prayer-acts. This is an important factor in understanding folk spirituality; it is especially significant in the spirituality of the Pennsylvania Dutch. As we shall see, much of the design and decoration for which the Dutch have gained renown have been forms of their communal spirituality.

A second characteristic of this spirituality is a kind of revelational transcendentalism. We may recall Professor Stoudt's paean that the "full-blown rose of mystical transcendentalism blossomed in Pennsylvania a full century before New England's scrawny plant began to bud." New England imported it second hand from German romanticism. But what Stoudt was calling "mystical transcendentalism" was part of the mind and heart of the Dutch, who found their European heritage curiously appropriate to their New World setting.

New England's variety of transcendentalism was hardly a folk phenomenon. It was elitist and highly literate, touching only a minority in American culture. While many of its precepts were in harmony with the eighteenth century Enlightenment and the developing mood of the American intelligentsia, it represented little in the soul of most Americans in its heyday. Yet even Sydney Ahlstrom states: "Anomalously or not, it was only in the land of the Puritans that American romanticism gained expression across nearly the full range of its possibilities."[18] Ahlstrom should have said that among *English-speaking intellectuals* only the land of the Puritans gave significant expression to American romanticism. There were German Americans in greater numbers than the English-speaking literati who were responsible for the development of a form of American romanticism known as transcendentalism. The predominance of English in the study of the history of American culture tends to stereotype our literature as Anglo-American. Nevertheless, the German language is an important ingredient in the study of American culture, well into the first half of the nineteenth century. And the transcendentalism of the Pennsylvania Dutch is of a different character than the well-known New England variety. It is folk transcendentalism, and much more culturally pervasive in its time.

For Ralph Waldo Emerson transcendentalism was idealism, which meant the superiority of the will and the mind over the senses. Objects confronting the senses are immediately transformed from a supposed external "out there" objectivity into elements of human consciousness. This led to the assumption that the divine was an ever-present reality in our consciousness. All around was the divine, the transcendent, waiting to be discovered by the divine propensity of mind and will. In some sense, New England transcendentalism may be understood as the domestication of the transcendent, which, of course, suggests pantheism and the loss of radical transcendence. Perhaps transcendentalism in its Emersonian form was a most inept and unfortunate term for the movement it signifies.

Which is what the Pennsylvania Dutch thought. Professor Stoudt informs us that the Philadelphia *Public Ledger* of 1856 defends the Dutch against the "crotchety, one-idead, dyspeptic, thin, cadaverous New England Brethren" with their "vagaries of pantheism." Pennsylvania Dutch transcendentalism was strongly revelational. What their poets and "mystics" saw in the realm of earth and nature was numinous, and cast in images that might well be obscure and esoteric to the ordinary rational mind. One saw the truth in nature with eyes provided by the Holy One. Knowing the transcendental world depended upon God's revealing selfhood. This is transcendentalism because it is turned toward this world as it is seen with the vision of God. It is expressed in often bizarre and exotic symbolism—the language of transcendence meant for the world. It is less contemptuous of the past, of tradition and scripture, than is Emerson's variety. At the same time it was in actuality a transcendentalism of the people in a manner that remained only an intellectual's dream for the "New England Brethren."

But if the spirituality of the Dutch was transcendentalist and phenomenological, it was also eschatological. The *Lilienzeit,* the time of the lily, referred to the millennium, the age of Christ's presence in a reign of peace. Perhaps the sturdy barns and robust stone houses of the Dutch were constructed to last a thousand years. There is little doubt that the time of the lily throbbed in the breasts of the Dutch well into the nineteenth century. But it was not a Millerite apocalypticism, except perhaps for some of the more ascetic Dutch communities, which lived in interim preparation for the great messianic marriage in a new heaven and new earth. For most of the Pennsylvania Dutch, the eschaton had to do with the visibility of God's redemption in this world. The rich imagery of the folk art and literature portrays a religiously and socially awakened world in the garden of Pennsylvania. The tulips, roses, and lilies were signs of the age to come.

"Europe's intolerance," writes Professor Stoudt, "had worked to select for migration to Pennsylvania those sects and individuals in whom the mystical spirit was most alive."[19] Yet the mystical character of Pennsylvania Dutch spirituality was not confined to the "sects" and the eccentric religionists like Conrad Beissel, who separated themselves from the churches in charismatic obedience to a new vision. It can almost be said that a new form of Christianity was in the making in Pennsylvania. Until the forces of modernization tended to the secularization of religion and the loss of Pennsylvania Dutch identity, the spirituality of those people was a truly Catholic phenomenon. For Schwenckfelder, Moravian, Lutheran, and Reformed people shared a mystical spirit and tradition derived from their common oppression and the ideas and symbols of medieval Catholic piety, Tauler, Eckhart, Boehme, Franck, the old German folksong and minnesong, baroque verse, Jesuit pastorals, and the works of French Quietism and German Pietism.[20] The spirituality is truly folk because it represents the natural inclination of people to find those religious expressions most favorable to their circumstances. While it lasted, it was a true flowering of a distinctive Catholic spirit. Pennsylvania German spirituality was mystical in the sense of its emphasis upon a holy longing (*Sehnsucht*), the necessity of some form of purification or renunciation in order to meet the claims of God, and the immediate experience of the knowledge and enjoyment of the divine. Extremes of asceticism, traumatic ecstasy, and erotic contemplation may be variables derived from particular social and subjective pathologies. However that may be, we are probably not in a position to exclude any of the divine madness of mysticism merely because it does not correspond readily to our conceptions of rationality. The folk spirituality of the Pennsylvania Dutch includes the mad and the exotic as well the tranquil and contemplative. What is held in common is a sense of participation in a mysterious universe where the earth shares secrets of creation that are more fully known by attention to the love of a transcendent reality.

The vocabulary and artistry of the Pennsylvania Dutch reveal their debt to a variety of mystical traditions and to forms of theosophy which may be traced to the Jewish cabbala. There are hymns to the Virgin Sophia, the heavenly Groom; there are allusions to the apprehension of mysteries that only initiates will understand, and a sense of humanity as microcosm of the universe itself.

Nevertheless, Pennsylvania Dutch spirituality maintains a basic loyalty to the Christian tradition and is stabilized by that fidelity. The holy scriptures provide much of the order and authority for the spiritual life. The iconography is frequently biblical, even if it has been complemented by associations and usage which are cabbalistic and Persian or Sufi. We must remember, however, that scriptures are used in many ways. For the "folk," the biblical material may be something other than, or in addition to, what the official church or the schoolmen say it should be. The hermeneutics which the people bring to their understanding and use of scriptures will be derived from varied contexts and needs. We are certainly familiar with the fact that the Bible becomes a sacred object for many people, so that it may be used for magical and spiritual purposes seemingly tangential to the conventional assumptions. Since the division of the text into verses it has also become much easier to identify "texts" which may be used according to the needs of individuals who seek "answers" that will serve their particular circumstances. The economically depressed and the politically oppressed use the scriptures in their special contexts. If they are sophisticated, they may seek themes of liberation which help them transcend or transform their existence. If, on the other hand, they are unsophisticated, they may seek texts, signs, or even use the Bible or its verses as magical symbols or formulas. Liberation theology and folk magic and superstition may not be that far apart. Together they demonstrate the manner in which we are all folk, using whatever offers us sacred potential in our quest for transcendence and transformation.

There has always been controversy between *Buchstaben* (the letter that kills) and *Geist* (the spirit which brings life). Allegorical and anagogical interpretations of scripture have sought to transcend *Buchstaben*. Wisdom has often insisted that these perspectives be maintained in balance with literal sobriety. Nevertheless, it is likely that our circumstances, the context in which we *use* scriptures, will be an important arbiter in the use of any of these approaches to interpretation.

The term "folk" tends to have a special meaning among the historians, the folklorists, and other scholars of culture. There must usually be some social reality that is at least partly definable. That is to say, we can talk about "folk" if we have some ethnic, regional, national, or other boundaries available to set limits upon the people we are calling into focus for observation. The scholars may, therefore, not like my previous use of "folk" in the rather broad, nonliterate sense in which I may refer to all of us as folk at some time or another. So it is appropriate that we return now to the more narrow vision of the scholars. For, when we observe the culture of the Pennsylvania Dutch and their spirituality, we are almost immediately aware of the fact that, in spite of their diversity, they are a people. The peoplehood is ethnic and regional; it is held together by the use of a dialect and a common religious heritage. But most especially, it is marked by the sense of community and communal reality that is found in a true folk culture.

The folk artist does not create a new thing. He is not an individual reaching forth out of personal anxiety and quest. He does not seek to express a private experience or search for a medium commensurate with his own egotistic requirements. Most of us are folk artists to some extent. Our culture, our religion, our families have provided us with a storehouse of images and ideas which find expression when we doodle or decide to draw, paint, or decorate—make "something fancy" or pretty. It takes no great twentieth century theoretician of the psyche to establish that insight. If we are contemplative beings, we *know* it. Certainly the craftsmen and farmers among the eighteenth and nineteenth century Pennsylvania Dutch knew it. Every person was an artist. Of course, some were better than others. The community recognized that and called upon those special folk to supply them with the "fancy" designs and equipment they needed. And there were artists among the folk who spent most of the time—at least their *spare* time—painting and crafting furniture and tools, bookplates and certificates.

The folk artist is free to make adjustments on his designs and ideas. He may prefer his own color schemes, and use some images more than others. But he is a community artist. The origin and conception of what he does are derived from his people, his heritage. "This is the way we do things," or "These are the things that are important to us" are functional modes of thought for the folk. The folk artist did not copy designs, he "remembered" them. When he wrote or painted, he did not produce what we would call "natural" or "representative" objects. Instead he expressed the intellect of the spiritual tradition of which he was part. Folk art speaks with the heart and mind. The eye that sees is more an eye of faith and mind than an eye of "natural" sensation.

The folk do not indulge in *self* expression but in personal reflection out of a fund of ideas. They trust only the insight they have been given, the ideas that have served to provide order, meaning, and transformation for existence. Reality is communal for the folk. The spirituality of the Pennsylvania Dutch is an ample demonstration of this fact. In a very real sense, the commercial production of design and idea which are supposedly representative of the Dutch leads to an altogether "foreign" result. The key chains and plaques bought in the gift shops of Lancaster County and along the stretches of interstate highway in Pennsylvania are obviously not folk art. Their designs are too regular, their messages too stereotypical. There are variations in line and image in folk art; even symmetry reveals slight asymmetry and deviation. For the folk artist is a community individual; but he is certainly an individual. In order to be a folk artist or versifier, you must have their images and ideas inside yourself. They must mean something to you. These ideas are not to be *imitated,* but given expression.

I should like now to defend artistry and craftsmanship as being forms of spirituality themselves. It may be relatively easy to accept devotional literature, proverbs, stories, poetry, and songs as spiritual expression. Perhaps it is not as easy to understand design, drawing, or construction as spirituality.

For some years I have maintained an interest in furniture reconstruction and refinishing. When I am engaged in such actions, I discover a certain contentment. I may not be aware of it while I am working, but my entire self is frequently lost in the activity. I am attentive to the present moment, not concerned with the successes or failures of the past, nor with future hopes or expectations. My mind loses its obsession with imaginary problems, worries, and desires that prevent me from living with the moment. Usually I am taking "thought for tomorrow"—not only with what I shall eat, what I shall drink, what I shall wear, but also with who I am, what I hope to achieve. The artist and craftsman both have moments when they forget themselves, when they are free from self-consciousness, and when they are open to the Christ nature, the mind of God. It is what the Buddhist calls mind-fulness—attentiveness to the action of the present moment. This does not mean consciousness of the "I" who is doing this, or doing that. It means being lost in the action or sensation itself.

When the Pennsylvania Dutch painters of illuminated manuscripts, barns, chests, and household articles, or the cabinetmaker or tinsmith were engaged in their activities, they opened their lives to the moment and permitted a flow of ideas and images that gave expression to the ultimate truth of reality. It was the time for the mind of Christ, the *Lilienzeit* itself, the visit of the Virgin Sophia. The work of the folk is frequently a form of spirituality, disciplinary spirituality that is as focused and attentive as meditation.

From all that we have said it should be clear that the Pennsylvania Dutch provide us with an important resource for the study of American spirituality and the understanding of the "American mind." It is folly to ignore the folk, whether we are engaged in intellectual, social and cultural, or religious history. My contention is that serious attention to the religiosity and spirituality of folks like the Pennsylvania Dutch may eventually lead to an altered definition or understanding of the Christian tradition. We begin to ask ourselves: what is Christianity? Perhaps it is all that Christians (as Lutherans, Presbyterians, Anglicans, Roman Catholics, etc.) believe, think, and do; not only what synods, theologians, and church historians circumscribe.

An exploration of the spirituality of the Pennsylvania Dutch permits insight into the workings of a unique culture. They are neither Germans nor Anglo-Saxons. They are a people fashioned out of special circumstance, and their dialect and way of life are rapidly vanishing before the flattening juggernaut of modern technocracy. Yet they have been in America since the end of the seventeenth century. Their culture has been formed as a society of the middle way. They have not been totally foreign enclaves, ethnic ghettos; instead they have been a non-English society in the midst of a dominantly Anglo-Saxon realm, influenced by that hegemony, but giving birth to a distinctively American way of life.

A word about our sources. When we deal with folk spirituality, the sources are difficult to justify. What, after all, is a legitimate source? A primary source would seem to be that kind of item which we discover in the course of what is called "field" work. I have done very little field work among the Pennsylvania Germans. For several years I visited with storytellers. However, the results of that work are not part of this book. On the other hand, there is a wide range of materials already collected and published by agencies like the Pennsylvania German Society. Many of these materials go uninterpreted—as is frequently the case among folklorists, who like to collect, preserve, and classify.

What are the sources which can provide us with some understanding of those religious ideas and practices which are not part of definitive and official doctrine and order? We can consult diaries or first-hand accounts of religious movements, of observers who sought to share their insights into movements and circumstances with which they were familiar. We can also turn to the work of historians and folklorists who have collected or preserved important documents and folk practices. However, the work of historians or folklorists may themselves be sources of understanding. How else, for example, can we begin to comprehend the people's observance of Christmas without the historical studies of a folklorist like Professor Samuel Shoemaker, whose work becomes a source for our own interpretation?

And, of course, the literary work of a twentieth century scholar like Cornelius Weygandt, reflecting upon his own roots in the Pennsylvania German culture, becomes a proper source for coming to terms with the manner in which these people perceive the ultimate order and meaning of their existence. After all, the most educated of us are of the folk as well as of the academic or intellectual elite. Many of our thoughts and actions belong to our status as human beings who belong to each other. We have many deep-seated preferences which are the values derived from our peoplehood. The most learned treatise or address will doubtless reveal something of the folk spirituality of which the individual is representative. Weygandt is a literary scholar. But he is also a "Dutchman" as I am. He speaks for his people both intentionally and unintentionally.

The sources for understanding the spirituality of an individual thinker are his writings and publications. These comprise primary sources. However, when we examine the spirituality of the folk, the sources are the extensive testimony and evidences of almost three hundred years of Pennsylvania German history. Our sources must be diverse—the work of historians, collectors, and interpreters. All such evidence as this has primary significance as we seek to learn something of the folk spirituality of the Pennsylvania Germans.

NOTES

1. Paul Tillich, *Systematic Theology,* Vol. III (Chicago: University of Chicago Press, 1963).
2. Jacob Needleman, *The New Religions* (Garden City, NY: Doubleday and Co., Inc., 1970), esp. 1–37.
3. William A. Clebsch, *American Religious Thought: A History* (Chicago: University of Chicago Press, 1973), 2.
4. Clebsch, *op. cit.,* 117.
5. *Ibid.,* 125.
6. Richard M. Dorson, *American Folklore* (Chicago: University of Chicago Press, 1959), 4.
7. *Way of a Pilgrim* (New York: Seabury Press, 1965), 44–45.
8. James York Glimm, *Flatlanders and Ridgerunners* (Pittsburgh: University of Pittsburgh Press, 1983), pp. 96, 97.
9. Glimm, *op. cit.,* 98–99.
10. Winston Davis, *Do-Jo* (Stanford: Stanford University Press, 1980), 84.
11. Paul Tillich, *Systematic Theology,* Vol. I (Chicago: University of Chicago Press, 1951), 86.
12. John Joseph Stoudt, *Pennsylvania Folk Art: An Interpretation* (Allentown: Schechter's, 1948), 50–51.
13. William T. Parsons, *The Pennsylvania Dutch* (Boston: Twayne Publishers, 1976), 34.
14. Parsons, *op. cit.,* 37.
15. Fredric Klees, *The Pennsylvania Dutch* (New York: Macmillan Company, 1950), 72.
16. Stoudt, *op. cit.,* xviii.
17. Frederick Franck, *The Book of Angelus Silesius* (New York: Vintage Books, 1976), 6–7.
18. Sydney E. Ahlstrom, *A Religious History of the American People* (New Haven: Yale University Press, 1972), 598.
19. John Joseph Stoudt, *Pennsylvania German Poetry, 1685–1830* (Pennsylvania German Folklore Society, 1955), xliii.
20. Stoudt, *op. cit.,* xlii.

# I

# THE PASTOR AND PREACHER

The story of how the Pastor became the Preacher is an American story. It is the story of the democratization of the clergy. Centuries of European ecclesiastical heritage were transformed by the tremors of the Great Awakening and the onslaught of nineteenth century revivalistic evangelicalism. The sense of religious leadership inherited from the great formation of Catholic Christianity and the European phase of classical Protestantism was changed by the fashioning of a new Christianity. There came into being an American Christianity that was born in a frontier setting, of a frontier spirit. There was little time for adherence to principles and practices of church order. From the time of Gilbert Tennent's "Dangers of an Unconverted Ministry" the stage was set for the performance of a new style of religious leader. America was to be the land of the Preacher. His story is yet to be told. The Preacher is the product of folk Christianity in a land that had no time for tradition, no patience with a life of mediated grace. All that was necessary was the person with a ready word on behalf of the Word, a loquacious midwife assisting in the birth of immediate salvation, readily and individually accessible. The Preacher is the creation of the religious needs of a folk with no time for the past and not much respect for formal education, whatever the reason.

When the Palatines arrived from their homeland, they brought with them a certain reverence and appreciation for their Christian heritage. But they were farmers, artisans, craftsmen. Or they were visionaries and those whose religious sensibilities ran counter to the establishments of their day. They brought few clergy and soon developed a religious life to suit their circumstances. When the ecclesiastical officials of Europe's churches sought to take seriously their responsibilities for the American settlers, they soon discovered a working spirituality that required some adjustment of their own working assumptions.

33

By the nineteenth century this democratic spirituality had gone a long way toward the transformation of pastor and priests into the Preacher, who was just one of the folks. The German Lutheran and Reformed churches fought this development by attempts to restore the confessional and catechetical structure of their traditions. However, the people retained much of their own democratic spirituality in spite of theological reaction. Among the Pennsylvania Dutch a tradition of "Parre Schtories" emerged. These are usually humorous tales, told about the pastor (*der Pfarrer* in German). They reflect a spirituality which is at once respectful, but meant to keep the pastor related to the same earth on which the drama of folk existence is staged. Pennsylvania Dutch spirituality is as earthy as it is iconographic and pious. And the "Parre Schtories" reflect a Christian world which has little room for a docetic Christ.

The folklore of the Pennsylvania Dutch also has reserved special honor for clergy like William Stoy, Henry Harbaugh, and Moses Dissinger. We include material from the biographical accounts of the latter two. Another section of this anthology will include short selections on Stoy. Harbaugh was a Reformed church pastor, very learned and gifted as poet, theologian, historian, and spiritual writer. He was interested in his people and was one of the first to use the dialect as a form of literary expression. He is truly a representative figure of folk spirituality even though he was an exponent of "high" tradition as well.

Dissinger is a true Preacher. In him the transition has been made from the classical traditions of Europe to the style of American religiosity. Dissinger was a member of the Evangelical Association of Jacob Albright, which may be seen as a formal denominationalizing of democratic spirituality with the aid of Wesleyan piety and ideology. Moses Dissinger was a real folk hero. His biographers could not refrain from idealizing him as a representative of the spirituality and aspirations of the people.

# MOSES DISSINGER: EVANGELIST AND PATRIOT

In this selection from the life of Moses Dissinger by Thomas R. Brendle we can detect the legendary inclinations of folk spirituality. Dissinger is a hero of the people, much like Davy Crockett. In the case of Dissinger, however, we see evidence of the kind of religious populism that has created the Preacher, the homespun religious hero who puts the powerful and unruly in their places. He is a personification of that distinctively American religiosity that has been called "revivalistic evangelicalism." This is America's contribution to the "new religions" of the world. It is the heritage out of which the televangelist has emerged.

*(The following is excerpted from* Moses Dissinger: Evangelist and Patriot, *Thomas R. Brendle. Proceedings of the Pennsylvania German Society, 1959)*

## Early Life and Conversion

The date of the birth of Moses has appeared in print erroneously as the year 1825. Although the records of the Lutheran Church at Schaefferstown give March 17, 1825, as his date of birth, we conclude that after considering all available evidence that he was born on March 17, 1824. He was baptized soon after his birth by the pastor of the Lutheran church at Schaefferstown. In his early youth he was hired out to farmers to work for his board and clothing, getting absolutely no schooling. He worked for a number of years on the Steinmetz farm, which adjoins Schaefferstown on the south, the home of Rebecca Steinmetz, for whom he held such a lifelong regard.

At the age of eighteen he was converted at the revival meetings held in the town and became a member of the Evangelical Association. The congregation with which he united passed out of existence about fifteen years ago and the meeting house has become a fire hall.

Up to the time of his conversion Mose was the "whoopee" boy of the community. He was the leader in mischief making, carousals, fighting and "packe"—catch as catch can wrestling. His good nature and ready wit, however, won for him tolerant consideration on the part of the community.

Coming home from drinking carousals or from frolics he would set all the dogs of the community to howling, make night hideous with his own tones, strike at fences with his club, waken sleepers by calling their names. But the good people wakened from their slumber, would only say: "It's all right: it's only Mose."

While preaching in Lehigh County in a country church, he was much heckled by a bunch of "Bully Boys" who made noises, imitating different animals. He turned to them and said, "Where I come from we keep the animals in the barn: here the people bring them to church." But the heckling continued till finally he called a member of the church to open the door and he threw them out one after the other.

\*   \*   \*

A letter from Mrs. Elizabeth D. Cornog, daughter of Reverend S. Neitz Dissinger, Mose's nephew:

Mose's first wife is buried in Schaefferstown, Pa. Her maiden name was Yocum [sic! Her name was Clark]. The second wife's name my father Rev. S. Neitz Dissinger can't recall but he, Mose, brought her to his [S. Neitz Dissinger's] parents' home. My father's mother said "Mose is she saved?" Whereupon Mose snapped, "Do you think I would sleep with the devil?"

\*   \*   \*

Mose used to say "that he had fought 17 battles before he was 18 years of age and won. But the last battle which he fought was the hardest." It was the battle with his own wicked nature—"seinre beesi naduhr."

After his conversion he was taught to read and write by his friends, two of whom were his grandfather's stepsister, Elizabeth, married to Abraham Brendle, and Rebecca, daughter of John Steinmetz, married to Daniel Brendle, son of Abraham Brendle. Years after when he had become prominently identified with the affairs of the Evangelical a scandal had arisen in the congregation. Among those called to bear witness was Rebecca Steinmetz. After she had spoken, Mose said: "That ends the matter, I believe Beckie Steinmetz more than the all of you put together." Rebecca Steinmetz was a sister of Reverend Dr. John Steinmetz, a prominent Reformed pastor of Reading.

When Mose worked on a farm not far from Schaefferstown part of his work was to drive the cattle to pasture in the morning and to bring them home at night. In the evening he went out, opened the bars and called the cattle, but they would not come. Wildly yelling he dashed among them, which made them run away as fast as they could. In this race he jumped on the back of a cow and stood upright and while the herd was running with all its might toward and through the bars, he gave another vigorous yell. The next moment he again stood on the ground. Then Moses followed the herd quite composedly. The next time he came to fetch the cows he simply opened the bars, stepped aside and bade them come and they came. This proved his favorite saying: "Wie mer sie ziegt, so hot mer sie [As you train them so they will be]." Such incidents may have given origin to the widespread belief that Dissinger once traveled with a show.

After his conversion he took an active part in the services of the congregation and also attended the services at Kleinfeltersville, a village several miles to the east of Schaefferstown, in the Millbach area, and the birthplace of the Evangelical church. His ready wit and fearless speech soon gained for him more than a local reputation. He felt called to the ministry. He was licensed to preach in the year 1853. A year later he was received as a preacher on trial at the conference held at Pottsville. In the year 1856 at the Conference held at Allentown he was ordained as a deacon and three years later he was made an Elder. Thus for a period of 25 years he preached in the First Pennsylvania Conference.

## On The Battle Line

When Moses was appointed to the Philadelphia station doubt was expressed whether he could adapt himself to the city. He enjoyed an immediate success. As Palm Sunday drew near one of his leading members told Moses that he was to preach a good sermon on that Sunday and that a new suit of clothing and a silk stovepipe hat would be given him for the occasion. When Mose returned to the parsonage, he said, "My, what a suit! I never expected to wear such a suit and I never had such a hat on my head before." He then inquired of Reverend William Yost who was at the parsonage at that time, "What did Brother T. say that next Sunday was?" "Palm Sunday," Yost answered. "Palm Sunday, Palm Sunday," he exclaimed. "They have curious Sundays here in Philadelphia. I never heard of such a Sunday. I am to preach a Palm Sunday sermon and don't know what it means. I am completely lost." And he asked Yost, "Can you help me out?"

As things turned out the sermon which Mose delivered on that Sunday was a powerful one. He, himself, said of it, "Never in my life did I preach better. The words could not come forth fast enough, they had to somersault over each other." After the service the brother who had seen to the appropriate fitting out of Mose for Palm Sunday came forward, drying away the tears, and said, "Thank God, Brother Dissinger, such a Palm

Sunday sermon was never preached in Philadelphia before, come to my store tomorrow. You shall also have a dozen white pocket hand-kerchiefs." The good brother had noticed that Mose used a colored handkerchief.

When Mose came to the conference from Philadelphia, some one asked him how he made out. The answer came, "Pocket full of money, church full of people and the devil whipped."

Moses recognized his strength and his weakness. He said: "I cannot preach like my brethren. When a carpenter, I used to hew close to the line, and so I must do in my preaching whatever knots there are in the way. I once tried to preach like my brethren, but my experience was that of little David when he thought he would like to fight the big-mouthed blas-phemer, in Saul's armor. He soon found out that if he were to fight in Saul's armor instead of slaying the giant the giant would cut off his head. But with the weapon to which he was adapted he knocked in the gable end of the big sinner. Only with the weapon the Lord has given me can I whip the devil, even if he does come upon me with stilts as high as a three story house."

During his early ministry he was invited to preach at what was then Millerstown, Lehigh County. There were rude people living there who purposely came to the meetings to create a disturbance. At the appointed time the hall was filled. Moses opened the services. Singing, praying and the beginning of the sermon took place without interruption. But all at once the crowd began to talk aloud and to create a nuisance. Mose stopped short in his sermon and proceeded to give the noisy fellows a lecture (in the dialect):

"Listen you fellows back there; you are all dog, every part of you, except the skin. You need only a dog's skin to let people see what you really are. If you didn't have a human skin on you, we'd know you better; but as it is, people still think you are human beings. I did not know that there are any of those accursed Gadarenes here in Lehigh County. You are as full of devils as were the Gadarenes. I'll tell you now what you will have to do; you must keep quiet or I'll come down and throw you out through the door that you'll break your necks. I can lick half a dozen such stuck-up chaps as you are. Dissinger is my name! And if you don't believe me, just stand outside when the meeting is over, and I'll show you."

Then he turned to the well behaved in the audience and with fine humor said: "But there are many orderly people here too, who have come to hear the word of God. I would advise you to secure carefully your hog stables, for if the devil should ever leave these Gadarenes and enter your hogs they will surely die, every one of them."

Scarcely had he said this when there entered a man who neglected to remove his hat. Him Mose addressed as follows: "And you old sinner, take off your hat or I'll teach you manners if you have none. I'll show you how to behave in places like this."

On another occasion young men disturbed the meeting by frequently going in and out of the meeting house. This Mose could stand no longer. Turning to the young ladies of the congregation, he said, "Young ladies, my advice to you is not to marry those young men. They're not well. They have weak kidneys. They'll die young."

Moses' sharp tongue could not always quell disturbances. A gang of drunken rowdies tried to break up a campmeeting held near Catasauqua. As they came on through the dark woods they drove the worshipers before them. Suddenly Mose leaped in upon the crowd, calling out, "Stand your ground, brethren, don't go back any farther." Quickly he seized the leader and hurled him to the ground. He seized another and threw him to the ground, then calling out "Brethren take clubs and sail into them." He seized another and turned him in a somersault to the ground. The rowdies disappeared and the services proceeded in peace.

An Allentown paper published a report of this meeting, stating that the ministers had earnestly endeavored by their preaching to convert sinners, but there had been one among them who wanted to convert them with clubs. "Des war gewiss dar Mose [That surely was Mose]."

Mose made terrific attacks upon the coldness of formal religion within and without his denomination. While making such a denunciation at Ironton, several persons got up and walked out, and Mose loudly observed, "Turn the windmill and the chaff flies out back."

At another time when he made a similar denunciation two men arose and walked out and again, and quick as a flash came the parting shot, "I have seen before that dogs lying around the stove jump up and run out when boiling water was squirted upon them."

Mose liked movement in his sermons and in the services. At a prayer meeting which dragged Mose broke out with the words, "You hem and haw like a set of old mill wheels when there is not enough water to keep them going properly."

At Bernville he came to a church which few persons attended. He boldly announced that he would fill the church. At his first service he preached while he stood with one leg hanging over the pulpit. That was the only time he preached to an empty church in Bernville.

Mose had been compared to Billy Sunday. There are those who regard him as the greater. The Billy Sunday campaigns were thoroughly organized in the community by the various churches with enthusiasm but the elements of spontaneity were lacking. One wonders whether Billy Sunday had ever heard of Mose. There was a Sunday family at Schaefferstown during the lifetime of George Dissinger and there were also Sunday families in the Womelsdorf-Bernville region of Berks County.

While Mose was preaching at Ironton, a Reverend Doctor sent his grandson to hear him. He told how one evening a paper was sent up to the pulpit with a text on it and the request that Mose preach upon it. He took the paper, looked at it, scratched his head and said: "This is a critical text, brethren, but it will be rightly preached."

The story is told that one day while walking along the road he came to two men working on a stone heap. They got into an argument and became rather heated about the matter and suddenly Mose pushed one of the men against the other which sent both sprawling on the ground. As they got up one said: "Parre Dissinger, is des Christenthum?" The reply came: "Ne awwer er iss en verstand gelannt uff en Schteehaufe" [Pastor Dissinger, is this Christianity? No, but it's teaching another understanding on a heap of stones].

While preaching at a "bush meeting" near Scheidy's Mose became very much wrought up. He leaped up into the air. Coming down he broke through the improvised platform to the ground. But immediately bounding back he cried out without a pause in his address, "Gott sei dank es is nedd in die Hoelle gange." ("Thank God it didn't go all the way to Hell.")

He admonished converted people not to remain in a lifeless church where there are no prayer meetings and whose members are mostly wicked people. "The Bible compares the wicked to swine and the converted to sheep. Now swine and sheep don't suit together. Swine like to wallow in dirt, while sheep do not. Swine eat rotten flesh, while sheep live on clean food; and where so many hogs are there is scarcely anything but hog food which the sheep cannot eat and so these have to starve. The hogs multiply too, faster than do the sheep. Moreover the hogs devour the young sheep. Thus the hogs in a short time would prevail so that no sheep could live among them. Such living together is unbecoming."

We know of one occasion at least when Dissinger was outwitted in the City of Lebanon. Reverend Johnson of the Reformed Church once met him on the street and said, "Mose we are going to put a cross on our church." "Is that so?" said Mose, "Why don't you put a mule there?" "We were considering that," replied Reverend Johnson, "but we concluded that you would be too heavy."

In one of his circuits Moses came into contact with an independent clergyman. One evening when a number of this man's followers were present he spoke thus, "If you were not such a low and ungodly people you would feel ashamed to have such a vagabond for your preacher. I will take a rag, dip it in whisky and drag it on the road for ten miles, and I will bet anything that your drunken priest will soon get the scent of it and will chase it like a hound after a fox, and you fellows all after him, for you all like to suck at the whisky rag."

In a short time Dissinger had driven the preacher out of the neighborhood.

This Boanerges frequently attacked the prevailing fashions. On one occasion while thus holding forth his wife entered the meeting house wearing a new hat. The preacher stopped, and then exclaimed, "And here comes my wife with the corner cupboard on her head." The explanation is that Mose sold a corner cupboard, maybe one that he, himself, had made, and his wife took the money and bought a hat with it.

In Allentown after a series of meetings he said, "Now I am going to do something that the devil never did in his life, I'm going to leave Allentown."

Mose had a habit of preaching against the devil, who was very real and very personal to him. One day in going down Hamilton Street in Allentown he passed a crowd of smart aleck loafers on one of the street corners, and as he passed they jeeringly asked, "Well Mose, how's the Devil today?" But Mose was ready for them and he replied, "Boys, I am glad to hear that you are concerned about the health of your father."

The Gadarene swine were a favorite illustration for Dissinger. Once when he was holding services in Northampton County a crowd of fellows created a disturbance in the rear of the room. He paused in his sermon to deliver this blast. "Once upon a mountain the devils which had been driven out of men went into swine, and the swine threw themselves into the depths of the sea. And lo these many years they have been lost, but now behold they are found. Back there they sit and the devils are still in them."

Dissinger on one occasion, in 1861, was preaching at Emaus (now Emmaus). A young man who had professed his faith found opposition to his action on the part of some person in that community. This brought forth the following:

"Here in Emaus there is a particular kind of a devil. Such devils as are found here I have not met in all my life. Here if a man seeks conversion, the devil certainly will set half a dozen dogs on him to drive him off. Up there, in yonder rum-hole they can lounge about and go on drinking day and night, and he doesn't care. But if anyone wishes to be converted, you can see him running about town carrying a cane and wearing gloves and almost wearing his legs off to his knees, trying to lead that soul away. It happens, as Luther said, when a herd of swine is eating in a stable, and you take one out and cut its throat, the rest will eat on and not even look around to see the fate of the one that is being killed. So it is here; they drink on and don't look around until they are down in hell. This is the truth and I'm not afraid to tell the truth, though the devil should come walking on stilts."

Mose reached the heights of his denunciatory eloquence in his attacks upon drunkenness:

"Just look at the drunkards! These the devil has ruined so fearfully that one might think they could never in a whole lifetime be restored. Many of them have not only drunk away all human sense of honor so that they can do anything mean and dirty that the dirty devil in hell wants them to do, without feeling any shame; they have also guzzled away their understanding. There is scarcely anything of a real man left in them. The devil has made them his shoe cleaning rags, he has made nearly all of them crazy and mad; a great many of them have almost drunk away body and soul, and so they drink on until the Devil carries them down to hell whither all drunkards go.

"Now, take a good look at their outward appearance. They have noses like red peppers, ears like Fasnacht cakes, bellies like barrels, and they make faces like foxes eating wasps; but in spite of it all, they go on drinking; they jump for the rum bottle like bullfrogs for red rags. If we did not know that Jesus Christ has received such degraded men and made honorable men of them, we could not hope that such drunken rumrats could ever be delivered from the devil of drink. But Jesus Christ has obtained grace for all sinners, and even those who are the most deeply sunk in the mire of sin are not excluded. By the power of the gospel the most wretched drunkard can be saved and gifted with power, so that he could swim in a stream of rum reaching to his mouth without the desire to drink of it; and even if the devil should offer it to him, he could, by the power of grace in the Gospel, resist the devil, and no devil in hell could force him to the accursed drinking of rum. Be ye, therefore, converted!"

Complaint was once made by a woman who was a member of the church that the minister never called at her house. It was an open secret that the reason for this was the filthy condition of her house. Mose said he would accept her invitation to dinner and see whether he could not induce her to adopt more sanitary methods. When called upon to ask the blessing at the table, he did it in this fashion:

"God bless this dirty woman; God bless this dirty food; and God bless poor Mose, who must eat it!"

At a campmeeting in Northampton county a clergyman of another persuasion took a seat on the side intended for women, the rules of that day, as earlier in New England, demanding a segregation of the sexes. During the singing he would not rise; during the prayer he would not kneel, showing utter disregard for the rules of the meeting. The next day Mose preached upon observing proper order in worship. "But I don't want you to do as that stupid ox did yesterday who sat among the women wearing his stovepipe hat, who did not rise for singing, nor kneel for prayer, nor even take off his hat. I don't want you to behave as that ox behaved."

Dissinger once went with one of his colleagues to the funeral of a young man who had lived a notoriously sinful life. The officiating clergyman preached on the text, "Because I live ye shall live also," and during his discourse cast aspersions upon the methods of working which were used by Dissinger and others. The sermon cut Dissinger to the quick and he had it made known that he would preach on the same text on the coming Sunday so that justice might be done to it. When the time came he opened up in this wise:

"Now I'm going to preach on the text which the priest out yonder chewed up so badly. God in heaven knows how much pity I have felt for this text. It has seemed to me just as if you had thrown a bag full of oats to a hog and left the bag tied up. The hog will sniff around it, smell that there is something there, but cannot get at it. Just so, that godless preacher went around his text, smelling that there is something there; he sniffed it over, chewed it all up, and yet he failed to find the grain. But, today justice shall be done to the text. God's eternal truth contained in the text shall now be preached."

### A Co-Worker Looks at Mose

Reverend William Yost, a life long friend, writes in his *Reminiscences:*

"His enthusiasm at revivals and campmeetings knew no bounds. Without any intermission he kept on singing, praying, shouting and working with penitents at camp meetings and quarterly meetings from morning till night, and during the night until the sun rose, being gifted with unusual powers of physical endurance.

"He became known throughout the church as a very singular man and everywhere people came in crowds to see and hear this marvelous preacher. He hurled divine truth with the force of a Titan. He was as bold as a lion and knew no fear. He was gifted with a marvelous memory. What he read and heard his memory retained, and he could use the knowledge acquired in his own peculiar manner. . . . What he learned from others was so mingled up with the product of his own mind that it seemed to come from its native mint.

"Though scarcely able in the first years of his ministry to read his text correctly, yet he would preach with such fluency, originality and power that it was a marvel to all who heard him.

"He was much given to prayer and study, spending hours, on his knees praying, or reading the Bible, and studying his sermons. Wherever he was staying, when the time for going to the service had arrived he would withdraw for secret prayer, saying, 'I must talk with the Father before going to meeting.'

"It was his custom to call praying, talking with the Father. He had a marvelous gift in prayer. I doubt whether I ever heard him pray in houses of worship and at campmeetings that the place was not shaken and the people simultaneously sprang to their feet while shouts of joy and cries of mercy filled the place. At family worship where he had lodged for the night, he would pray until every converted member of the family was either leaping for joy or shouting aloud the praises of God. He frequently made the remark, the devil must be whipped before breakfast. He will then easily stay whipped the whole day! In company with him at camp-meetings, when the time approached that he was to preach he would say to me, 'Let us go out in the woods. We must talk with the Father. I am to preach and you know I'm only one of the Lord's sprinkling cans: if he doesn't fill it with water fresh from the throne, I am walking around the garden endeavoring to water the Lord's plants with an empty can and the devil would laugh at me. I can only give to the people what the Lord gives to me.'

"His sense of humor and his sarcasm were manifest on numerous occasions. At a campmeeting where he knew members were much opposed to fashions he preached from the text, 'Deliver us from evil,' and said: 'You will observe that these words do not apply to the ungodly who are as full of evil as a dog is of fleas, but to the Christians, and teaches that they have evils from which they must be delivered. Here is pride by which some, especially women, so transform themselves that they look anything else than human beings, and frighten horses on the road.'

"His words brought forth a chorus of amens. It was the day of hoop skirts. Mose continued: 'There is another evil, the greatest of all and the root of all. It is stinginess.'

"The pews were silent. The amen corner was still. Mose continued: 'Brethren, what's the matter? Why don't you shout amen? When I preached about pride you shouted amen as if your throats would burst; now when I preach about stinginess, the highest of all evils, you hang your heads, and pinch your lips so closely together that a man could not drive a hog bristle through with a sledge hammer.' "

### Character and Traits of Dissinger

His was a most remarkable personality. Rev. William Yost said of him, "He was a unique character, and extraordinary man, both in body and mind, gifted with tireless energy, an original, peculiar personage, the like of which our church has never had and never again will have in its ministry." He embodied in his character such singular eccentricities, such original and peculiar traits that it is wholly impossible for anyone, we believe, to make a clear satisfactory statement about a man like he was, that such a character as he possessed defies formal analysis, because some things in life must be perceived rather than expressed in order to communicate them. So in this topic we shall not attempt to analyze his character nor make an estimate of the works and influence of his life, for such a life as he lived cannot be measured by any rules formulated by mere man. What we would do is only to discuss the characteristics and traits that Moses was endowed with, that permeated his whole being, and which manifested themselves in his every word and deed,—that so endeared him to all who knew him.

Only a few words of an outstanding physical trait: his great strength and unbounded nervous energy. Moses would himself say to his older children that at times he felt that he was a head taller and possessed of unusual strength. He told them how, in his youth, he would climb to the top-most branches of trees, swing on them by his hands, then allow his body to drop through the air and catch hold of another limb beyond, just as one sees circus performers swinging from one trapeze to another. These unusual physical exertions and activities of his body and limbs, as a growing boy, undoubtedly gave later life; qualities he retained until to his last illness, for his habits of living were regular, cleanly and with no let up in doing exercise of some kind. That he was a natural born athlete is evidenced by his ability to easily vault over the back of a horse even at 50 years of age. Being far stronger than the average man, he delighted at times to show it; not in the way of a braggart, but in a natural feeling of elation in being able to lend a helping hand to some seemingly impossible task. He was prone to relate incidents of such a nature to his children, seated on his knee, and would chuckle at the recollection of these incidents,—for he never laughed aloud, only a low suppressed laugh. We may relate here several such incidents that he told his children. He once came upon a laborer unsuccessfully trying to move a heavy log. Telling the man to seat himself upon it, Mose lifted both man and timber moving it to the desired place. Then he related of a place in Penna. where the bully of the town was present at church services and caused much disturbance while prayer was going on. So Moses took the fellow by the nape of the neck and seat of his trousers, yanked him down the aisle, and threw him bodily through the door with a tremendous heave, so that the fellow landed prone on the ground with an audible thud. With the usual chuckle, Moses then added how this same man had invited him to dine in his home several days after the affair; which Moses did!

He had a great sense of humor! never forced. Its originality made it irresistible and flowed naturally from his alert mind. He loved to tell a good story, and delighted in harmless little jokes. For instance, while holding one of his grandchildren on his knee, he would suddenly pull off his wig, and the surprise shown on the face of the little one would amuse him immensely. As a dispenser of cheer and gladness he was hard to excel, and in his inimitable phrasing of the Penna-German dialect in uttering both words of a humorous or serious nature, he has never been even equalled. Though his humor was at times sarcastic and critical, as well as grotesque, when he thought that such was deserved, yet never was it coarse nor vulgar. His manners in this respect were beyond reproach, for though he was never proud nor "high-hatted" yet he possessed of a very refined nature. To see him smile, to hear his words of cheer made weary people laugh and forget their fatigue, made sad people smile and, for a time, forget their sorrows, made people who were straying from the fold to have a renewal and strengthening of faith; and made men holding different views forget them, for the moment, and listen attentively to his eloquence.

Even his voice and speech had the stamp of his marked individuality. His voice was not gruff, nor was it shrill; yet it was very penetrating and possessed great carrying power. Rev. John Wuerth, of Kansas, said that he once heard Moses pray with such power that he surely thought the walls of the church would collapse, for they seemed to tremble as from an earthquake. It is also related that in Lehigh County, Penna., in a campmeeting grove, Moses yelled so fearfully that the horses were frightened and had to be held and calmed by their owners. Then his enunciation was very clear and distinct; also decidedly rapid, when we consider that he always spoke German, which is a rather drawling tongue.

Shortly before his last illness, in a sermon on the Redeemed Multitude (mentioned in Revelation Chapter 7), he became quite dramatic. Kneeling over the pulpit steps, he illustrated how the redeemed would dip water out of the stream of heavenly life; and when he uttered these words, "and God shall wipe away all tears from their eyes,"—he stepped off the pulpit and drawing forth his handkerchief, he wiped the flowing tears from the face of an aged man. This gesture made an overwhelming impression upon the congregation, who sat spell-bound, their moist eyes riveted upon the solemn dramatics so unconsciously played by their minister.

On another occasion, Moses preached to a vast throng at the campmeeting. His theme was the Translations of Elijah, this being one of his favorite texts. In this sermon he gave a very vivid description of the heavenly chariot with its fiery steeds sweeping down to earth from the

Heavens. Just as the chariot reached the earth, Moses, in imitating the prophet, stepped forward toward the chariot. At this very instant he removed his coat, and, like a flash, tossed it about his shoulders as one would a cloak. This being significant of the mantle of the prophet, Elijah. Then stepping into the imaginary chariot, with his face directed toward heaven, and with a burst of sunlight suffusing his sober features, he repeated solemnly the lines of a German hymn, beginning with the words, "Von fern glaenzt mir mein Kleinod zu." (From afar shines my salvation upon me.) The people sprang to their feet, and rushed forward over the benches to kneel at the altar as if drawn by a mighty, irresistible whirlpool.

### Reverend Dissinger Pays His Respects to Two of His Cloth
He never ignored facts nor lied about them.

Reverend B., a Lutheran minister and a publisher of children's papers and German almanacs, and Reverend A., a Baptist minister, had criticized him about this, which was perfectly natural, for it is not the tree casting the longest shadow that is dubbed and stoned the most but the one that has the finest nuts or the most luscious fruit on it. He made many a scornful dog eat dirty pudding; there was always savor and flavor in his denunciations. He had no regard for formal and lifeless preachers and of course his sermons were never so polished as to be pointless. One evening after he was tuned up he relieved himself in this wise: "I have been and am slandered by my own kith and kin. When I preached at Cedarville there was a red devil that persecuted me saying that I had been a clown in a New Jersey circus. I have shaken him off and when I came here I had thought that I was rid of all persecutors. But, Oh I had thought that I was rid of all persecutors. But, Oh No! For the first thing I knew, a certain minister in this city commenced to hound me, you know who he is, he is an almanac maker and prints a children's paper. Well I downed him and I expected that I would have rest but, No! The next thing I knew this water dog down here (meaning the Baptist minister) is after me. But so it goes in this wicked world. If you get rid of one devil you will have two new ones in his place. "Great fleas have little fleas upon their backs to bite them, and little fleas have lesser fleas so ad infinitum!"

While preaching to a mixed audience among whom were a lot of unseasoned young men—speckled rowdies—on wailing and gnashing of teeth and the damnation of the wicked, and a half dozen of the young, defiant of decency, who had no regard for the words, "My son hear the instructions of thy father and forsake not the law of the mother," demeaned themselves badly, he said, "Please give me your undivided attention for a few minutes and I will tell you the direct road to hell." They got up and started for the door. He continued, saying, "I see you know the route already, when you come home tell your mother who gave you suck when you were babies, that when I proposed to tell you the route to hell I learned that it was not necessary because you knew it already. Proceed my young knickknackers, you are going in the right direction." The boys were fully convinced that the parson was champion at stone throwing.

# Parre Schtories

The following anecdotes, jokes, or stories were told by Professor Albert F. Buffington in a column in the Allentown *Morning Call* during late summer and fall of 1961. Professor Buffington served as guest columnist for Professor Preston A. Barba of Muhlenberg College, who regularly edited " 'S Pennsylvanisch Deitsch Eck, Devoted to the Literature, Lore, and History of the Pennsylvania Germans." Buffington was a professor of German at the Pennsylvania State University and later at Arizona State University. He was a specialist in the nature of the dialect, also a collector of stories, songs, and sayings.

I have translated these stories from the dialect. However, Buffington reminds us in his introductory comments that the "jokes" usually "sound funnier when told in the dialect. There is something in the nature of the Pennsylvania German dialect itself which tends to make the jokes funnier." The reader is encouraged to read the stories in the dialect, which is not difficult to master once one settles on the orthography.

The stories were collected by Professor Buffington over many years in interviews of country stores and inns (*Wattsheiser*), and at various Dutch "Versammlinge." What is of special interest to us are the "Parreschtories." These are stories and jokes told about the Pastor/Preacher, who was so close to the everyday life of the people. The stories reveal a certain attitude toward the sacred that belongs to the democratic spirituality of the Dutch.

Here is a translation of Buffington's own introduction to the "Parreschtories": "The Pennsylvania Dutch like their pastors. That is, of course, the reason why they tell so many stories about them. If they did not like their pastors, it would have been no fun to tell stories about them.

"One of the first of the Pennsylvania Dutch tellers of "Parreschtories" was Parre (Pastor) Daniel Miller of Reading, and several of the stories that he told in his books of 1903 and 1911 I have heard told (sometimes in different forms) in almost all of the counties where Pennsylvania Dutch is spoken. . . ."

In this way Professor Buffington reminds us that many of those responsible for the preservation of Dutch culture and spirituality were the pastors. They were often the storytellers and the collectors. They told stories about their own profession because they knew that the people wanted to remember that they were human, that the good Lord was no respecter of hierarchy or "highfalutin' " people. He loved the simple folks who enjoyed the earth and learned to live with tears as well as laughter. The Dutch like the saying: "Wie Gelehrter, wie Verkehrter" (The more learned, the more mixed up).

*(The following stories are translated from their dialectic versions in the Allentown* Morning Call.*)*

### A Blabbermouth

One Sunday morning as the Pastor was making his way to Hill Church, he passed by Charlie Boyer's house, and there in the orchard he saw Charlie burning brushes. This made the Pastor feel very bad, especially since Charlie was a deacon in the church.

So the Pastor tied up his horse and walked over to Charlie. "I never would have expected this," said the pastor. "You should be in church and here you are burning brush."

"Yes, I know," replied Charlie, "but I didn't believe that you would see me."

"That wouldn't make any difference," said the Pastor. "There is one above who would've seen you anyhow."

"Yes, that's true," answered Charlie, "but he isn't a blabbermouth like you are."

### Too High and Mighty

Several years ago there was a church in Lancaster County that was very, very snobbish. The members of this church were understood to stick their noses much higher in the air than other folks.

Well, Sam Lattschaw heard about this church, so when he sold his farm and moved to Lancaster, he wanted to join it. He went and talked to the Pastor about it. The Pastor told him he would discuss it with the deacons and then tell Sam what had been decided.

So the Pastor talked it over with the deacons, but they were all opposed. Sam was not really aristocratic enough. The Pastor called Sam and told him what had happened. He also told him he should call upon God for counsel and advice. Well, about a week later the Pastor met Sam, and asked him whether he had called upon God for advice.

"Yes," said Sam, "I have, and do you know what God said? He said I shouldn't feel bad about it; he himself had tried to get into that church for twenty years."

### Too Much Christianity

This is a story that I have heard very often over in Macungie. The story is supposed to be true.

Years ago there was an old doctor by the name of Katerman, who lived over in Macungie, who had sent his son away to school to study to be a doctor. The old doctor was already quite old, and had thought it would be nice if his son could take over his practice after he couldn't get around anymore. So when the young man graduated from medical school, he came home to help out his father.

The first day that the boy was home, the old doctor said to him: "Well, Henry, today I will take you with me as I make my rounds to see my patients. At the first place, I will take care of things and you can watch the way I do it, then at the second place you can handle things."

Well, at the first place they came to, there was a man sick in bed. The old doctor examined him, then said to him: "The trouble is you have too much patent medicine in you. You have to give that stuff up, and you'll get well again."

When the old doctor and his son were outside again, the young man asked his father: "Say, Pop, how did you know that that man is taking too much patent medicine?"

"Oh," said the old doctor, "you must keep your eyes open a little better. Didn't you see all the empty bottles standing around?"

"No," said the son, "I didn't notice that."

Well, about that time they came to the next place. There was a good looking woman sick in bed. The young doctor examined her, and after he was finished, he said to her: "The trouble is, there is too much Christianity in you. You have to give it all up, then you will be well again."

When the young man and the old doctor were outside again, the old man asked him: "What in the devil made you tell that woman she had too much Christianity in her?"

"Why," asked the son, astonished, "didn't you see the pastor lying under the bed?"

*(The above three stories are from the Allentown* Morning Call, *August 5, 1961.)*

### An Easter Story

Once there was a Pastor down in Lancaster County who wanted to do something special for a beautiful Easter service. So he went to the janitor and said: "Harry, I'd like you to go over to the Boyer's and ask them for a white dove. Then bring it over here on Saturday evening before Easter, and take it up in the church tower and leave it till the next day. Then, when it's time for the service, go up into the tower, get the dove, and when

I say in my sermon: 'And the Spirit of the Lord descended like unto a dove,' open the little window that opens into the church, and let the dove fly."

Well, all the arrangements were made. Sunday morning the Pastor began preaching. When he came to the words: "And the Spirit of the Lord descended like a dove," nothing happened. So he repeated the same words, but much louder. But nothing happened. Then he shouted again: "And the Spirit of the Lord descended like a dove," and finally Harry stuck his head through the little window and shouted down: "Pastor, the black cat ate the white dove last night—shall I throw the cat down?"

### Be Quiet, Old Man

One Sunday a father said to his son: "John, today you are going to church, and I want no arguments."

"But Pop," answered John, "you know that I've never been in church. I don't know how to act."

"Well," said the father, "you just go in and sit down where no one else is sitting. All you have to remember is not to talk, or else they'll throw you out."

"Well, okay," replied John, "I'll go once." But John was a little late, and when he arrived at the church, all the seats were full. There was only one place empty, and it was up front in the chancel, where the preacher was supposed to sit. But John walked right up and sat down. After a while the Pastor came up to the chancel, and when he saw John, he asked him: "How is this? Am I to preach today, or are you going to do it?" At first John kept very quiet and said nothing.

Then the Pastor asked again: "How is this? Should I preach today or do you want to?" Then John leaned over and whispered in the Pastor's ear: "Old man, be quiet, or by damned they'll throw the both of us out."

*(The above two stories are from the Allentown* Morning Call,
*August 19, 1961.)*

### No Hurry

They tell a story about another Pastor who also lived down in Lancaster County. He was very nearsighted.

Well, one Monday afternoon the Pastor went to visit some of his members who lived on a large farm. When he got there, there was no one around; they were all working out in the field. So, in order to pass the time, the Pastor decided to walk around the yard a bit, but because he couldn't see especially well, he accidentally fell into a well. Fortunately it wasn't a very deep well, and there wasn't a whole lot of water in it. However, the Pastor immediately began shouting and screaming as loud as he could. And the people in the fields heard and came running to see what was the matter. When they found the Pastor in the well, one of the fellows was sent to fetch a rope. But the Pastor became very impatient and shouted up: "Tell him he should hurry!"

"Ach, Pastor," shouted one of them, "be patient! We really don't need you until Sunday."

(Allentown Morning Call, August 12, 1961.)

# LIFE OF HENRY HARBAUGH

As stated in the introduction to this chapter, Henry Harbaugh was the German Reformed pastor who is in many ways the quintessential Pennsylvania Dutchman. Unlike Dissinger, he was educated at Marshall College and the German Reformed Theological Seminary in Mercersburg, Pennsylvania. He had been raised on the family farm near Waynesboro, just eighteen miles east of Mercersburg. Like Dissinger, he was also of the folk. But he was of a family that was closely linked to its Reformation heritage. Harbaugh was restless as a farmer, and wandered into Ohio, where he worked as a carpenter and sang in the choirs of neighborhood churches. When he returned to Pennsylvania to seek formal education and ordination, he began a career of profound contribution to American religion and the life of his people, the Dutch.

Harbaugh was a unique representative of the high tradition of the church, as it combined and embraced the more romantic and sensual piety of folk traditions. He was a successful pastor in Lewisburg, Lancaster, and Lebanon before becoming a professor of theology at the seminary in Mercersburg. Harbaugh had learned a great deal from his old mentor, John Williamson Nevin, and became a spokesperson and interpreter of Mercersburg theology. He was gifted as a liturgist, poet, and preacher; and became a champion of the folk culture. It was the eminent historian, Philip Schaff, who encouraged Harbaugh to publish poetry in the dialect. Prior to this, all writing and publication among Pennsylvania's Germans had been done in the Hochdeutsch, the High German language of European ancestry. An entertaining storyteller, Harbaugh may be considered quintessential of those Lutheran and Reformed pastors who were to become the primary conservers and transmitters of Pennsylvania German spirituality.

*(The following three selections all appear in the* Life of Henry Harbaugh, *by his son Linn Harbaugh, Esq. The first is from the Introduction by Nathan C. Schaeffer to* Life of H. Harbaugh, D.D. *Philadelphia: Reformed Church Publication Board, 1900)*

I saw and heard Dr. Harbaugh but once. It was a rare privilege. It deepened the impression which his articles in the *Guardian* had made, and greatly enhanced the high estimate which I had formed of his genius. The occasion was the commencement banquet of Franklin and Marshall College in the year 1866. We undergraduates were not allowed to participate in the feast; but when the part of the program which consisted of toasts was reached, the alumni adjourned to the main auditorium of Fulton Hall (since converted into an opera house), and this gave me the opportunity to hear Dr. Harbaugh's response to the toast, "The Mercersburg Review." Its humor and delivery made a deeper impression than the oratory of all the eminent men at home and abroad whom I have had the good fortune to hear at banquets, in the pulpit or from the rostrum. This may be due to the fact that the speech was delivered in the dialect of my boyhood. He had shown the poetic possibilities of the Pennsylvania German in the pages of the *Guardian;* he was now to prove its power and fitness for the purposes of an after-dinner speech. When the toast was announced, he attracted attention by walking forward after the manner of an old farmer, pulling off a slouch hat with both hands, and catching a red bandanna handkerchief as it dropped from his forehead. His first sentence,

"Es gebt gar greislich gelerente Leut, und Ich bin awe aner dafun,"

(There are some very learned people, and I am one of 'em,) sent a flash of merriment through the assemblage. When he proceeded to enumerate the learned languages—

"Es gebt sieva gelehrte Sproche, Englisch und Deutsch, Lateinisch und Griechish und Hebraeisch; sell sin funf. Die sechst haest Pennsylvania Deutsch, die sievet is German Reformed,"—

(There are seven learned languages, English and German, Latin and Greek and Hebrew; these are five. The sixth is called Pennsylvania German, the seventh is German Reformed,—)

there were shouts of laughter over the entire hall. The merriment reached its climax when he referred to the venerable Dr. John W. Nevin as

"Der Chon Nevin, do navig mir."
(John Nevin, here beside me.)

The applause then was like that of a great convention and lasted for some time. The impression made by his enumeration of the contributors and by his description of the work it accomplished before its publication was suspended is evident from the fact that the *Review* was revived, and under different names its publication has been continued to the present time.

Dr. Harbaugh was a typical Pennsylvania German. The dialect and its range of ideas he acquired at his mother's knee and from the companions of his childhood and youth. His powers of work and his love of fun were developed under the tutelage of the old farm and under the influence of its customs, traditions and forms of speech. He was thoroughly familiar with the homes and habits, the social and religious life of the Pennsylvanians of German ancestry. He knew their merits, foibles, and shortcomings, their peculiar ways and superstitions, their highest hopes and noblest emotions. He admired their frankness and simplicity, their thrift and industry, their honesty and integrity. He shared their fondness for good meals, their sense of humor, their hatred of every form of sham and humbug. He summed up in his personality and exemplified in his life the best characteristics of these people. Of all the men whom they have given to the world, he was the most gifted and the most productive from a literary point of view. Even in his criticism of the common school system he reflected their views, their fears and their prejudices. Had he lived to our time he would have accepted, as a fixed fact among all civilized nations, schools supported by taxation; and he would have been untiring in the effort to put into these schools teachers of the highest skill and the most unblemished character.

Dr. Harbaugh was more than a Pennsylvania German. He mastered the English so well that his style was envied and admired by many whose mother tongue was English and who had enjoyed far superior educational advantages. Such was his command of Anglo-Saxon words that many of his sentences consist almost entirely of monosyllables. . . . He always aimed to make his discourses intelligible and had little patience with those who cannot or will not make their ideas clear to their audiences. His assimilation of the fruits of scholarship and sound learning was thorough and rapid, yet he never drifted away from the common people. He voiced their sentiments and aspirations in prose and poetry, and sought to bring absolute and eternal truth within the comprehension of the humblest. His talks to children made a lasting impression upon all who attended his Sunday School. Several of the hymns which he wrote have come into general use and are now helping to stimulate the hopes, to enrich the devotions, and to elevate the aspirations of Christian worshipers wherever the English language is spoken. The best thoughts of the best men were his special delight. Everything human and divine had an interest for him. By taking up into himself the best things in literature and the humanities he became a representative of humanity in the best and broadest sense of the term. Jesus Christ was the centre of his thinking, his affections, his purposes, and everything that he wrote and spoke was intended to build up the Kingdom of God.

As a preacher he had few equals and no superior in the Reformed Church. His sermons were fresh, interesting, instructive, and edifying. An audience composed largely of students and professors is very hard to please and very difficult to hold. Of their own accord the students of the college flocked to his church and filled its pews. With pleasure and profit they listened to his lectures on cultus and on the Heidelberg Catechism as well as to his regular sermons. . . .

The letters which he wrote at different periods form a very interesting study, because they show how a boy of Pennsylvania German parentage may gradually acquire the graces of style and diction in another tongue. The life which is here given to the public is from the pen of his son, with whom it has been a labor of love. In my judgment, the most glowing tribute ever paid to the genius of Dr. Harbaugh is from the pen of his life-long friend and successor in the chair of dogmatic theology, Dr. E. V. Gerhart, who has at my request consented to its publication in this memorial volume. . . .

*(From "In Memoriam to the Rev. Henry Harbaugh, D.D.," by the Rev. Emmanuel V. Gerhart, D.D., L.L.D., March 2, 1868; also from Linn Harbaugh's life of his father.)*

Dr. Harbaugh challenges our attention as *a man.* Born in a Pennsylvania German family consisting of twelve children, of whom he was the tenth; brought up on a farm at the foot of the South Mountain; trained by an honest and industrious father, and by a gentle, pious, and noble mother; moulded by the customs, manners and habits prevailing in the social life of our German population; baptized into the communion of Christ's mystical body; carefully instructed in the doctrines and duties of our holy religion, and gifted with a rare combination of extraordinary natural endowments, he grew up into youth and manhood in the element of German *Gemuethlichkeit,* sanctified by the grace of the Christian Church. He realized in his person, in body, mind and spirit, the richness and beauty of the German character, as strengthened by genius and ennobled by living faith in Jesus Christ.

He was a representative man. This he was in relation to the race. The true idea of a man, or the ideal type of manhood, was individualized in his spirit and character. So it is in a measure in every man. But in Dr. Harbaugh the individualization answers more fully to the generic type than is common, even among devoted ministers of the Gospel. Nature and feeling were held subordinate to understanding; understanding to reason; reason, to faith. Mind ruled the body; spirit ruled the mind; and Christ ruled the spirit. . . .

But his character as a man, true as it was to the generic type, was just as distinctive of the *national* life in which he stood. Dr. Harbaugh was a German; not an Englishman, nor a Scotsman, much less a Frenchman; but a German, an American German, from head to foot. The blood of a Pennsylvania farmer flowed in his veins, and with his mother's milk he drank in *das tiefe gemuethliche Wesen* [the profound congeniality] of the German farming population. In all his moral and religious instincts he was one of themselves. He understood their prejudices, lived in their modes of thought, shared their feelings, and sympathized with them in all their religious and educational needs. He loved their language, their peculiar homely dialect, and rescued it, as Burns did the Gaelic dialect, from death and oblivion by the baptism of his genius. Of all the sons of the German fathers of Pennsylvania who have sought the halls of learning and entered the sphere of the liberal professions, he is the first one, that, seeing the capabilities of a dialect, before only neglected and despised, and laying hold of it with new-creating energy, wrought it into the genuine forms of living poetry and breathed into these forms the genial spirit of their own social life, thus at once ennobling the dialect by consecrating it to the spiritual ends of fine art, and clothing it with honor and immortality. To him belongs the honor of being, as he has been called, the poet of the American German people. He is their true representative man, the representative of their genius on the elevated plane of religion, science, and art. . . .

The most prominent trait in his Christian character was devotion to the person of Jesus Christ, and to His mystical body, the Church;—devotion to Christ as God manifest in the flesh, really present and living in His mystical body on earth throughout all the ages and in the midst of all the contradictions and convulsions of time;—a devotion that was intelligent, intense, exclusive, all-absorbing, steady and unfaltering, always fresh and always vigorous. Devotion to Christ and devotion to the Church were inseparable. The Church was the original human life created anew by the Holy Ghost and perfected in the person of Christ; perpetuated by the same divine agency through the sacrament of Holy Baptism; nourished and matured by the preaching of the Gospel and the Communion of the Body and Blood of the Son; existing on earth, in time and space, in the form of an organized kingdom, which as to its constitution is both divine and human, as to its manifestation is both visible and invisible. It was the true and only Noachian Ark to which all men must flee for deliverance from the overwhelming curse of sin. To labor in the Church and for the Church, was, for him, to labor for Christ. The notion that a man may either come to Christ, or labor for Christ, apart from and outside of the Church, was a delusion, fraught with tendencies towards infidelity. . . .

Paradoxical as it may sound, yet it is but the simple truth to say, that Dr. Harbaugh had but little, or no concern about his personal salvation. He took God at His word. He believed Christ and His salvation to be sealed to Him in the sacramental acts of God; and he believed this so firmly that the dark shadows of doubt or fear rarely, if ever, disturbed his peace. His was the objective assurance of salvation. He did not look into himself for the evidence of forgiveness. He did not analyze his spiritual feelings to find out whether he was a Christian, just as he did not analyze his natural feelings to find out whether he was a man. To him one process was as vain as the other. But relying on the word and sacramental acts of Jesus Christ, who can neither lie nor deceive, he felt himself standing as on an immovable rock, and he looked forward to his resurrection from the dead and his ultimate glorification in heaven as certain and necessary facts, rejoicing in hope with unspeakable joy. . . .

I shall conclude by merely summing up the results of this review of our sainted brother's life.

The central idea may be expressed by saying that the spirit and genius of Dr. Harbaugh were in the true sense representative. He was a representative personality under every prominent aspect of his character. Whether we consider him simply as a man, an individual member of the race, or as an American German, an individual member of this particular nationality, the assertion is valid. He was a genuine man, realizing the rich truth of a noble manhood. He was a genuine Pennsylvania German; the best type, taken all in all, of German life, of German geniality, and German modes of thought, that has come to view in our day.

*(From* The Life of Henry Harbaugh *by his son Linn Harbaugh, Esq.)*

"Shame on him who will know nothing of his parentage," exclaimed Dr. Henry Harbaugh from his pulpit at Lancaster, Pa., in 1851. "Shame on him who disowns his ancestry; he reproaches the blood in his own veins. Both shame and sin on him who is ashamed of his countrymen; he brands himself as a hypocrite in the eyes of all nations! Yet there are those still who seem to think that he who speaks German is necessarily ignorant, and that he who understands two languages knows less than *he who knows but one!* This lowest of all prejudices is certainly held with consistency by the descendants of those who in 1727 remonstrated with Governor Keith against the naturalization of the Swiss and German settlers on the Pequea, urging among other things against them *'that they had resolved to speak their own language!!!' O jam satis."*

Upon another occasion he wrote:

No country lies so near heaven as Switzerland. Her eternal Alps are her fit monuments, at once the symbols of power and freedom; while the quiet valleys which they shelter and shade speak to us forever of peace and blessing.

It is intended herein to trace briefly the lineage of Henry Harbaugh, from the ancestral home in Switzerland down to his own life and times, and to offer something in support of the proposition that his deeply religious and poetic life, if nothing more, sprang through the influences of heredity from the very heart of the Swiss mountains.

In the Land Office at Harrisburg, Pa., there is a deed of record in which it appears that in 1739, *Joost Harbogh* was the owner of a tract of land of one hundred acres in what is now Berks County, three miles above Maxatawny creek. He came from Switzerland about the year 1736, and lived on this tract for about four years. After this he moved to the new settlement of Kreutz creek, west of the Susquehanna, where he cleared the land and built a substantial log house which was yet standing in the year 1836. It was forty feet square and the logs were of the choicest timber, all nicely hewn, some of them being as much as two feet broad. Westward from the site of this old house there is a gentle slope downward towards the spring; directly south of the spring was formerly the garden. Not many years ago there still grew some parsnips and larkspur along the fence which once bounded the old garden plot—the degenerated and lingering relics of ornament and use. Their dying and reviving each year seems to be a picture of how memory lingers and struggles to keep itself alive around the spot to which its fondest associations are bound.

Numerous German settlements were made on the banks of the Kreutz creek as early as 1736. Exiles from the Palatinate, they sought a new home where they hoped to live in peace; martyrs to the cause of Protestantism, they fled from the cruel religious persecutions of France and Germany, and expected to find a dwelling place where they could build anew their homes and their churches.

But in the place of receiving them kindly for their own sakes as well as for the sake of Him in whose cause they had suffered so much, the magnanimous government of Penn denied them a home for a time, and then after relenting so far as to allow them to remain, subjected them to great annoyances for many years.

The mode of life and surroundings of these early German settlers were truly primitive, simple, and severe. Here the young man and wife with a calm courage born in part at least of a hope for material prosperity, blazed a pathway through the forests and braved the dangers of the time.

Upon their arrival from the fatherland the first want of these hardy pioneers was to found a home. To clear away the forest and erect a good strong house of logs was the labor to which they first addressed themselves. Their furniture and conveniences of the household were of a rude sort, and their dress was simple, consisting of tow cloth almost wholly, until later when wool came to be an article obtainable in the markets. But there was a long time during which even a mixture of tow and wool was regarded as an article of luxury, and fortunate was he who could have it as a means of comfort in the winter months. In all that district around Kreutz creek there was neither shoemaker nor tanner, and shoes were brought annually from Philadelphia to supply the settlers. The mending was done by an itinerant cobbler who carried his little pack of leather used in the mending, with his tools, from one farm house to another. Tailors and blacksmiths were also itinerants. The same inconvenience attended the introduction of schools. The first schoolmaster was known only as "*Der Dicke* (thick) *Schulmeister*" and it goes without saying that he was crude in his art and often mercenary in his motives.

The privileges of the church could only be enjoyed by going to Lancaster, where a Reformed Church was built as early as 1736. It is said that "ministers from the other side of the river" were wont to come over once or twice a year to baptize the children. However, the lot for the Kreutz Creek Church was taken up October 27, 1746, and there was a church erected soon thereafter. The settlers maintained their religion and church services, though at times they were disheartened and scattered, only to be brought back again and provided with shepherds by such heroic missionaries as Zinzendorf, Muhlenberg, and Schlatter. . . .

Almost within the shadow of South Mountain, on the Pennsylvania-Maryland boundary line four miles southeast of Waynesboro, Pa., stands the old Harbaugh homestead. The house is a double front stone structure whose substantial walls, built in 1805, bid fair to weather the storms of another century, while its less durable companion piece, the school house at the creek, "right next to Daddy's House," lives only in the song of the "Harfe." Here amid the homely scenes of Pennsylvania-German country life, George Harbaugh and Anna his wife lived and reared their children, and here it was that Henry was born on October 28, 1817.

In after years, when visiting the old home, he was wont to stroll through every corner of the house from cellar to garret. Rummaging among the old lumber, usually stowed away in the garret, his eye fell upon the cradle, which he thus describes:

> There is one piece of furniture in the corner of the garret, the sight of which touches us more strangely than all the rest, and awakens feelings of a peculiar kind. It is the cradle in which we all—the boys and the girls—were rocked in infancy. It is of the old fashioned make, and never was capable of the long, gentle sweep and swing of the modern cradles. Broad and flat, with rockers well worn, it hath little grace in its motion, but waddles clumsily, like a duck. Yet sweet in it was the sleep, and pleasant were the dreams of infancy; and over no cradle, no, not in palaces, has a warmer mother's heart, or a more watchful mother's eye, ever hung and sighed, smiled, prayed, and wept. . . .

In "The Annals of the Harbaugh Family," Henry Harbaugh drew his own picture of his mother:

> In personal appearance she was not tall, but heavy. She always enjoyed good health; and even in her last years, retained a ruddy color, and when exercising freely had rosy cheeks. She was industrious, mild, and kind hearted to her children, and always good to the poor. At the time of my mother's death, I was in Ohio, and did not hear of her sickness till I heard of her death. I had spent the summer in Harrisonville and returned to Massilon in November, 1837. My cousin, residing there, had just received a letter containing the sad news for me; it having been directed to him because it was known at home that I expected about that time to be there. He immediately asked me to take a walk with him. We found our way into a woods south of town, where he opened to me the touching news. Her image came up to me, not as dead—for I could not see her so—but as she stood leaning upon the railing of the porch in tears, when I was entering the carriage to leave for the West, over a year before. In this way, and

in no other, have I seen her ever since. In this position only do I desire to see her—it is the best picture of her true character, always affectionate, bearing tenderly upon her heart of hearts the temporal and eternal good of her children. I cherish this image of my weeping mother. I can so easily transfer this recollection of her to the state of the glorified in Heaven, where all the beautiful is permanent. So will I see her, till I meet her in the bloom of immortal youth, clothed in the pure white robes of the sainted, in our Father's house above.

She used to say, "Give to the poor and you will always have." I suppose she learned this from an old Book that used to lie on the corner of the mantel, and over which she used to pore full many an hour. It pleaseth me greatly that I can recollect this of my mother, now that she sleeps in yonder grave. I never heard my mother boast of what she had done; when she gave, it was all so natural with her, and she did it so quietly—just as it is with a tree when it shakes off its ripe fruit.

My mother used to read the Bible and go to church. It seems as if I could still see the carry-all move round the corner of the orchard, towards the little village in which stood the church where our fathers worshipped. It was a plain way of going to church, but it was the way my mother went; and I verily believe she went with a good object in view; and it is doubtful in my mind whether it ever entered her mind that it was a shame to go to church in a carry-all. It is a long time since then, and times and customs have greatly changed, but still it giveth me much pleasure to think of the old Book on the end of the mantel, that my mother used to read on Sunday afternoons after she returned from church. I cannot get rid of the idea that it was her church-going, in connection with that Book, that made her so good a mother.

So Henry Harbaugh passed his boyhood, in the winter months at the school house by the creek; in the summer turning the hay rows or following after the grain cradles in the broad acres of the harvest field. Perchance he would steal away to the mountain side, there to commune with nature or to ponder over his well-thumbed book, away from the thoroughfares, far away from the towns where only the faintest din of the noisy work is heard and the tallest spire of the distant town is almost hid. Many an hour he spent watching the glistening surface of the winding stream or the tall poplars swaying in front of the quiet mountain brow afar off. An ideal place indeed for reading and study, where physical health makes meditation vigorous, and where separation from the great flow of busy life makes interruptions few.

Into his quiet retreats there crept many a rude, disturbing element, and when duty called him back to the farm he grasped the handles and plodded along behind the plow with a cheerfulness of spirit that sustained and strengthened his reluctant hand. But he was not simply a dreamer. Between brain and brawn there was a goodly balance wheel. He had no apology for idleness, which he characterized as a burden to oneself, a trouble to others, and an offense to God. But in the rhythm of nature he had an enduring part, and the ordinary incidents of labor led to reflections of mind. . . .

There were about 130 students at Mercersburg at the opening session of Marshall College and the Seminary in the fall of 1840. Henry Harbaugh was not regarded as one of the most promising among them. . . . He became a member of the literary society, which was conducted in the German language, and also one of the rival English societies. In *Die Deutsche Literarische Gesellschaft* he found opportunity to supplement his study of the German language, to exercise in the sound German words, and to become more fluent in the use of them. Criticism on the part of the various members was unsparing, and Henry Harbaugh was severely brought to frequently on account of his tendency to drift into the use of the Pennsylvania-German dialect—the language of his home.

He became a member of the Diagnothian Literary Society, in which English was used, and around which much of the charm of college life lay for him. . . .

He accepted an urgent invitation to go to Lewisburg, Pa., to preach for the people with a view of becoming their pastor. The former pastor had resigned owing to his inability to preach in the German language, and the people were rejoiced at the prospect of having a minister. Mr. Harbaugh's impressions of the town and country were very favorable. He pronounced it a beautiful place, and the people received him with a warmth and kindness that never abated in the least during his seven years' pastorate among them. . . .

He began his ministry in December, 1843, and was ordained on the 24th of January following. He found Lewisburg to be a town of considerable size, pleasantly located on the west branch of the Susquehanna river, about ten miles above the forks. It is in the historic Buffalo Valley in central Pennsylvania, amid fertile farm lands, bounded by the Blue mountains in the distance.

He found the German language difficult, especially in sermonizing, and once in a while his sermon was made singularly emphatic by a little hesitation and then the introduction of a broad, crisp Anglo-Saxon word in place of the German one that could not be recalled. After ten years of pulpit experience and no small amount of translating of the German language, he still found it something of an effort to preach the German, and a welcome relief to resort to English. . . .

The characters of Nevin, Schaff, and other men of the Mercersburg movement are not easily susceptible of comparison. In personality they differed widely. In their habits of work and thought they were far apart. Nevin was a teacher of teachers; Harbaugh was peculiarly a teacher of the people. Schaff and Nevin were to the church what an upright man should be in the national senate. Harbaugh was a commoner. Just as the ideal senator concerns himself with the great questions of state and thereby reflects back to the people a more perfect form of government, so Nevin championed the cause of Christ on the floor of the synod. Harbaugh came forth directly from the hearts of the people and brought their needs and interest up with him. The influence of great theologians tends from the seat of deliberative bodies back to those who created them; the influence of Harbaugh's life and teachings, on the contrary, originated in the homes and hearts of his people, and forged its way to centres that were even beyond the confines of his own branch of the church. But the attributes that were predominant in either of these fathers of the church were in a large measure common to all, and in their personal lives they were devoted and affectionate friends. . . .

If the tenderest theme of Dr. Harbaugh's whole life were capable of expression in one word, it would be *Home.* In fond recollection, it was the home of his childhood that found expression in "Heemweh" [home sickness], and other poems both in English and German, as well as in almost every number of the *Guardian,* during the early years of his ministry. In present enjoyment and affection, it was the family home—the sympathy and companionship of the wife of his mature years whom he called "the home of his heart."

In his deepest contemplation and spiritual longings, it was the heavenly home of which he said at the conclusion of his first published volume, "The Sainted Dead":

> Here I lay down my pen, but here do I not end my meditations on the heavenly land. My thoughts, and feelings, and hopes crowd onward still. Along the misty Jordan, which bounds the future side of this mortal life, I continue to walk up and down, crowding upon its awful confines, and looking anxiously across, till the fog breaks.

Then from the German of Stilling he quotes:

Blessed are they that are homesick, for they shall come to their father's house. . . .

The first published volume, "The Sainted Dead," grew out of a series of sermons which he delivered at Lewisburg as early as 1845, and after several years' meditation on the subject, he published the work in 1848. In gathering information on this interesting subject he was surprised to find that so little had been written directly on it. . . .

When he had finished the work it was laid unreservedly before his friend and teacher, Dr. John W. Nevin, with the request that he exercise critical censorship on the work without mercy. In the July number of the *Mercersburg Review* (1849) Dr. Nevin reviewed the book. . . :

A very popularly written volume on a popular and interesting theme, which needs only to be known generally, we think, to find many readers, and which, when it is seriously read, can hardly fail to leave behind it a salutary religious impression. The work of course is more practical than philosophical, designed to serve the purposes of believing piety rather than to minister food for curious speculation. At the same time the writer shows himself to be possessed of a good deal more learning, and philosophy too, than we meet with in many who put forth much larger pretensions in this form. Mr. Harbaugh is constitutionally a thinker, and not a mere dull retailer of other men's thoughts.

The habits of the preacher and the pastor, both vocations in which he is known to excel, are not allowed with him to mar the sympathies and affinities of the scholar; and the present production, in this view, is certainly very creditable to his literary character and powers, and carries in it also good augury for the time to come. The author has a certain advantage for the popular discussion of the subject he has taken in hand, in his temperament and age. The first includes a broad dash of mysticism; to the second he is indebted for an exuberance of imagination, which riper age will be apt considerably to tame, both qualifications well suited to help the mind forward, in such an excursion as is here made over the confines of time and sense, into the world of unseen mystery that lies beyond. There is nothing dark, however, nor particularly transcendental in the style of the work. Its poetry is not prose run made, or mounted on stilts into the region of the clouds, but clear, sensible thought and speech which as a general thing all sorts of readers may readily enough comprehend. Mr. Harbaugh uses a pen which is at once both fluent and correct.

After discussing the work on its theological side somewhat at length, Dr. Nevin closes with these words:

On the subject of the Church, as we have before said, as well as in its whole Christological theory, the little volume before us is far enough removed from the abstract spiritualism which has become so common in our modern divinity. One great object of the writer seems to be indeed to expel such spirituality of the mere intellect from our minds, and to make us feel that the mystery of the new life, as it is unfolded to us in Christ, is no less real and concrete and near to the world as it now stands, than are the palpable existences that surrounded us in the sphere of sense. . . .

The following words are taken from Dr. [Philip] Schaff's memorial sketch of Dr. Harbaugh, in the *Christian World* of January 9, 1868:

As the poet in the Pennsylvania-German dialect, he stands alone, if we except an isolated attempt made before, namely, the touching evening hymn, *"Margets scheent die Sunn so schoe* [the sun will shine beautifully tomorrow]," which was written by a Moravian minister (the late Rev. Mr. Rondthaler), and published, with some alterations, in Schaff's *Kirchenfreund* for 1849. I first directed his attention to his piece of poetry, and suggested to him the desireableness of immortalizing the Pennsylvania-German in song, before it dies out, as the Allemannian dialect has been immortalized by Hebel. He took up the hint and wrote his "Schulhaus an der Krick [schoolhouse by the creek]," which he modestly submitted to me, and which, when published in several newspapers, produced quite a sensation among the Pennsylvania-Germans, and found its way even to Germany. The "Heemweh" and other pieces followed from time to time in his *Guardian,* and were received with equal favor. These poems can, of course, only be fully appreciated in Pennsylvania; but in originality, humor, and genuine *Volkston* they are almost equal to the celebrated Allemannian poems of Hebel. They are pervaded, moreover, by a healthy, moral, and religious feeling.

# II

# JOURNALS AND OBSERVATIONS

The folk culture was in formation almost from the beginnings of German settlement. As a people being liberated from the hardships and oppressions of their European homelands, they were a pilgrim people wandering in a landscape where familiar boundaries did not exist. They were a marginal people living on the wilderness margins of a European world. No cathedral towers and town halls gave them perception. What they remembered of their church life and folk piety seemed quite removed and even inappropriate in this Land Promised to the Saints in the legends of home. They lived with memories and precious documents that survived the terrible transit of the Atlantic Ocean. They sought to adapt their spiritual and ecclesial life to the awesome circumstances of a world without markings.

Often their pilgrimages were exotic, sometimes frustrated. In this chapter, we gain insight from the writings of some of these pilgrims. Mittelberger observes spiritual chaos, sectarianism run amok. He discovers curious religious practices and the beginnings of the tradition of the American "preacher," that common person, the voice of the democratic religiosity of the people.

On the other hand, the mystical and theosophical heritage of Europe found a home in the New World wilderness. America in the early eighteenth century was charged with apocalyptic expectation. This mysterious land seemed to be the providential setting for the eschatological dreams of the unsettled centuries. Ancient wisdom combined with apocalypse in the creation of communities of the new age. However, the language of these holy experiments was a language that spoke to the needs of many who were not part of their activities. Ephrata was a symptom. It expressed the symbols of liberation and hope that have continued to reside in the folk spirituality of the Pennsylvania Dutch. The symbols we find in both art and poetry are drawn from the exotic iconography of Christian mystical and theolosophical tradition. The pelican, the lily, the dove, the unicorn, and the rose were the life-giving images of the people of eastern Pennsylvania. It is well for us to understand something of this early manifestation of folk spirituality. Much of the leadership and constituency of these movements was of the folk.

\*   \*   \*

No exploration of Pennsylvania Dutch folk spirituality would be complete without an introduction to the hermits and cloistered communities that gave themselves to prayer, contemplation, sacred music, holy work, and the cultivation of healing herbs. These were not Roman Catholics, but drew their spirituality from a wide variety of sources. They found meaning in the texts of the medieval mystics and in the writings of Jacob Boehme and Angelus Silesius. They listened to the esoteric chords of theosophy and watched the cherubic ascent of the cabbala. They were Pietists, Quietists, Dunkers, and independent charismatics; and they represented all walks of life and many levels of education. The followers of Johannes Kelpius who in 1694 settled on the banks of the Wissahickon Creek, just west of Philadelphia, were students of the occult as well as of confessional Christianity. The community that emerged from the settlement of Seventh-Day German Baptists in Ephrata in the 1720s had much in common with Kelpius. But it was shaped more radically and given stability by the forceful leadership of Johann Conrad Beissel, who arrived in Germantown from the Rhenish Palatinate in 1720. Beissel was essentially self-educated, a journeyman baker whose natural intelligence and philosophical genius were accompanied by great eccentricity. His ideas of spiritual discipline and the nature of sacred music are an important element in the folk history of America. He is a truly folk religious figure.

Serving as prior of the Brotherhood at Ephrata was John Peter Miller, a highly educated German Reformed clergyman. Known as Prior Jaebez and Agrippa, he is responsible for the completion of *Chronicon Ephratense.* We present selections from Kelpius' journal, the *Chronicon Ephratense,* the journal of Ephrata Brother Ezechiel Sangmeister, and Beissel's treatise on music from a preface to the "Turtel Taube" of 1747. Not only do these selections provide evidence of the spirituality of certain eighteenth century Dutchmen; but they share many of the ideas and symbols which continued as part of the folk tradition.

The final selection of the chapter is a twentieth century document, reflecting the thoughts of a latter-day Dutchman who sees himself as a pilgrim in the contemporary world. In this case, the author is one of the educated Dutch, who nevertheless knows his own folk-essence.

# JOURNEY TO PENNSYLVANIA

*(Although Gottlieb Mittelberger is not a primary example of Pennsylvania Dutch spirituality, his words provide interesting observations about religious life among the Germans in Pennsylvania. America was not to Mittelberger's taste. Many of his thoughts are negative and sardonic. He journeyed to Pennsylvania in 1750, returned to Germany in 1754. This selection is from his* Journey to Pennsylvania, *translated by Carl Theo, Eben, Philadelphia: John Jos. McVey, 1898.)*

Coming to speak of Pennsylvania again, that colony possesses great liberties above all other English colonies, inasmuch as all religious sects are tolerated there. We find there Lutherans, Reformed, Catholics, Quakers, Mennonists or Anabaptists, Herrnhuters or Moravian Brethren, Pietists, Seventh Day Baptists, Dunkers, Presbyterians, Newborn, Freemasons, Separatists, Freethinkers, Jews, Mohammedans, Pagans, Negroes and Indians. The Evangelicals and Reformed, however, are in the majority. But there are many hundred unbaptized souls there that do not even wish to be baptized. Many pray neither in the morning nor in the evening, neither before nor after meals. No devotional book, not to speak of a Bible, will be found with such people. In one house and one family, 4, 5, and even 6 sects, may be found. . . .

There are . . . many churches built in the country; but many people have to go a journey of 2, 3, 4, 5 to 10 hours to get to church; but all people, men and women, ride to church on horseback, though they had only half an hour to walk, which is customary also at funerals and weddings. Sometimes one can count at such country weddings and funerals 300, 400, and even 500 persons on horseback. It may be readily imagined that on such occasions, as also at the holy communion, no one appears in black clothes, crapes, or cloaks.

I will give a somewhat more detailed account of the funeral customs. When some one has died, especially in the country, where on account of the intervening plantations and forests people live far from one another, the time appointed for the funeral is always indicated only to the 4 nearest neighbors; each of these in his turn notifies his own nearest neighbor. In this manner such an invitation to a funeral is made known more than fifty

English miles around in 24 hours. If it is possible, one or more persons from each house appear on horseback at the appointed time to attend the funeral. While the people are coming in, good cake cut into pieces is handed around on a large tin platter to those present; each person receives then in a goblet, a hot West India Rum punch, into which lemon, sugar and juniper berries are put, which give it a delicious taste. After this, hot and sweetened cider is served. This custom at the funeral assemblies in America is just the same as that at the wedding gatherings in Europe. When the people have nearly all assembled, and the time for the burial has come, the dead body is carried to the general burial-place, or where that is too far away, the deceased is buried in his own field. The assembled people ride all in silence behind the coffin, and sometimes one can count from 100 to 500 persons on horseback. The coffins are all made of fine walnut wood and stained brown with a shining varnish. Well-to-do people have four finely-wrought brass handles attached to the coffin, by which the latter is held and carried to the grave. If the deceased person was a young man, the body is carried to the grave by four maidens, while that of a deceased maiden is carried by four unmarried men.

It is no unusual thing in this country to hear a totally unlearned man preaching in the open field, for the sectarians say and believe that the scholars of the present day are no longer apostles, and that they are only making a trade of their learning. Nevertheless, there are many excellent preachers in Pennsylvania who, by the grace of God and by their indefatigable toil, have converted many souls to the Christian faith; I myself have witnessed how our evangelical ministers have baptized and confirmed many adult persons, both white and black. Such an act is always attended by a large concourse of people. But I am sorry to say that there are also quite unworthy preachers who give offense to many people, and who furnish the sectarians with arguments, to the great annoyance of our ministers. I will quote here an example of such an objectionable preacher. One by the name of Alexander, of Oley township, said in a meeting of young farmers, with whom he had been drinking and carousing, that he would preach so that all his hearers who stood in front of him would weep, but those that stood behind him must all laugh. To this effect he bet a considerable sum with said young farmers. On the appointed day he appeared at a church-meeting, took his stand in the middle of the people, and began to hold a touching and pathetic sermon. Seeing that his hearers were moved to tears, he put his hands behind him, drew his coat-tails asunder, exhibiting a pair of badly-torn breeches through which his bare posterior, which he scratched with one hand, shone forth, so that those who stood behind him could not help roaring with laughter. Thus he had won his wager. This disgusting affair was published in the English and German newspapers of Philadelphia. The sectarians said often to those of our own faith that such men were the false prophets that went about in sheep's clothing, but were in fact rapacious wolves. But this is a source of great annoyance and vexation to all righteous teachers and good pastors.

There are at present many good English, Swedish, Dutch and German preachers of the Lutheran and the Reformed churches in Pennsylvania, of whom the following are very well known to me. Among the English, the three brothers Tennent and Mr. Datt. Three Swedish ministers who are very closely associated with our preachers and hold yearly conferences with them. But the German Evangelical Lutheran preachers are: Mr. Muhlenberg, senior, in Providence township and New Hanover. Mr. Brunholz, in Philadelphia. Mr. Handschuh, in Germantown. Mr. Kurz, in Tulpehocken. Mr. Wagner, in Readingstoun (Reading). Mr. Heinzelmann, in Philadelphia. Mr. Schulz, Mr. Weygand, Mr. Schrenk, Mr. Schartel, in the Blue Mountains. Mr. Hartwich, in New York. Mr. Gorack, in Lancaster. Reformed ministers are: Mr. Schlatter, Mr. Steiner, Mr. Siebele, Mr. Weiss, Mr. Michael, Mr. Streitter, and Mr. Laidig, without mentioning the Dutch and others whose names are not known to me.

The preachers in Pennsylvania receive no salaries or tithes, except what they annually get from their church members, which varies very much; for many a father of a family gives according to his means and of his own free will 2, 3, 4, 5 or 6 florins a year, but many others give very little. For baptizing children, for funeral sermons and marriage ceremonies they generally receive a dollar. The preachers have no free dwellings or other *beneficia.* But they receive many presents from their parishioners. The same is true of the schoolmasters. But since 1754 England and Holland give annually a large sum of money for the general benefit of the many poor in Pennsylvania, and for the support of 6 Reformed English churches and as many Reformed English free schools. Nevertheless, many hundred children cannot attend these schools, on account of their great distance and the many forests. Many planters lead, therefore, a very wild and heathenish life; for as it is with the schools, so it is also with the churches in the rural districts, because churches and school-houses are usually built around at such places only, where most neighbors and church members live.*

---

* In an English publication, which treats of the condition of the immigrants who have settled in Pennsylvania, Virginia, Maryland, etc., the following is reported among other things: From the most trustworthy accounts which we have of these provinces, it appears that the number of immigrants there has increased exceedingly within the last few years. They consist for the most part of Palatines, Franconians, and Swiss. In the Colony of Pennsylvania alone there are over 100,000; of these about 20,000 belong to the Reformed, nearly as many to the Lutheran, and about 1700 to the Roman Catholic religion. The rest consists of Ana-

The preachers throughout Pennsylvania have no power to punish any one, or to compel any one to go to church; nor has any one a right to dictate to the other, because they are not supported by a *Consistorio*. Most preachers are hired by the year like the cowherds in Germany; and if one does not preach to their liking, he must expect to be served with a notice that his services will no longer be required. It is, therefore, very difficult to be a conscientious preacher, especially as they have to hear and suffer much from so many hostile and often wicked sects. The most exemplary preachers are often reviled, insulted and scoffed at like the Jews, by the young and old, especially in the country. I would, therefore, rather perform the meanest herdsman's duties in Germany than be a preacher in Pennsylvania. Such unheard-of rudeness and wickedness spring from the excessive liberties of the land, and from the blind zeal of the many sects. To many a one's soul and body, liberty in Pennsylvania is more hurtful than useful. There is a saying in that country: Pennsylvania is the heaven of the farmers, the paradise of the mechanics, and the hell of the officials and preachers. . . .

The many sects lead people astray, and make them heterodox, especially many of our young German folks who are easy to seduce, because they have often many years to serve with them, so that they even forget their mother-tongue. Even many adults and old people have changed their faith, merely for the sake of their sustenance. I could quote many instances, but as this would lead me too far, I shall content myself with relating a single case. I was well acquainted with an old German neighbor who had been a Lutheran, but had re-baptized himself in a running water; some time afterwards he circumcised himself and believed only in the Old Testament; finally, however, shortly before his death, he baptized himself again by sprinkling water upon his head.

I cannot pass over another example of the godless life of some people in this free country. Two very rich planters living in Oley township, who were very well known to me, one by the name of Arnold Hufnagel, the other named Conrad Reif, both arch-enemies and scoffers of the preachers and the divine word, often met to ridicule and scoff at the

---

baptists, Moravians, Brethren of Zion, Rondorfers, and other Separatists. As among the latter almost every one is his own teacher, it may be said of them that they have their tenets (if the inanities of these people may be called so) better by heart than many of the other denominations; for although not a few pious and illumined Christians may be found among the latter, by far the majority live in the deepest ignorance, which must be ascribed to the want of sufficient preachers and schoolmasters, the inhabitants lacking the means for their support. The author of this publication closes with the wish that the nation of Great Britain might duly consider the condition of their brethren, both in a spiritual and worldly aspect, and do for them what is necessary to have in them a constant bulwark in America against all their enemies.

ministers and all the church people, and to deny heaven and future salvation, as well as eternal damnation in hell. In 1753 these two scoffers met again one day, according to their evil custom, and began to speak of heaven and hell. Said Arnold Hufnagel to Conrad Reif: "How much will you give me for my place in heaven, brother?" Said the other: "I will give you just as much as you will give me for my place in hell." Said Hufnagel again: "If you will give me so and so many sheep for my place in heaven, you shall have it." Replied Reif: "I will give them to you if you will give me so and so many sheep for my place in hell." Thus the two scoffers agreed on their bargain, joking blasphemously about heaven and hell. On the following day as Hufnagel, who had been ready to part with his place in heaven on such cheap terms, was about to descend to his cellar, which had always been his heaven, he suddenly dropped down dead; while Reif was attacked in his field by a flight of so-called golden eagles, which would surely have killed him if he had not cried piteously for help, when some neighbors came to his assistance. From that day he would not trust himself out of his house; he was taken with a wasting disease and died in his sins, unrepentant and unshriven. These two examples had the visible effect of arousing the consciousness of other scoffers. For God will not permit Himself to be scoffed.

On the first and second days of the month of May there is general merrymaking in Pennsylvania, in which the unmarried persons of both sexes chiefly take part. All amuse themselves with playing, dancing, shooting, hunting, and the like. Such unmarried persons as are born in the country adorn their heads with a piece of the fur of some wild animal, together with any painted animal they may choose. With these the young men walk about the city, crying "Hurrah! Hurrah!" But no one may put such a token on his hat except those born in the country, and these are called Indians.

In Pennsylvania the following custom prevails among all people, high and low, in the city and in the country. When any one enters a house, or meets another, he first presses the hand of the father and mother of the family; then he salutes in the same manner with his hand all other persons, as many as there may be, and it happens sometimes that he will find a whole room full. Such salutation and handshaking is customary with strangers as well as among the most intimate friends, and the mode of addressing each other is among the English as well as the Germans: "How are you, good friend?" And the answer is: "So middling." This pleasant custom springs in part from the many English Quakers in Philadelphia, and in part from the Indians themselves, who were the first among whom this custom prevailed. To speak the truth, one seldom hears or sees a quarrel among them. Even strangers trust each other more than acquaintances in Europe. People are far more sincere and generous than in Germany; therefore our Americans live more quietly and peacefully together than the Europeans; and all this is the result of the liberty which they enjoy and which makes them all equal. . . .

The cultivation of music is rather rare as yet. In the capital city, Philadelphia, no music is made either in the English or in the German churches. Some Englishmen give occasional concerts in private houses with a spinet or harpsichord. I came to the country with the first organ, which now stands in a High German Lutheran church in the city of Philadelphia, and which was built in Heilbronn. After this work had been set up and tuned it was consecrated with great rejoicing, and delivered to the Christian St. Michael's Church for the praise and service of God. At this great and joyous festival there appeared 15 Lutheran ministers with the entire vestries of all the Evangelical churches. The crowd of hearers was indescribably large; many people came from a great distance, 10, 20, 30, 40, and even 50 hours' journey, to see and hear this organ. The number of hearers, who stood inside and outside the church, both German and English, were estimated at several thousands. On the 2nd day of this solemn festival of rejoicing a conference was held by all the assembled Lutheran ministers and vestries, and on that occasion I was appointed schoolmaster and organist. As I became more and more known in Pennsylvania, and the people learned that I had brought fine and good instruments with me, many English and German families came 10, 20 and 30 hours' journey to hear them and to see the organ, and they were greatly surprised, because they had never in all their lives seen or heard an organ or any of these instruments.

At the present time there are 6 organs in Pennsylvania—the 1st is in Philadelphia, the 2nd in Germantown, the 3rd in Providence, the 4th in New Hanover, the 5th in Dulpenhacken (Tulpehocken), and the 6th in Lancaster, all of which came to the country during the 4 years of my sojourn there . . . .

Three great roads have been laid out in the province of Pennsylvania, all of which lead from Philadelphia into the interior of the country as far as it is inhabited. The first road runs from Philadelphia to the right hand by the Delaware to New Frankfurt (Frankford); the second or middle road runs through Germantown, Rittingston (Reading) and Dulppenhacken (Tulpehocken), extending across the Blue Mountains; the third road runs to the left hand toward Lancaster and Bethlehem, where there is a monastery and nunnery of Dunkers, inhabited by brethren and sisters. The men do not shave their beards; many a one among them has a beard half an ell long. They wear cowls like the Capuchin monks, in winter of the same cloth and color, but in summer of fine white linen. The sisters dress in the same manner. These people are not baptized, which is done by immersion in deep water, until they are full-grown and can give an account of their faith. Instead of Sunday they keep the preceding Saturday. Their convent-sisters aforesaid frequently bring forth living fruits in patience.

# THE JOURNAL AND LETTERS
## OF JOHANNES KELPIUS

*(From the Journal of Kelpius.* The Diarium of Magister Johannes Kelpius, *edited by Julius Friedrich Sachse, Lancaster: The Pennsylvania German Society, 1917.)*

J.N.J.

(IN THE NAME OF JESUS)

A.D. 1694.

On the 7th of Jan., I, convinced by God, resolved upon going to America, my companions being: Henry Bernard Coster, Daniel Falkner, Daniel Lutke, John Seelig, Ludwig Bidermann, as well as about 40 other companions, some of whom were numbered (mustered), and other convicted by God, in Germany, had as yet in the preceding year, resolved upon that voyage.

On Feb. 7th I engaged for them the ship, "SARAH MARIA," of good hope, Captain John Tanner, an Englishman, the vessel being hired at seven (7) English £ of Silver, which I paid out on board the ship on the 14th of this month, having embarked on the 13th, but the rest had embarked on the 12th.

This first day was passed tranquilly on the Thames river, by our people, by me (in this manner) for the greatest part. At night-fall a dispute arose concerning the arrangement of the beds, which dispute kindled the zeal in P. G. (puellis, Germanis—German girls?), so that disappointed in the pacific union of heart, I deemed my zeal for obtaining a single bed the heaven of Christ, (zelum and coelum, being here a jeu de mots). The lewdness might have increased (?) until Maria (solitaria, a spinster, lone woman) brought in an Ethiopian virgin, who would previously inform herself concerning the purity of an European maiden, before she consented to marriage. But George was afflicted with a most severe illness, the condition forbids me here, enough, wherefore in this manner he slept alone.

The second day, 15th Feb., was lucky for us (secunda and secunde—

79

2nd & lucky, another jeu de mots). But the third was destined fatal. My apprehensive mind presaged evils with a fortunate outcome. Falkner said the same of himself. We were visited first by the impress-gang of the king. Then we were driven towards sand-banks by a contrary and turbulent wind; wishing to escape these, we sought safety in our anchor, whereby we should have perished if not Divine providence had made it, that the great weight of the metal, which, under our ship, would have perforated the same had not the anchor been broken itself. Our anchor being lost in this manner, we were at length borne upon the sand-banks by the whirl. All, saving a few, feared the end was at hand. The Captain, having fired off four cannons, called those who were near to the rescue, but took pity on none of us. We furled the sails and committed the vessel to the turbulent billows, whilst the sailors were despairing. I had hold (of) the turtle-dove, that is not to be deserted, about the middle (waist) from the beginning (Feb. 16) of the storm, a divine witness, when already I saw our pilot despairing in the midst of our distress, when I was admonished, likewise, that by bearing witness concerning the most certain aid of God, I should raise his faith and hope, but being agitated myself, I kept my thoughts for myself. I was admonished a second time, but seeing him intent on other matters and turned away from me, I held my peace in turn. All were despairing and invoked the name of Jesus, as if about to journey into another life. Then being admonished (divinely) for the third time, I said to the pilot: "Have faith in God, who certainly will save us." The pilot rejoiced, for he was not so ignorant of divine matters. He pressed my hands and said: "God alone can help me everywhere, on Him shall I hope." Said, done (No sooner had he said these words than they were fulfilled). The storm began to drive the ship away from the sand-banks into deep water, where casting anchor, we praised God in safety. Meanwhile Coster, with the rest, had been pouring forth strong supplication to God (and indeed, about that time, when I began to collect my thoughts) as soon as I was admonished for the 3rd time, inwardly, and addressed the pilot, he had changed his entreaty to a prayer of thanksgiving, being sure his wish had been granted, though not knowing what just now was being done by us (with us).

I went below, rejoicing in our deliverance, to announce the glad tidings. I told them what had been done by me just a little while ago, and they, in turn, related their experience; therefore I no longer wondered at the divine virtue in me while I prayed, (their prayers had so powerfully aided me). I went up on deck and explained the matter more fully to the pilot, who began to praise the Lord with folded hands, especially when I added, *that still more dangers were imminent (threatening), but that I was fully convinced of the final aid of God.* Going below for the 2nd time, I also disclosed this matter to my brethren, when Falkner, filled with spirit of God, poured forth fervent thanksgiving: Praised be the name of the Lord for ever! Amen! Hallelujah!

LETTER TO HEINRICH JOHANN DEICHMAN,
LONDON, ENGLAND.
COPY OF A LETTER FROM PENNSYLVANIA TO LONDON,
TO MR. HEINRICH JOHANN DEICHMAN.

February 24th, 1697.

*Faithful Fellow Champion Deichman!*
Your esteemed favor received with joy, and there resounds from "The Call to Wisdom," which you enclosed, such an echo in our spirit, as though wisdom herself had meant us. We behold the harmony of divine discipline by virtue of a sympathetic agreement of your centre with ours, and although the radiant roads from and to the latter, cross each other in an endless manner, yet with all this diversity, the aspect of the upper huts of our mother, manifold wisdom, becomes more dear and joyous. Therefore we are not angry because of your cross and opposition roads, just as you, we hope, are not angry with ours, because, indeed, from the stroke of the cross, the bright colors of the sign of peace must be born, just as Solomon from David. The radii of our cross are directed at present from the centre exteriorly, when, however, the Lord is willing to unite these outward-turned extremities of our cross in their central point, He alone knows, and to Him alone this is possible. Hence it is not my intention to pen with ink of our color the letters Y. L. (Your Love), because your love is sealed in its place. We only long for the revelation in and from out of the heart of the love of God, and the more anxiously we bear, the more carefully the Lord hides us from the dragon, that watches so carefully for the birth, in order to devour it. . . .

LETTER TO HEINRICH JOHANN DEICHMAN,
LONDON, ENGLAND.
TO THE SAME, MAY 12th, 1699, THROUGH JAN VON LEWENIGH
(DELIVERED).

*Faithful brother and fellow of the tribulation, of which at this time, all partake that hope in patient and longing waiting for the glorious appearance of our Lord and Saviour Jesus Christ.*

I hear with special joy, how you show in your last letter, happily delivered together with a package by Mr. Schaeffer, your heart unto us as in a mirror, and how you permit us to see in what manner you are being purified in the furnace of the covenant, even so, that you feel that your experience was not the lot of the children of God for many centuries. Just as I have made mention in my first letter to you, of similar experiences of ours, but especially of mine own, concerning such as the Lord from the beginning to this hour uniteth more firmly; but, afterwards, for upwards of a whole year, my experience is such that the water hath not only often encompassed my soul, as you say of yourself, but I have even sunk in the deepest and bottomless slough of despond. So you, too, at the beginning of that state, did compose a lay of woe, sent to me through Falkner, so that I must conclude that the entire body of Christ is now suffering on earth, nor do I understand this to be an ordinary suffering, but rather such as extendeth from Gethsemane to Golgotha; yea, what shall I say, it hath not yet come to the . . . branch! The worst, the thrust of death, is still behind, when I shall atone before no common one . . . on the cross, or Jebusite, as Herod, or mystic imagination and dreams (but I am not speaking) (will reveal the right mystic way, which the world did hide) but of a real, where, essentially, this is done once and for all time, and from out of which a necessary transmutation as to body, soul, and spirit resulteth. I have, indeed, heard and read much of many that have died, risen, ascended, yea, descended with a virgin body, and now filling therewith their former body in such a manner, than the new covereth the old, as hides or pelts cover the hut of Moses, etc., the worthiness of which I do not impeach; yet sad experience hath hitherto taught that most men, after such advance, have not only not outstripped the others, but some have been made subservient to others, and have, in part, become unlike themselves in a deterior altitude. The words of Partus (Plato ?) are clear indeed, on which my faith is founded, that none in this life is preferred before another, much less, that one shall be the cause efficient of another's resurrection. Great speculations on this subject are of no avail. . . .

But, worthy brother, forgive me if I continue as an unbelieving Thomas to present to your mind the example of our dearest Saviour Jesus and his precursor John, not to speak of others, as I only represent a biga (two-horse-chariot) of eternal grace, because, at present and heretofore, men have always been speaking of Z.* However much these kept themselves hidden before their assumption of office, however silent they were concerning their future, but they kept themselves in all things in a virgin silence (whereof in the Old Testament, the virgins always remain at home,

---

* Z = possibly an astrological character.

and a going out in disguise representeth something properly) until that hour which was destined for them in the calendar of eternity, and then she stepped forth not with pen and ink, but in strength and might, which no foe could withstand, there you see how very much such a biga of eternal grace, even for our times and longer yet (availeth?), but this excessive boasting hereof in the streets of Babylon is somewhat suspicious to me. The cry: "See here!" "See here!" not to speak of the idle personal applications. In a word, the affair will come to pass quite differently than one or several men, yeah, even Jesus Christ himself imagines, and though we have revelation hereof, this revelation oftentimes cannot comprehend the spirit of the instrument, and often falls upon a false application of its person, and, if this will not do, it must be called a figure; now, inasmuch as many have practiced carnal lust in faith, or, at least, have brought about a spiritual mixture. How often, for pity's sake, have these things happened, and still happen even in such through whom it was hoped salvation should burst forth; and we may perhaps not be so much mistaken in the application, as were the two disciples that journeyed to Emmaus, though we cannot demonstrate it to them, for those unto whom we can re-monstrate it, so that they may know it themselves even without remonstrations, these also stand in just as great danger as the others, in whom it appeared spiritually before God, but did not come to a bursting forth. As then the mystery of the holy gospel (when children that tie a string about a bird's foot and permit it to fly upward, and the bird thinking its freedom attained, but the children may pull it down to them at will) is fulfilled, wherein the spirit of evil permits them to soar on high in knowledges and visions, caring little about their freedom of ascension, if only he can make them descend at will by means of the rope fastened to their feet and incorporated with their earthly dwelling.

Dearest brother! Unto your opened wound, oil may be perhaps more agreeable than salt and pungent wine? which oil you would fain choose and expect of me as, doubtless, you are bruised and dejected in mind sufficiently, and, believe me, that I am loth to swim in this element, as I would rather enjoy and gently glide with my beloved on evening clouds, but I am loth to storm with the north wind through the garden of God! But, faithful heart, when I consider the dangerous place where you are, and in spirit see how some by bland gifts . . . seek to gouge out your eye and to bind your hands, after having shorn you of your locks of liberty, I would rather see you with Samson turning the mill-stone of exterior hard work (as we have done and at times still do, rather than see you basking in the lap of your beloved spiritual Delilah). . . .

I deem myself too paltry and miserable to teach anything, because I am so fain to see that, being rid of all teachers and martinets, we might be taught, enlightened and inspired and directly united with the head, the only high priest of our salvation, which, of course, cannot and will not be accomplished without previous dearth, discipline, temptation, cross (or whatever we may call it, as previously indicated by me), nor without the final lunge of death, although thereafter nothing shall take us captive and detain us; hence, we cannot but expect the bursting forth of salvation from Jesus Christ, in, from, and through us all, because we all are but one body, and He, Jesus of Nazareth, remaineth the glorified theanthrope, from whom the life of the Father welleth and bursteth forth. Behold, dear brother, this manifest and through His apostles manifested truth is not unknown to you; inasmuch, however, as we see so many and various pseudo-saviours in the theatre of these our revolutions, it were not strange if our countenances were somewhat turned away from the only true one, and if we looked infatuated upon another guest-brother's beauty, yea, angelic and cherub-like clearness, and thus forsook our truest and most beautiful bridegroom amongst all, and if we became faithless or even adulterous and would thus contaminate our virgin garment or even lose it; we recognize, indeed, among all these forms, the proximity of salvation, but so that we may not embrace some folly because of too great ardour and heat of desire, as some men and women in their too ardent and passionate devotions have done, soaring perhaps too high, and then being humiliated, they took heed, as then the danger is truly and ineffably great, but not so great as when we in spirit desert our most true and loving Jesus for the sake of others (though they were angels). . . .

LETTER TO STEVEN MOMFORT IN RHODE ISLAND.
TO MR. STEVEN MOMFORT IN LONG ISLAND* IN AMERICA.

1699, 11. December.

*Dear Friend and Brother:*

In fellow-fighting in that Free and Royal Spirit which strives for the Prize of the first Resurrection when in this Midnight the Cry of the Bridegroom's coming is sounded forth among the Virgin waiters for the Preparation of the Temple Body, wherein the King of Glory and Father of the coming Eternity is to enter. Your great desire for to be a little further informed of the Principles and Practices of those People that go under the Name of Pietists, what they hold as Doctrine differing from others, what their Discipline is and what Methods they use in their own Country; this

---

* Should be Rhode Island.

desire I will hope, doth not arise from the Root of that Anthenian Curiosity to hear some new thing; But rather you being one among thousands in
Juda, who sees how since that glorious Primitive Church of Christ Jesus
the Apostacy hath run in a continual current till this very day, and though
this Stream hath divided itself in many smaller Rivulets, under several
Names of more reformed Purity, yet you are not ignorant how they derive
their Emanation from one Spring and tend to the same end, Viz. that the
Woman in the Wilderness might be carried away by the Flood. Therefore
you, as a Remnant of her seed, long for to see your Mother and groan for
the Manifestation of her children. No wonder then, if your continual
Gazing upon this Supercaelestial Orb and Sphier from whence with her
Children causeth you to observe every new Phoenomena, Meteors, Stars
and various Colours of the Skei, if peradventure you may behold at last an
Harbinger as an Evidence of that Great Jubelee or Restitation of all things
and glorious Sabbathismos or the continual days of Rest without intervening or succeeding Nights, whereof God hath spoken by the mouth of
all his Prophets since the world began (Acts 3, 21) and whereof both the
Testaments prophesie in every Title and Iota. If now this late Revolution
in Europe (not to speak of that in other parts) which in the Roman
Church goes under the Name of Quietism, in the Protestant Church
under the Name of Pietism, Chiliasm, and Philadelphianism, If I say this
together or one in Special purtends any thing to this effect. I do not
question, but it will be your as well as my desire, who would rejoice not
only to give you full satisfaction as to this, but to see with you, yet in our
days, that happy day, which when its new Earth swallows all that foremen-
tioned Floud and where its glorious Sun causeth all other Stars and
Phoenomena to disappear, no Night succeeds it, but that the Night is
swallowed up in ye, Day, Darkness into Light, Death into Life, Judgment
into Victory, Justice into Mercy, all imperfect Metals into Gold, and Gold
itself is refined seven times, and all Churches and Virgins comprised into
the one Dove (Cant. 6, 9), then all the Sons of God will shout for joy as
they did in the Beginning, when God was all in all, as he will be all in all,
when again the End hath found its Beginning. Amen! Halleluiah! . . .

*(Kelpius published a little book on the method of prayer. The first
edition was printed in 1700, the second by Franklin in 1756. Following is
an excerpt of the text.)*

For as much as internal Prayer is so Weighty a Point, that one may
call it the only means to attain to Perfection in this Life, and to kindle the
Pure and disinterested Love in our Hearts; and as all Christians (who will

indeed be such) are Called to this State of pure Love and perfection, and will, by the power of this call, have the necessary Grace offered to them to attain such a State. So this inward prayer suits all persons, even the most Simple and ignorant, who are also capable of performing this Order or Manner of prayer.

This brings us soonest to the Union with and Conformity to the Will of God!

Let us ascend the Mountain with Jesus Christ, let us pray as he has prayed; let us contemplate, let us love; so shall we perform God's prayer.

O divine Jesus! I join with thee in the Prayer which thou hast in Solitude by Night prayed, in this prayer of God; grant that we may perform no other Prayer.

O God! send this internal Spirit over the whole Earth; so will it be anew created, Let this Spirit rest on the Waters of thy usual and wonted Grace, which thou offerest to all Men; so will it distribute an overflowing Fruitfulness. O give us new Hearts. Amen, O Jesus!

# CHRONICON EPHRATENSE

*(From* Chronicon Ephratense, *A History of the Community of Seventh Day Baptists at Ephrata, Lancaster County, Pennsylvania, by "Lamech and Agrippa," translated from the original German by J. Max Hark, D.D., Lancaster, Pa.: S. H. Zahm & Co., 1889.)*

The Superintendent* first saw the light of the world in the year 1690 at Eberbach, a village on the Neckar, belonging to a sub-bailiwick of the domain of Mossbach in the Palatinate, and bore the family name, John Conrad Beissel. His father carried on the trade of baker, but was so given to drink that he sank all he owned down his throat, and then died, leaving behind a poor widow with a numerous family. This, his youngest son, was born two months after his death, and was therefore a true *opus posthumum;* by which orphan-birth the Spirit indicated his future lone condition, and that, as one pre-ordained to be a priest after the order of Melchizedek, he should derive little comfort from his natural kindred. His mother was a godly person, and, with the help of his other brothers, raised him until his eighth year, when she also died. From that time on he led a sorry life, after the manner of the country, until he was old enough to learn a trade. With his growth in years he displayed extraordinary natural gifts. He showed a wonderful facility in learning many things without any instruction, merely by his own reflection; so much so that his oldest brother often said to him: "Your studying will make a fool of you yet." By his orphanlike birth, moreover, he was given so small a person that he often said, if his oldest brother were to have been as small as himself, he would have had to have been born again. At length he was apprenticed to a baker, and as the latter was also a musician, he learned from him to play the violin, and had the opportunity to display his bright disposition at weddings, at which, when exhausted with fiddling, he would betake himself to dancing, and from this again return to the former; so that the wonder was all the greater when afterwards it was said he had become a Pietist.

---

* Johann Konrad Beissel, also known as the *Vorsteher.*

His conversion took place in the year 1715, therefore in the twenty-fifth year of his age; but ere the spirit of penitence came upon him, his reason became so enlightened that he could easily solve the most intricately involved matters. He turned his attention to mercantile calculation, covering all the walls of his back room with his cipherings, and mastered it without any help. Soon after, however, the awakening-Spirit knocked so loudly at his conscience that his whole being was thrown into the utmost perplexity, and so the foundation was laid for his conversion, which followed after, wherein he attained to such superhuman faithfulness to God that he may well be regarded as a great miracle of our times. The beginning of his conversion was directly from God, without any human instrumentality, and its fame has spread everywhere. . . .

At that period, according to the custom of the country, he began his travels as a journeyman at his trade, though he got no further than Strasburg, for the Spirit hindered him. It is a remarkable circumstance that, though he intended with four hundred other journeymen bakers to go to Hungary, he was prevented from doing so by God's providence and to his own good fortune, as they were all killed by the Turks. He finally entered the service of a man in Manheim, Kantebecker by name, where he was temporarily brought low in the spirit; for his master, who had marked in him a specially godly simplicity, loved him exceedingly, whereas his mistress was so displeased at this that she broke out into violence. For this he called her a Jezebel, and on that account was obliged to leave the house. At the same time the drawings of the Virgin above were so strong within him, that it was deeply impressed upon his heart that a man who intends to devote himself to the service of God must, at the beginning of his conversion, renounce Adam's generative work, for which reason he bade good-night to earthly woman at the very commencement. On this account also the tribes of the earth expelled him from their fellowship.

From Manheim he turned to Heidelberg and engaged himself to work with a baker by the name of Prior. Here he found greater access in the Spirit; for there was a great awakening going on, and there were many Pietists who were already beginning to be persecuted. . . .

At Heidelberg he met a learned scholar named Haller, a strong suitor of the Virgin Sophia, and also a correspondent of Gichtel, although at last he for all took to woman. This man made him acquainted with the Pietists in Heidelberg, who all maintained a hidden walk with God. . . .

Haller observed a large measure of the Spirit in this new Pietist, and foresaw that their awakening would not be of sufficient import to him. He therefore advised him to betake himself to the friends in Schwarzenau, which was at that time the Pella and rendezvous for all the pious. This advice was re-enforced by the persecution in Heidelberg, which shall now be described. At that time he still was staying with his master Prior, and as by his illumination there was also given him a strange insight into the secrets of nature, he in a short time became the most celebrated baker in the city. His master, too, received a blessing from this; for Christians and Jews ran after him, and the other bakers had little to do; he even sent of his wares to Frankfurt. . . .

After this latest part of the inhabited earth had lain waste for over 5000 years, it was resolved at a council of the Watchmen to impart unto it a fruitful evening rain, which fell upon Pennsylvania in particular, as shall now be demonstrated. The Superintendent speaks thus of it in his 5th Epistle: "Asia is fallen, and its lamp is gone out. For Europe the sun hath set at bright midday. America sees a lily blooming whose perfume will spread unto the heathen. The evening and the morning will again make a day (Gen. I). The light of the evening shall send its brightness even unto the morning; and the last promised evening rain shall come to the help of the morning, and bring again the end unto its beginning whereat Jacob shall be glad, and Israel rejoice." His purpose in this journey really was to spend his life in solitude with God. That in America he should again dive into the ocean of humanity was something of which at that time he probably did not even dream. . . .

The Superintendent arrived at Germantown; but kept very quiet as to his projects for a solitary life, for many, who had maintained a very proper walk in Germany, had here hung up their holy calling on a nail, and, what was worst, would give no one credit for zeal or diligence. Among these were several who in the Palatinate had let themselves be driven from house and home, but here left great wealth behind them after their death. . . .

In order to carry out his purpose, he went, in the autumn of the year 1721, into the upper country known as Conestoga, now Lancaster County, which at that time was inhabited by but few Europeans, and there, with the aid of his traveling companion, Stuntz, erected a solitary residence at a place called Muehlbach,* where they lived happily for a while.

Ephrata is situated in Lancaster County, thirteen miles from Lancaster, eighteen from Reading, and sixty-five from Philadelphia, in an angle where two great highways intersect each other, the one from Philadelphia to Paxton, the other from Reading to Lancaster. The Delaware Indians, who inhabited this region, named it and the stream that flows past Ephrata, *Koch-Halekung,* that is Serpents' Den, on account of the many

---

* Mill Creek, in what is now Lebanon County.

snakes found there. The Europeans kept the word, but pronounced it Cocalico, which is also the name of the township. The inhabitants did not value the land as being unfruitful. A Solitary Brother, Elimalech* by name, was the first one to build on this barren spot; and he gave his little house to the Superintendent when the latter fled thither. Thus it appears that the founding of Ephrata sprang entirely from a providential occurrence, and not from the premeditated will of man. . . .

Here in this wilderness he fixed himself as though he intended to live apart from men to the end of his days. He cleared himself of a tract of land, and cultivated it with the hoe, and in general made such arrangements that, in case men should again deliver him up, it would not be any loss to him. It is easy of belief that in the short period of his seclusion, during which men left him in peace for awhile, his addresses to the virgin Sophia were redoubled, for it was then he composed the beautiful hymn, "O blessed life of loneliness when all creation silence keeps." He often told what pains it cost him in the beginning to free this region from the evil spirits which hold dominion over the whole earth. If this seems strange to anyone, let him read Otto Clusing's Life of the Fathers in the Desert; there he will find more about such things. . . .

About this same time the Solitary Brethren also made up their minds, and moved after their spiritual leader, and built, in the winter of 1732, the second house in the Settlement. Their names were Jethro, Jephune,** and Martin Bremer, the last of whom was the firstling of those who fell asleep in Ephrata. This was not the end of it, however. Soon after, two of the Sisters who had earlier been devoted to virginity, A. and M. E.,* also came and asked to be taken in. The Brethren, who went according to the Fathers in the Desert, of whom it was known that they did not tolerate such a thing among themselves, protested against it to the Superintendent as being improper and perhaps a cause of offense. But he was not of their mind. It seems that he foresaw in the spirit what would be the outcome of the matter. The result was that a house was built for them on the other side of the stream, into which they moved in May, 1733, and where they lived until the Sisters' Convent was founded. In the following year another house was built for two brothers, Onesimus and Jotham,** otherwise called Eckerlin. This was followed by the common bake-house, and a magazine for the supply of the poor; with these building stopped for a while.

---

\* Emanuel Eckerle.
\*\* Jacob Gast and Sam Eckerlin.
\* Anna and Maria Eicher.
\*\* Israel and Gabriel Eckerlin.

These matters created a terrible stir in the land, especially among the neighbors, who were partly degenerate Mennonites and partly spoiled church-people. . . .

After the Solitary in the Settlement, however, were lodged in their convents, the schools of the solitary life began, where such lessons had to be learned that one often almost lost sight and hearing, and to which the oldest Solitary ones had become as little used in their hermit-life as the novice who had been received only the day before. And now the cause became known why the hermit-life came to be changed into the communal; and that the holy fathers in the desert had erred when they maintained that the foundations of the Solitary life were to be laid in the convent, but that its perfection would be reached only in the desert. The Superintendent now so managed with the good that while everyone might partake of it, yet no one could gain selfish possession of it. He was on his feet day and night, and whoso wanted to be rid of him had to lock his door at night; for he was often accused by his calumniators of being under the spur of his natural spirit. There was accordingly a constant stir in the Settlement, so that if anyone were absent but for three days, he became a stranger, and had much trouble afterwards again to work his way into the order of affairs. No one would have been able, even though he had lived in the Settlement for many years, to give a correct description of the course of events there; it was inconceivable, and at the same time highly offensive to the mere reason. Falling and rising alternated continually; he who to-day was exalted on spiritual heights, to-morrow was laid low; and this was unavoidable. He whom the Superintendent took into his confidence was elevated on high; he from whom he withdrew it, sank down again, sometimes even into the darkest depths, where then he was nailed to the cross; which things happened frequently. Here was the post of danger, where many of his followers were offended in him, and afterwards closed themselves against him, some of whom, through God's grace, were loosed again upon their death-beds. . . . Divine worship he appointed for the most inconvenient time, at midnight, and took special delight in the spirit if he could carry it on until daylight. If anyone offered him refreshment, he often said, "It gives me none," for his emaciated body was nourished by the Word that proceeded out of the mouth of God, otherwise he could not have endured such severity. When, constrained by love, he was often seen to eat during the day, it nevertheless made no change either in his body or his spirit, for he was a living skeleton until his death. Whenever he went into the Sisters' convent the whole house was moved; and when out of every corner they called to him, he was pleased with this open-heartedness, and said: "The young birds have the same simplicity when their provider comes to feed them." He was most careful to maintain the equilibrium of the Settlement, for God had placed the balances in his hand; and although, during the revolt of Korah, he was for a time deposed from the government, still finally it all fell into his hands again. His house was an asylum and city of refuge for all widows, orphans, and destitute ones; and whoso could reach its borders was safe against the avenger of blood. . . .

The Superintendent in those days was lifted above the world of sense, and had surmounted time with its changes. His hymns composed then are full of prophecy, and belong to the evening of the sixth time-period, that is, to the holy Ante-Sabbath. They represent the mysteries of the last times so impressively that it seems as though the kingdom were already dawning. It appears that it was the intention to set upon a candlestick the wonders of the last times through the revelation of the heavenly Virgin-estate and of the Melchizedekian priesthood in America; for that these hymns were given unto him in visions he at times betrays, when he adds, "This did we see in the spirit." . . .

# THE MUSIC OF THE EPHRATA CLOISTER

*(From* The Music of the Ephrata Cloister *also Conrad Beissel's* Treatise on Music *as set forth in a Preface to the "Turtel Taube" of 1747, by Julius Friedrich Sachse, Lancaster: 1903.)*

## THE TURTEL TAUBE OF 1747.* FOREWORD.

It is written, "Behold a Tabernacle of God With men." Rev 21. There is a dam broken of the heavenly ocean, through the forthcoming of the Church, which from eternal ages remained concealed in God, as between Father and Son, but in due time appeared among men, and has now as in the last days, shown forth herself anew, with vigor and strength as in the early ages.

This holy Church, having through the heavenly dove, which in the early days descended upon our high head Christ, at his baptism, appeared in the world, and from time to time drawn souls unto herself, who under her protection, remained steadfast unto the end in their calling, we believe the Church to possess a renewing, reviving, and sanctifying power. And that all, spoken of by the prophets and apostles, which should come to pass in future ages, finds its beginning in the Church; in which all the wonders and powers of future glory are found concealed. Whosoever, therefore, honoreth the Church, honoreth God: for God is in the Church; and he that abideth in the Church, abideth in God, and has his free city, where he may find protection when pursued by the blood-avenger of the powers of darkness. Deut. 19.

After the same manner in which God reveals forward into eternity through the Church all his mysteries, it also remains for him to receive from the Church praise, and the glorifying of his name, unto everlasting ages. In accordance with this, it was ordained by the spirit of the Church, or heavenly dove, that the talent of singing should be added unto spiritual services, and be employed in outspreading the praise of God unto endless ages.

---

* Original English version

93

By the use of this talent the holy angels made known the near approach of the Church when they at the incarnation of him who was the heart of the Church, entered within her borders, and by singing gave honor unto his appearance in the flesh. . . .

We nevertheless found, upon entering into the Church, a contrariness of things, between ourselves and the spirit, preparing the way to a newness of life. For as said before, God having ordained that through the church his name should be glorified, there were required voices, hymns and music written for the use of the singers. . . .

Now as such a selection of hymns and music adapted to the worship of God was not to be sought in our own abilities, nor in the power of the unsanctified mind (for by the unsanctified mind, heaven is constantly being locked up) but in the abilities which God bestows, so we found it necessary constantly to renew our diligence in practicing self-denial, if at all heaven should again be unlocked at our natural state, and the praise of God from thence brought out. . . .

On the contrary, so far as consolation is sought in the amusements of the visible world, so far we lose communion with the Church, the spirit of singing, as the heavenly dove retreats, and the praise of God is no more heard. It is therefore of the greatest importance to be always engaged in laboring for the prosperity of the church; and it cannot well be expressed in few words, what attention must be paid to a careful walk of life, and what acquirements are necessary to establish excellent church music. . . .

The spirit of the Church, having taught us in the course of our spiritual labors to place a high estimation upon the hymns of the followers of Christ, brought forth in their trials under the cross; and believing them to be instructive, we have concluded to secure them as treasures, and have in the compilation as well as in the print of this work, applied our utmost care that no errors might occur through which occasion might be taken to give our labors a low estimation.

But to speak yet further of the compilation of this spiritual work, it is a field of flowers, grown forth of many different colors, and of various fragrance, as they were produced by the spirit of the Church, out of the *Mysterio* of God. In some the spirit of prophecy soared above all mountains of the cross, bidding defiance to his enemies, setting forth as present, the future glory of the Church. In others, the spirit trod into the inner court, and exalted his voice in the holiest of all. Again, others have the pleasant odor of roses; others, on the contrary, sprung up upon the myrrh mountains.

Now as the Church hath extended herself, so also have the voices increased in our own spiritual school, in which our hearts were the praise of the great God. And any one who has had only a limited experience in this, our spiritual school, can readily perceive that in this entire work can be found naught that reminds one of human effort or wild fancy, but that the words of the spiritual songs herein contained, sprang from many and varied emotions.

Here we would conclude our foreword, did not an important matter still remain. For after having come into possession of so rich a treasure for the praise of God, it became a question in our spiritual school how our voices could be cultivated for spiritual song; hence such a matter of spiritual practice became imperatively necessary as would bring the voices into spiritual harmony and at the same time make our sacrifice of praise conformable to good common sense. . . .

Let us now proceed directly to the subject, and show, as briefly as possible, by what means and opportunities we may, both spiritually and physically, attain to this art of high degree, and then consider further whatsoever things the circumstances of the case may require. In the first place, be it observed that divine virtue must be viewed from the summit of perfection, and occupy the first place, if one would become the right kind of pupil and thereafter a master of this exalted and divine art.

Furthermore, both pupil and master ought to know how necessary it is, in addition to all other circumstances, to embrace every opportunity to make oneself agreeable and acceptable to the spirit of this exalted and divine virtue, inasmuch as according to our experience and knowledge it has within itself the purest and chastest spirit of eternal and celestial virginity.

This naturally requires compliance with the demands of an angelic and heavenly life. Care must be taken of the body, and its requirements reduced to a minimum, so that the voice may become angelic, heavenly, pure and clear, and not rough and harsh through the use of coarse food, and therefore unfit to produce the proper quality of tone, but on the contrary, in place of genuine song, only an unseemly grunting and grasping.

At the same time it is especially necessary to know what kinds of food will make the spirit teachable, and the voice flexible and clear; as also what kinds make it coarse, dull, lazy and heavy. For it is certain that all meat dishes, by whatever name known, quite discommode us, and bring no small injury to the pilgrim on his way to the silent beyond. Then there are those other articles of food which we improperly derive from animals, e.g., *milk,* which causes heaviness and uneasiness; *cheese,* which produces heat and begets desire for other and forbidden things; *butter,* which makes indolent and dull, and satiates to such an extent that one no longer feels the need of singing or praying; *eggs,* which arouse numerous capricious cravings; *honey,* which brings bright eyes and a cheerful spirit, but not a clear voice.

Of bread and cooked dishes none are better for producing cheerfulness of disposition and buoyancy of spirit than *wheat* and after this *buckwheat,* which, though externally different, have the same virtues in their uses, whether used in bread or in cooked dishes.

As regards the other common vegetables, none are more useful than the ordinary *potato,* the *beet,* and other *tubers. Beans* are too heavy, satiate too much, and are liable to arouse impure desires. Above all must it be remembered that the spirit of this exalted art, because it is a pure, chaste, and virtuous spirit, suffers no unclean, polluted, and sinful love for woman, which so inflames and agitates the blood of the young as completely to undo them in mind, heart, voice and soul; whilst in the more mature it awakens excessive desire after the dark things of this world, and consequently closes heart, mind, and voice to this pure spirit as its haven.

As concerns *drink,* it has long been settled that nothing is better than pure, clear water, just as it comes from the well, or as made into soup to which a little bread is added. Every other manner of cooking, however, whereby the water is deprived of its healthgiving properties and turned into an unnatural sort of delicacy, is to be considered as a vain and sinful abuse; just as other articles of diet, which we do not deem worthy of mention in this place, have, through many and diverse lusts, been turned from their natural and harmless use into delicacies. Of those who gormandize we cannot here speak, for we are concerned only with those who are already engaged in the spiritual warfare, and who in all respects strive lawfully. With those who walk disorderly and unlawfully we, therefore, have nothing to do. It of course stands to reason that the power to exercise divine virtue is not to be sought in the selection of this or that particular diet; for, were this the case, we would wish, if it were possible, to be entirely relieved of eating, so that we might lead an Enochian, supernatural, and supersensual life. Then this heavenly wonder-song would of itself break forth, without the addition of any of those things that are only transient and never reach eternity. . . .

We have now imparted, as well as we are able, the secret of our spiritual song. Although in this work (the *Turtel Taube*) we are more concerned with hymns than with tunes, and a well-informed person might ask why so much has been said about music when none appears in the book, we have yet thought it proper to write this introduction, partly because from music the hymns in this volume derive their attire and adornment, and partly because it will stimulate lovers of this noble and paradisiacal art to inquire further into its secrets.

# MYSTICAL SAYINGS OF BEISSEL, 1730

*(From* The Ephrata Cloister, An Introduction, *Eugene E. Doll, Ephrata, Pennsylvania: Ephrata Cloister Associates, Inc., 1958–1983.)*

The following sayings of Beissel are from his *Mystische und Sehr Gehymne Sprueche,* published by Benjamin Franklin in 1730. In 1771 Peter Miller, replying to a letter from Franklin, included a translation of the *Sprueche,* with the comment: "I offer the whole to your Freedom, either to burn or publish the same, or to make such alterations as you think best: . . . for I am a Foreigner to the Idiotism of the Language." The present author, in making the following selection for publication here, has also made bold to exercise the privilege extended to Franklin, by personally mending a few of Miller's Germanisms.

1. To know truly oneself is the highest Perfection; and to worship and adore rightly the only, everlasting, and invisible God in Jesus Christ is Life eternal.

2. All wickedness is sin; yet none is so great as this: to be separated from God.

5. All works which a man worketh bring him to that end for which they are calculated, either for God's or his own self's sake.

7. Carry no fire in a wooden vessel, lest it burn thee; but build an altar of new stones, and put thereon good frankincense, and let the fire of Divine Love penetrate the same. Then shall a pleasant fragrance arise before His holy nostrils.

8. Be always humble and little in a high station, and raise not thy building high before thou hast measured the depth: lest thou mightest in thine ascending come above the measure, and thy building be destroyed.

10. Fight with nothing which proves too mighty for thee: yet keep a good watch, lest thou mightest be killed by thine own domestics.

15. Be not lazy in thy doings, that thou mayest fill thy measure, either in good or evil; yet prefer always the best.

20. Neither the heights nor the depths are yet measured; but he hath seen both which thinketh little of himself.

31. The same is great and highly learned, who always willingly occupieth the lowest station.

37. Whosoever buildeth his own house with the goods of others gathereth fire for its destruction.

40. Let none praise or blame thee but thine own works, which were begotten in thy soul.

53. Wisdom is a fine thing; yet hath she not many courtiers, for she is chaste.

65. If thou dost see the sun setting, look not after her, as if she would rise from thence again, else darkness will catch thee, for the same followeth always the light. But turn thy face toward the East: then shall her clear light again surround thee, and thou shalt be refreshed with a pleasant morning dew.

96. Be not wise in thyself before thou hast travelled through the way of folly, lest thou mayest possess folly for wisdom.

# LIFE'S DESCRIPTION

*(From the Journal of Ezechiel Sangmeister, entitled* Life's Description, *Ephrata: Joseph Baruman, 1825. Although Sangmeister was somewhat estranged from Beissel, his journal reveals the spiritual struggles of a simple carpenter of Pennsylvania. The translation is by Barbara Schindler, published as the* Journal of the Historical Society of the Cocalico Valley, *Volume IV, 1979.)*

## EZECHIEL SANGMEISTER'S LIFE AND BEHAVIOR

I, poor pilgrim, was born into this miserable world in the year 1723, on the 9th of August, in the afternoon at 2 o'clock. My father's name was Stephan Heinrich Sangmeister and my mother's was Anna Margaretha Bergen, a native of Hornburg in Prussia. Both were of the Lutheran religion and they had such a peaceful marriage, the likes of which I have never seen. They lived in a village called Beddig about one mile from Wolfenbuttel, where my father was a schoolmaster. This profession was in our family from our grandfather and great grandfather.

In the manner of the Lutheran religion, my father was a very pious and upright man. (For in my time I have heard nothing of awakenings in this country.) He was especially compassionate toward the poor and the sick. Therefore he strongly urged us to fear God. Mother, on the contrary, very strictly urged us to outward works, for she unfortunately was more inclined to the world and the accumulation of wealth than my father was. However she was not unjust, but rather tried to be frugal so that they also lived comfortably and were well off. There were six children, four sons and two daughters (in addition to an orphan which they had taken in out of pity to raise it.) My parents' marriage was almost always accompanied by constant burdens, sickness, and distress. For this reason my father used to say that if we could, we should stay single. The brother closest to me in age was bewitched by an old woman, and he had to suffer with terrible headaches for a year and a half. Then when a remedy was finally found to help him and as soon as he was better, she did it to my father in the same way. After much distress and misery, which lasted for about one and a half or two years, he finally died as a result of this condition in great peace in the 42nd year of his life. Since shortly before his death my two sisters and my youngest brother died soon after another and very unexpectedly, my mother was so affected that she almost gave up hope. Day and night she cried until her fountain of tears was totally drained and no more tears were to be had. Often she did not know how else to recover but to look at her earthly treasures that she possessed and put them back in their place.

Although my father had nothing but misery in this world, especially in the last two years in which he had to endure a great deal, he bore this not only with great patience but he also ordered, and earnestly at that, the mentioned woman, the witch, to diligently give alms which she carried out up until his death.

My mother was now a widow with three children and as I mentioned she encouraged us in good discipline and work. Since I was about nine years old when my father died and I had already learned so much (because I was very quick to learn) that I could go to communion, she did not let me go to school anymore, but rather as it is said: the wheels on the carriage stayed still (which also may have been fate) so that I might not lose myself even more in pride. I did what I could at that time, and so it remains.

In order that I finally begin with discussing myself, I know well to remember that when I was a small boy I played many games and was very haughty. Among other things I had a special evil about me, namely stone-throwing with which I often took care to do harm. I was often corrected for it by my parents, but unfortunately it didn't help much since I was often out of their sight. One day out of force of habit as I had a stone in my hand ready to throw it, I felt an internal reprimand whereby suddenly the passage came to my mind, Whatsoever you do, remember the end, and you will never do amiss. This internal reprimand went so deeply into my heart that I immediately dropped the stone. Afterwards I was seldom struck by this evil.

Now it also happened about this time that I was drawn and internally driven in a powerful way to prayer and a different life, so that particularly at night when others slept I prayed for a long time. Sometimes I would experience an internal state of extreme well-being. At other times, however, I was plagued with terrible, horrible visions and imagined phantasies. During this time I also found such an internal love within me that I almost could not bear. Therefore I knew of no other pleasure than to be alone with children like myself, to enjoy them, and to hold discussions with them about good and godly things. We had a garden by the house where I took care to make huts here and there in order to be alone with other children. Also passages from the Holy Scriptures came into my mind since I had no real clearness and explanations of how I should understand it. I mention this only so that one might see what can take place with children in tender youth since at this time I may have scarcely been seven years old. I did not have the heart to tell my parents or to ask them anything about what was going on with me. In spite of that, my father finally noticed it, that a great change had occurred in me and he developed a special love for me, when he had always preferred my younger brother to me. He spoke very affectionately with me alone and exhorted toward goodness, and this continued up to his death.

When my father's unheard of headaches became worse and worse in addition to his weakness, he endured this with unusual patience and calmness. On different occasions, however, he would say that his end was near, which he had guessed correctly. Right after his death, an illness came over me. I believed that my father was pulling at me because I had a great inclination to die. For this reason I demanded to be given communion. The preacher himself came to me and tried to talk me out of it since I was so very young. So I had to content myself. Hereafter I lay still in bed until the next day. About noon I looked out the window and looked at the sky. It seemed as though I came out of myself. Two angels came to me, took me between them, and led me to a small door at heaven, but they said to me that I could not come in yet. With this I came to my senses and began to scream loudly: "I'm dying! I'm dying!" Out of both fear and joy I sprang from the bed in a cold sweat, whereupon everyone came running and wondered. Hereupon I got better unexpectedly in a short time.

I forgot to mention before that my one sister, of about six years of age, took her end in her last illness with an extreme devoutness. This child could pray the most beautiful passages from Scripture to comfort herself, so that one and all were astonished and everyone was moved to tears.

After my mother had lived as a widow with us three sons for a while, she sent me to my cousin's upon my request to undertake the carpenter's trade although I was still small and very young. The trade was difficult for me and I did not have enough to eat, so that to a certain extent it went for me like the children of Israel in Egypt, who sighed under their hard work. Because of this I finally forgot completely the goodness of my God and I stopped praying, reading, and singing. When my years of apprenticeship were over, I had unfortunately learned very little (with the exception of the required work). However, I received more freedom now to follow the vanity of the world and pretty soon thereafter I set out on my travels. I was about 16 years old when I left. At my departure my mother said to me, "I will never see you again as long as I live," and so it happened too. When I traveled quite a stretch through Germany, heard and saw much, and got no satisfaction within me and things were going quite badly for me, finally I got a great urge to travel to America, while I was in the Wurtemberg region. For I searched everywhere for peace and security outside of God, but I could find it nowhere, for my conscience frightened and nagged me day and night so that often I did not know how to endure out of great fear. Especially when I heard thunder it went through all my bones. When I saw clouds climbing in the sky at night as I was going to bed, I could not sleep the entire night. When it started to thunder I immediately ran to people and sought refuge out of fear that if I were alone, the storm would kill me. The good Lord let all of this happen in order that I would turn to him again, but unfortunately I was so stubborn that I was afraid of prayer. Oh what a misery it is for a person who is burdened with an evil conscience. Ah you, my Lord and my God, didn't you let all of this happen just so that I would turn to you again, but I was so far away from you and so stubborn that you were truly a terrible God in my eyes. Therefore I could never pray in the midst of all such fear and fright, for when I wanted to pray the spirits mocked me. They said that it was no use and I should just let it be, God would not hear me anyway. And so, I put it off again. If I went to church or to communion, I did this only for appearance so that the people would just be satisfied with me and might not consider me as being overly wicked. Otherwise it was always like this, that I always believed that it would only further serve my judgement and damnation. Unfortunately I spent many years of my life in this miserable condition. I searched for pleasure in many types of vanity, but I could never find it. It was all in vain. Sometimes the thoughts occurred to me that if I gave myself totally to Satan, then I could lead a truly cheerful life like Doctor Faust. I dared not let this evil suggestion be known to anyone, for they were becoming an unbearable burden for me. It finally happened then as I was working as a journeyman in the Wurtemberg district, that I made up my mind to travel to America in the hope of finding joy in the new world. I set out on foot. I had little money for traveling because my master [in the trade] owed me a considerable amount of money. Since he did not have much money and also wanted to come to this country, he went to sea and promised to give me what was rightfully mine in Holland. I went to him, but received little from him. Then I went along to sea where I spent time with the sailors and helped climb the masts since I was especially healthy and fit. I was surrounded by many people, so that I felt absolutely no longing within me for land. Finally after a voyage of six weeks and a few days we arrived in Philadelphia from England. . . .

When we arrived in Ephrata we were received with great love and kindness, and Peter Miller, a learned man, washed our feet. Hereafter we were brought to C. Beissel's house and were baptized the following day. Of course I asked to postpone the matter a little in order that one could first prepare oneself for it, but his answer was, "Strike the iron while it is hot."

And so I had to let it happen for he was extremely hungry and eager for souls since he was in a constant state of working and driving for his own fulfillment. I even took a garment along with me to Ephrata as a precaution that if I should find that Ephrata does not suit me, I would go to New York, and from there to Germany. After being there for several days, a poor man came to the door. Unhesitatingly Brother Gideon Eckstein ordered me to get my garment and give it to the poor man. I found this a little harsh, but I did not let it show, and so I was completely undressed. But I say, wasn't it you, my God, who did this so that I would not come into temptation thereby to leave? My tools were also taken from me.

We came to the Brothers at a good time, for since the mill was burned down, I was immediately appointed to do joinery in order to help to build the new one. Anton was appointed cook for the Brotherhood in their kitchens.

After this I found that my old vices and habits strongly adhered to me and held me captive. One morning it was said within me, either you must live a righteous life now, or run away. However my old habits were so deeply rooted that it was almost impossible for me to relinquish them. Often I did not know where I should put myself. Each of us had a small room, of course, but I could not spend my time in it for it was too close for me. I visited one Brother after the other throughout the entire house, but found no satisfaction from any of them. (For at that time Agabus lived at Hans Velten's.) Finally I hit upon the idea that without a doubt I would find what I was searching for with Conrad Beissel since he was extremely praised and considered by everyone as being a saint. I visited him often in the hopes of acquiring a portion of his holiness. I committed myself to his prayers at all times, but he used a style of language which I could not understand. With might and main he referred me to the sensual* life by way of love feasts, going to meetings, going to matins, notesinging, and Fracktur-writing. I was foolish and followed him, but found little peace and pleasure in doing so.

Once while I was alone in my room I thought to myself what the best thing would be for me to do in order that I might succeed to a different life. For what Conrad Beissel had recommended, namely learning note-singing, Fracktur-writing, and painting, it occurred to me that I could learn these quickly, but what then? All of these things were not adequate to satisfy my great hunger. Suddenly it came to my mind that I would have to apply myself to prayer and make this my main foundation. . . .

As I mentioned, my leader forsook me and at precisely such a time

---

* The author uses this word to refer to externalism, outward ritualism.

when I had (according to my thinking) needed him the most. I did not want to burden him, but rather pulled myself away and held myself all the more closely to my good God, who was always unchangeable, yes always one and the same. Here one sees how little human supporters help in a time of need.

Now since I was alone on all sides, the good God let me come to the test from within and without, for since I had to unavoidably go along to all the meetings, services, and love feasts, it was no different for me on such occasion than as if I were on the rack, the spirits tortured me so severely in a magic way, which I have not yet understood. If I went into my little bedroom where I usually took care to have so much goodness, such horror came over me, that I often had wanted to wish for death. Thus, I was tormented day and night in a gruesome way. I was very stupid in the beginning and did not know that people could torture one another in a magic way. This was my fortune, for in this way I could not blame anyone or go against anyone unlovingly. Therefore I took the blame upon myself and always thought that it came from my own evil and corruption that it was going so badly for me. For this reason I asked God all the more fervently in prayer to stand by me and help me, for now I had no other means but to endure. I would gladly have taken it upon myself to keep watch for the Brother in waking them for matins if only I did not have to go inside, (and never was it worse than when Conrad Beissel was there) for the more I went in [to the services] the harder it was for me only because I did not want to pray aloud or disclose how it was each day in my inner life, whereby he could judge the souls through their actions. Otherwise I did all that I was told. For a long time I was the reader. I had to begin [the Services] on my knees for a long time. I had to order the songs for the singing for a long time, and so on and so forth. Brother Agabus could accommodate himself well in order to ignore suffering. He said a little prayer, which almost always was the same in the manner of a small boy, but I came into distress when I wanted to make such a change in praying or thinking up new words. As was mentioned, I had no other comfort, nor help, nor refuge than praying. Mornings I remained on my knees for one hour without fail, another hour at noontime, another hour after leaving work, and if I possibly could, before we went to midnight services, so that I awoke early enough to be on my knees for a while, and once again another hour after the services, etc.

When I told it to Brother Agabus after quite some time, he told me to kneel each time only for a half an hour. What the reason was I do not know, although I did notice that I was getting thinner, but I was still afraid to go against him. When time came for a love feast, which we often had two or three times a week, I asked God heartily on my knees not to let me enjoy it unworthily. The more fervent my prayer, the greater was my suffering, for the speeches which the Vorsteher made flew at me like arrows, of which I want only to mention a few for example:

No man has any right to come alone before God, and all such prayer is foolishness, for then God will attend to each fool or broom-cutter separately (He called me a broom-cutter because I was a carpenter.) For that reason it is said in the Lord's Prayer, our Father, not my Father, for everything depends on the community, so that man has absolutely no right to come to God for himself. . . .

The entire country is blessed by this community, and whoever lays but a finger on this (Ephrata) community will never again be free now or in eternity, for it serves to his advantage and restoration. If ever there was a separatist, it was I, but I realized the deception, for all of our goodness lies in the community.

# THE RED HILLS

*(Inside Cornelius Weygandt's* The Red Hills, *the cover page reads "A Record of Good Days Outdoors and In, With Things Pennsylvania Dutch." There is a quotation, unidentified: "Good-bye, proud world! I'm going home." Weygandt was a scholar, a professor of English literature at the University of Pennsylvania. However, his book is a spiritual document, a twentieth century homecoming that belongs to his folk.* The Red Hills, *Philadelphia: University of Pennsylvania Press, 1929.)*

There are things that are of the earth earthy; there are things that are of the earth racy; there are things that are of the earth sweet. The Pennsylvania Dutch, like other people, have their share of these sorts of earthiness. We make no pretense that we have not, no matter what our degree. The poor whites among us, the hillmen of the remote upland farms are closest to the soil, but their earthiness is no more pronounced than that of certain groups of villagers and townsmen. There are some of us of higher orders, too, who are very much like the hillmen in habits, despite our feelings of superiority over them. Even the professedly godly among us can run riot on occasion. A Sunday school festival may turn orgiac and a camp meeting pass through phases of the Dionysia. There are those among us, on the other hand, who are simply and unaffectedly good, day in and day out, and no inconsiderable number who from generation to generation have followed the code common to gentlemen the world over. Whether weak or strong ourselves, we are tolerant of weakness in others, one and all of us.

We are unashamed, almost to a man, of such earthiness as is ours, and of whatever kind. There are few of the "unco guid" among us, and still fewer of a sickly conscience. We are not afraid of our appetites, and we are willing to accept, when we surrender to them, the consequences of such a surrender.

We are famous trenchermen, most of us, and we are frank to admit that the table is one of the chief joys of life. In all America's broad land of plenty there are no places of greater plenty than a thousand and one places in the "Dutch" counties. At the onset of winter the outdoor ground-cellars of our country homes are crowded with many sorts of food, milk products, vegetables, fowls salted down. Smokehouses are filled with cured meat, hams and sides of bacon and burlapped sausages hanging there as thick as bees on the comb. Cupboards groan under crocks and jars of preserves and jellies. Hanging shelves and wall racks in the house-cellars are stacked to their capacity with jugs of cordial and bottles of wine, homemade all of it. A row of cider barrels, fifty-gallon fellows, is ranged along the wall under the racks and shelves, in every well-conducted home.

The importance of food is writ large on the buildings about the farm-house. . . . The food which is prepared for table or storage, and housed in these buildings, is largely for home consumption. . . . It is feast day every day on the typical "Dutch" farm, and in the typical "Dutch" town home, too, for that matter. My grandfather, who turned vegetarian about 1840, was regarded as surely mad, and his son, my father, believed to be a martyr by his aunts, my grandfather's sisters. . . .

We are, on the whole, tolerant and kindly. We do not expect too much of humanity. Even the Puritan sects among us are very mildly Puritan, Puritan generally in externals and in a few prejudices against ultra-worldly ways. We accept human nature as it is, and we rejoice in all the instincts that it gives us. We can, like other people, drink hard on Saturday, and pray hard on Sunday. . . .

We are stout church-goers, whether Lutheran or Reformed, or of the Separatist sects, but we are kindly to the sinners among us, and we outlaw very few for the sins of the flesh. Mennonite bonnets and Amish broad-cloth do not necessarily mean the suppression of the natural man. If children should by chance be born out of wedlock they are not as a rule banished to some orphan asylum, but are brought up, with little prejudice against them, in the mother's family. If the child's father is a married man, or if either one of the parents should not care to wed the other, the young mother may still make a happy marriage with some neighbor who knows her story and who accepts things as they are. Such bye-blows are more usual among the Busch Deitch, but should they occur among families with pride of place and cherished traditions the unwanted youngsters would still be kept at home and treated as if they were legitimate. . . .

I have never heard of a Venusberg in the Red Hills, but the Wild Huntsman rides them on certain dark nights of all seasons, and we cele-brate harvest home with many of the rites of Johannisfeuer. Even at such mild festivities as those of an apple-butter party we can grow quite lively with the throwing of the blumsock.

There are more high jinks among us now on Hallowe'en than at any other season of the year. So it has been in certain places for two genera-tions at least, but back in the country Christmas Eve was once the time for such carryings-on. Even now in certain places Belsnickel and "Kriss Kinkle" call together, and raise quite a ruction with their rewards and punishments.

Hallowe'en is almost too well organized now to seem a folk custom. We have still the old tick-tacking on the windows, the ringing of doorbells, the stealing of gates, and, when their survival makes it possible, the lofting of buggies and old wagons to almost impossible places. In old days the young man's horse and buggy was even more the symbol of his affluence and eligibility as beau than the car is now. It was indeed a triumph for his neighbor to get the buggy up on the carriage shed that housed it, or on the cowshed of the barnyard, or on some springhouse roof off in the meadows. Often, of course, this lofting involved the taking off of the wheels and their restoration again when the wagon body had been gotten up to its high perch. . . .

I was brought up in familiarity with a hundred and one superstitions. I was not brought up to believe in them, but I followed, as if by instinct, many of their admonitions, and I rejoiced in omens of good fortune. I was happy when a cricket chirped on the hearth in winter; or when a black cat came of her own accord to live with us. I always "ate" the bubbles on the coffee; and as faithfully threw salt over my left shoulder when I spilled it at table. I still feel in my pocket for silver when I see a new moon over my left shoulder, and wish upon it if I find it there; and I look for rain after I see spiders' webs on the grass in the morning.

You have only to scratch the veneer off any man to find all sorts of primitive things beneath. With us, a regard for the supernatural is quickly uncovered by such scratchings. The supernatural is as instant to those of us who live in back country places as it was in medieval times to our ancestors in Germany. It is more than a portent, it is a sure sign of disaster to come, if a snowy owl bumps his solid self against one's bedroom window. Those wild eyes, and outstretched beating wings, and fluff of white feathers close pressed against the glass mean that he who sleeps within is no better than a dead man.

That doomed man, nevertheless, will go about his work as usual. He will start in the close dark next morning for that ride of thirty-five miles to Philadelphia. He will sell smoked sausage and scrapple, butter and eggs, fresh pork and fowl as phlegmatically as usual. He will be so tired from the long drive in the wintry air and the long marketing that he will sleep soundly, despite the city noises and his foreknowledge of his doom. On his way home he will be more than usually watchful at all railroad crossings. He will pass them all safely until he comes to the last one of all, within hail of his home. Then, because he is a fated man, he will, for all his striving, fall asleep, and be run down by an engine, under white flags, that is running wild, to relieve its fellow broken down twenty miles beyond. And in the awakening moment of death he will be glad that the horses escaped, and he will be resigned to his own doom because the omen of the fowl had foreshown it to be inevitable. . . .

The doctor's son was talking. "Yes," he said, "father has been nonplussed entirely by some of the witch doctoring." There was a woman up toward the Welsh Mountains who had burnt her hand badly with the hot juice of huckleberry pie. He was called in and dressed it and told her it would be three weeks before she could use her hand again. He saw she didn't like that forecast of his, but he didn't know what her pursed lips meant. He told her he would be back again the next day to see that no infection threatened. When he got there he found the wound surprisingly improved. He let a day go and called again. This was on the fourth day of the case. He couldn't believe his eyes, the hand was so much better. He had used on it the old country salve he had always prescribed for burns, and he laid the rapid healing to that. He saw, however, that the woman was nervous about something, and seemed to want to get him out of the house. He saw her looking out of the window, and then he heard wheels. The woman saw that the issue had to be met, so she said to him: "Would you mind meeting the other doctor? There he comes now."

It was the powwow man, of course. Father was interested, you know, in all that sort of hocus-pocus, so he said that if the other doctor didn't mind he would like to see his treatment. For once a powwow doctor was willing to show off. He had brought a salve, but that, he said, was not so efficacious as "sympathy" and the rest of the treatment. The fellow said what seemed to be a mixture of "Dutch" and dog-Latin over the burnt hand and he rubbed on his salve. Father said it looked and smelt exactly like his own, but that it couldn't be that if the salve was what had worked the healing. The two doctors went out together most amicably. The powwow man was happy because his treatment worked better than the trained doctor's, and father was absorbed with curiosity to see how quickly the hand would heal entirely. Father had told the woman, of course, that he would withdraw from the case, but she didn't want him to. So he agreed to call again four days later when the other doctor would make his next visit.

When father reached the place that day the powwower was there, and father discovered that he had been there every day from the very evening of father's first visit. I needn't tell you that the wound was now covered with new skin and the hand almost ready for its old hard work. Father asked for the formula of the salve, and the fellow gave him a formula, very like his own. It never worked for father any better than his own old salve.

Father was convinced that the powwow man had used the remedy well known through the countryside but with some healing substance in it that he kept secret.

An incident such as that reveals a pleasant side of "hexing." There is another and less pleasant side. That is the kind of "hexing" that brings misfortune to the "ferhexed." In Lebanon county when I was a boy there were two farms side by side where Trout Run slides along under Second Mountain. The richer farm, of course, was in the valley, the poorer up on the side of the mountain. The hill man worked for the valley man at most seasons of the year. They had a disagreement finally, not a very serious one, the valley man thought, but serious enough to make the hill man throw up his job and to refuse to come back to it even after a rather humble visit of his old employer.

Shortly after this, hogs of the valley man sickened and dropped off one by one until six were dead. Meanwhile one of his mules was mired and broke his leg and had to be shot. A cow died of milk fever after calving. The valley man went over the mountain to consult a famous powwow man in Schuylkill County. The powwower told the valley man that the hill man had bewitched his stock. That was what the valley man had expected to be told, for the hill man had been regarded by some of the neighbors as having certain ways of a "hex." The witch doctor told the valley man that if he went to one of the great wooden uprights in the underground stable of his barn he would find a hole in it with a wooden plug and hair of the pigs and mule and cow behind the plug. He found a hole bored out with an auger, and plugged, of course, and a wad of hair at the back of it. After the removal of the hair no more of the stock died.

The valley man had no more bad luck that winter, but by spring he was so uncomfortable living there under the "hex's" eye, with the water from the "hex's" place running down through his pasture, that he sold out and moved down into the Tulpehocken valley. What really drove him out was the light he saw every night in the hill man's attic. The valley man thought there was magic being made there that would end in more trouble for him and his. Just before the light appeared the hill man had gone to Reading, and on his way back home he had shown at the last tavern a copy of Albertus Magnus. In his cups he had boasted of the great power of witchcraft in the book. Then came the light in the attic window. The richer and stronger and better man thought it the part of discretion to move. That was more than thirty years ago, but the hill-man "hex" still lives, and still at night you can see the light in his attic, certainly up to and past twelve o'clock. Neighbors who have sat up to watch it say that sometimes it is not out until three o'clock in the morning. . . .

In all the sects* much is made of birth, marriage and death, and in those churches that have baptism, that, too, is celebrated with befitting ceremony. Great preparations are made at home for the expected child, and its birth is an occasion throughout all the family even to the outer degrees of consanguinity. The birth is carefully recorded in the family Bible. Yesterday it was recorded, too, in a *geburtsschein,* and baptism in a *taufschein,* in illuminated writing, and the records framed and hung on the wall like a sampler. Sometimes the birth certificate was combined with the baptismal certificates as *geburtsschein,* and *taufschein.* This is the form in which most of the printed certificates appear.

There are a hundred sayings about what one must do with the new-born child to make it successful and fortunate. It must be carried upstairs before it is carried downstairs if it is to have health and happiness and riches in after life. It must be decked with jewelry at baptism if it is to be "highminded." Often a part of the jewelry has been worn by many generations of the family at baptism, as has been a certain rhinestone that I know set in silver and with a cross cut into that side worn next to the breast. This talisman was certainly made in Germany, and maybe in pre-Protestant times.

If you wish the child to have rosy cheeks you must throw water from the baptismal bowl over a rosebush in your dooryard. To do this you have to take some utensil to church in which to carry home the *taufwasser.* So deeply implanted is a sense of the importance of everything connected with this custom that a Stiegel cup has been used in a family I know for this purpose and this purpose only down the years.

The baptismal vessels of country churches are often of unique design, a set being made, apparently, for a certain church and never repeated exactly for another. A good many of these vessels are of pewter, though the choicer silver is to be found in churches that were rich in old times, and the humbler toleware in the little and poor churches back in the hills. A painted tray I have is evidently that used to carry the baptismal bowl. It bears on its bronzed background a font in white and red, picked out in black, and draped with a long wreath in green. Below the front, from a sod of green, two plants in yellow spring up with all their leaves swirled to the left, the leaves being in number, as so often in "Dutch" art, the mystic seven. The border about the eight sides of the tray is in the familiar red and yellow and green. . . .

It is a funeral, however, that we make most of, of all family functions.

---

* Here Weygandt refers to the Anabaptist, the "plain" Dutch. (REW).

Our own folks, even to fourth cousins, make every effort to attend the services, and the "baked meats" prepared for their consumption are many and weighty indeed. In the old days before automobiles, the cousins would sometimes have to set out on their journey the day before the funeral to get to the home in time for it. It was the country custom for everyone to come with his own team, and, after the services at the house, join in the procession to the graveyard.

Years ago I attended such a funeral in upper Bucks. The man who was being buried had been murdered, and hardly a stone's throw from his house, and on his own land. He was a Mennonite, and his people, traditionally opposed to going to law, and to any dealings with lawyers or police, had not been willing to co-operate with the local authorities in ferreting out the murderer. He was unindicted after it, though suspicion as to who he was was very strong. The tragic circumstances of the death helped to swell the crowd that gathered for the funeral. Large as the home was, only a small proportion of those who attended were able to get inside to hear the service. Groups stood about outside, near the house, by the barn, and along the road, and talked together in low tones. The services over, their members found their way to their carriages, and fell into a procession of more than three hundred teams. There was everything from a market wagon to, literally, a one-horse shay in that long line.

It was more than six miles from the home of the dead man to the graveyard where he was to be buried, and it took that cavalcade a full two hours to reach it. As the team in which I rode neared the meeting-house the smell of coffee boiling was very present on the air. There were great copper kettles swung by chain and trammel from stout saplings laid across between the lower limbs of the oaks and hickories of the meeting-house grove. Long fires of logs were burning beneath the kettles. There was coffee for all. Many of the people had brought doughnuts and sandwiches and cakes, so that after the services the grove looked almost like a Schwenkfelder Thanksgiving.

It was a day of late November, with the ground frozen hard and little windrows of snow gathered along the fences. An east wind rustled the leaves still hanging to the oaks to an uneasy and cold murmur. The grave was sunk in red soil, and in the offing the blue line of the Durham Hills greyed in the darkening light. The people, many of them plain-clothes folk in bonnets and broadbrims, stood about in little groups after the services, and talked, more noisily than at the house, but still with the decorum proper to the occasion. Their horses stood, carefully blanketed, in the many sheds of the meetinghouse yard, or in the protection of those sheds, resting for the long pull homeward that lay before many of them. The kettles were still boiling, and the bracing smell of coffee was mingled now with the friendly smell of horses. The crowd was slow to disperse, and the longer it lingered the more animated grew its talk. There was bustle and confusion and loud talking as the dispersal began. It was strange to think that death had brought all this life to so quiet a countryside. . . .

All my life the ways northward and westward to the Red Hills have been familiar ways, ways that my people have trod. Everywhere throughout the Red Hills went John, great-great-great-great-grandfather of mine, on his futile mission to reconcile and unite all the many German sects of Colonial Pennsylvania. To that end he compiled a catechism and had Franklin print it, which, he thought, embraced all the fundamentals of Protestant Christianity and would afford a basis on which all the sects could combine. To that end he preached here, there, and everywhere, in churches of any denomination which would listen to him, a man of German Reformed faith whom Count Zinzendorf won to Moravianism.

# III

# FOLK CHRISTMAS

The late Professor Alfred L. Shoemaker of Franklin and Marshall College was an eminent folklorist of things Pennsylvania Dutch. His study of folk Christmas, gleaned from newspaper records and conversations with those who had special knowledge of early practice, is a seminal, although popular, work on the subject. Shoemaker's work helps us to see the manner in which the Pennsylvania Dutch fashioned a religious observance, quite of their own making, out of the resources of earlier tradition and the demands of life in rural Pennsylvania in the nineteenth century.

From Shoemaker we may observe how the Catholic substance of European Christianity continued to manifest itself well into the nineteenth century. The effects of the Reformation had not completely eliminated the residue of attitudes and practices which had been part of the centuries-old habits of Christian Europe. Especially among the Lutheran and Reformed Germans in Pennsylvania there remained a sense of the church and the mystery of God's Incarnation in the common world. This residual Catholicity was conducive to festivity. Although the teachings of the church may have sought to retain a purity of observance associated with the Nativity of Jesus, there was a folk wisdom that knew this was an occasion of joy, of sociality, and of celebration. God had taken upon himself the life of the people! He had been born into their world.

However, in America the Germans found themselves in an environment that was dominated by the austerity of Puritanism and the angelistic tones of Pietism. Here there was a conflict between the need of the folk to express their joy, and the American propensity to deny the efficacy of anything not prescribed in Scripture and to deplore the rejoicing of carnal existence. Here the High Church Lutherans as well as the Puritans were likely to oppose too much Christmas festivity. This was particularly true when commercial America began to sanctify human greed by fashioning Santa Claus out of the earlier traditions of Christ-child and Saint Nicholas.

However, the folk will have their way. Their spirituality may retain its loyalty to the reverential claims of the Nativity, but it will also help the people to relieve their sense of oppression and take joy in the fact that God embraces them in their ordinary existence. The Sunday School movement, which very quickly became a lay institution, often associated with the churches but sometimes not, was also the setting for folk religiosity to assert itself. The writer remembers, as a boy, attending Sunday School in a German Reformed church on the Sunday closest to Christmas. It was an occasion of receiving candy, oranges, and a gift from the teacher, and a time of festive programs and singing that set the tone for other church and family observances. The poor were not to be forgotten, but the folk expressed joy in their own God-given existence. Sunday schools had begun their development of folk Christmas early in the nineteenth century, as Shoemaker demonstrates.

The folk Christmas was a time of miracle and magic. Many of the practices retained by the Dutch were reminiscent of medieval spirituality, in keeping with the residue of Catholic substance still in evidence (although hardly acknowledged as "Catholic"). Christmas was a time of talking beasts, a moment to search for portents of good fortune or ill fate. Weddings, deaths, and the well-being of family and farm animals were affected by the proper celebration of Christmas.

The folk also understood that Christmas is a double-edged blessing. Had not the Advent season always reminded the "church" people that penitence was a necessary preparation for the birth of the Christ? On Christmas Eve, there were two visitors to the family hearth. First came the Belsnickel, who playfully separated the "sheep" and the "goats" from among the children. Those whose behavior had been less than exemplary heard the crack of Belsnickel's whip as he prevented them from gathering nuts and candies until they confessed their bad deeds and promised to do better. Only after his visit, when the children were safely in bed, did the more benevolent figure of the Krist-Kindel (Christ-child) make his visit, bringing some gift symbolizing his love for fallen humanity.

Readers will encounter these varied nuances of folk spirituality as they reflect on the following selections from Shoemaker's book.

# CHRISTMAS IN PENNSYLVANIA

*(From* Christmas in Pennsylvania: A Folk-Cultural Study, *Alfred L. Shoemaker, Kutztown, Pennsylvania: Pennsylvania Folklore Society, 1959.)*

The Lutherans and Reformed in Pennsylvania had a double basis for their Christmas. Because they came from Protestant traditions with a liturgical base, traditions that paid more than usual Protestant attention to the church-year, Christmas was defended by the ministry. This pro-Christmas attitude on the part of Lutheran and Reformed religious leaders allowed the people, in the first century and a half after the first settlement (1700–1850) to establish and develop a folk-Christmas of their own, most elements of which had been brought from the Rhineland.

In the second half of the nineteenth century, when a significant proportion of the Lutheran and Reformed clergy had become either Puritan or High-Church in outlook, when also the folk-Christmas showed some signs of taking over in the Sunday School—when, as the church papers put it, Kriss Krinkle and Santa Claus began to crowd out the Christ-Child —the clergy and the clergy-dominated church press changed their tolerance of the folk-Christmas into opposition.*

To illustrate what happened, let us look at the case of "Second Christmas."

---

\* Before 1840 we [Prof. Shoemaker] located but three references to Santa Claus in our Pennsylvania Christmas literature. The earliest is from the Philadelphia *Saturday Evening Post* of Jan. 7, 1826. The very next one is from the Lancaster *Union* of Dec. 27, 1836: "... and when the Christmas trees have all been wondered at ... 'St. Claus' and his tiny chariot and horses will have ceased whirling through the brains of our little readers." The third is from the Philadelphia *Herald and Sentinel* of Dec. 25, 1837: "... where that old gray-beard, 'Santa Clause,' or St. Nicholas, finds so many beautiful articles which he afterwards distributes in his rambles."

A definitive article on the origin of Santa Claus in America is Charles W. Jones' "Knickerbocker Santa Claus," in the New York Historical Society Quarterly for October, 1954, pages 357–383.

## Second Christmas

If the English celebrated Twelve Days of Christmas, as the carol has it, the Gay Dutch* celebrated at least two, Christmas Day and "Second Christmas," which was the day after Christmas itself.

In general Second Christmas was a day of relaxation, not quite so much of a religious holiday as Christmas. Ezra Keller, Lutheran minister in Hagerstown, Maryland,** German communion I appointed on the second Christmas Day," he tells us; "this displeased some, who although they deem it proper to observe the 26th as a holy day, yet do not think it as holy as the 25th." A Lancaster news item from 1849 gives us the popular attitude to Second Christmas: "On the second day of Christmas we had a fox chase and other amusements . . ." (*The Pennsylvanian,* Philadelphia, January 2, 1849).

In the attempt to sanctify Second Christmas, other ministers held church consecrations and Sunday School exercises on the day. William A. Helffrich, the widely-known Reformed leader of Lehigh and Berks Counties, tells us in his autobiography of the consecration of the new Longswamp Church on Saturday and Sunday, the 25th and 26th of December, 1852: "Preached on the first day . . . The church was at that time the finest in the country. I thought on Christmas, when frost and snow covered the earth, that the sutlers would stay away—but no! even though in not such large numbers, yet the Devil brought them hither. There they stood, behind their 'ginger cakes and sugar sticks' [Lebkuchen und Zuckerstangeln], stamping their feet and pulling their coat-collars closer on account of the frost, and used all their arts to entice buyers."

What is significant about this is that the people were reacting in the old traditional ways. Second Christmas was to them a day of relaxation. Even though they answered the call of their minister to gather at the church, they wanted to make it a social affair. The sutlers [Marketender] with their cakes and wares reacted also in the traditional manner. It was much like the traditional Kerwe (Kermess, Kirchmess) of the Rhineland villages from whence the Gay Dutch forefathers had emigrated a century before.

The people, then, reacted in their usual way. The clergy too, perhaps, were acting in what was a traditional role for them. With their fear of the secular, with their growing dislike for the folk aspects of the culture, they forbade the popular practices.

---

* Gay Dutch is a term referring to those whom we have called "Church Dutch." (REW)
** Hagerstown, Maryland, was on the expanding periphery of the Dutch country, which moved through Washington County, Maryland, into the Shenandoah Valley of Virginia (REW).

## The Church Versus Santa Claus

While the Sunday School Christmas festival was not of course part of the Gay Dutch folk-Christmas, it did become increasingly popular in both Lutheran and Reformed parishes in the second half of the nineteenth century. This again produced tension between the layman's interpretation of Christmas (the Sunday School was a typically American layman's church organization) and clerical attitudes. Increasingly in the 1880's, the Lutheran and Reformed leadership became critical of some of the practices of the Sunday School celebration. While the *Lutheran Observer* for January 26, 1883, comments approvingly on the "Santa Claus pails," full of candies and dates, which were featured at a recent Christmas celebration in Blairsville, *The Lutheran and Missionary* of Philadelphia—representing the High Church wing of Pennsylvania Lutheranism, in a stern article on "Christmas Presents for Sunday Schools"—urges the giving of *religious* gifts rather than clay pipes, jumping jacks, and other secular delights (*The Lutheran and Missionary,* December 9, 1880).

The folk-Christmas practices were bitterly opposed by the Lutherans of the growing high-church school. "Let it be *Christmas* indeed," writes the editor of the *Lutheran and Missionary* in 1881, "and make Christ prominent everywhere. It is His Day, and old and young should remember it. The sooner you present the *Christ child* to your children, the better. Do not suffer this lovely picture to be hidden by the hideous caricature of a Kriss-Kringle, that odious corruption of the German expression *Christkindchen,* or *Christkindle;* and do not substitute for the Babe of Bethlehem, the figment of a Santa Claus . . ." (*The Lutheran and Missionary,* 1881).

Even the *Lutheran Observer* was ready to attack the Sunday School celebrations by 1883. It did so in an article entitled "The Heathenism of Christmas. A Protest Against Santa Claus," signed by "Germanicus" and written expressly for its columns. After giving a biography of St. Nicholas, whose birthday, more than incidentally, was pointed out to fall on "Luther's birthday too," "Germanicus" continues as follows: "The curious customs of St. Nicholas eve, as they obtain in the old country, are interesting and pleasant, and they do not at least partake of the nature of sacrilege. But when the Dutch brought their Sante Klaas to this country, and the German during this same month celebrated the feast of the *Christ-Kindlein,* the Christ-Child, they came in contact with people who gazed in astonishment on these superstitious customs. The New England Puritans had for years been forbidden by law to celebrate Christmas, and even the adherents of the English established church were accustomed to look upon Christmas as a day of feasting and jollity, rather than as a sacred religious festival."

"Thus it was natural for them," he continues, "to combine the customs of the foreigners, the Dutch and the Germans; and Santa Claus and Kriss Kringle, as in their barbarous ignorance of the language they called the Christ-Child, became hopelessly intermingled in the American mind. The festival for both gradually came to be fixed on Christmas."

And now our correspondent gives us his view of the state to which the American Protestant Sunday School Christmas Festival had attained by 1883:

And now, in a week or two, we shall read notices like the following:

Santa Claus in the flesh—The merry time made by his appearance in the Fourth P. Q. Church—How Christmas was kept— Santa Claus held a reception and made a special distribution of gifts in the Fourth P. Q. Church last evening. An army of children was present, whose faces shone with anticipation. The exercises began with a Christmas carol entitled "Who comes this way so blithe and gay?" after which Master William Robinson marched boldly to the front and delivered a speech of welcome. Little Miss Florence Montague then told a story of her last doll, which caused much amusement. Miss Genevieve Parkington then recited the beautiful verses.

'Twas the night before Christmas
When all through the house.

The Hon. Willard Brown then read a letter from the good saint, expressing that gentleman's perfect satisfaction with the Fourth P. Q. Sunday-school, its minister, its superintendent, and all its children.

At this moment a great commotion was heard outside. The rattle of sleigh bells was heard, and suddenly Santa Claus himself came dashing into church, and with a hop skip and jump stood on the platform, amid the wildest cheers and shouts of the children. After giving a history of himself he began to distribute presents to the children.

After the distribution the children sang the following beautiful hymn:

Oh, this is Santa Claus' man,
Kriss Kringle with his Christmas tree.
Oh ho, Oh ho, ho, ho, ho, ho, ho, ho, ho, ho,
Then jingle, jingle, jing, jing, jing,
Right merry shall we be,
Then jingle, jingle,
Come Kriss Kringle,
Come with your Christmas tree;
And welcome, welcome, welcome Kriss,
Right welcome shall you be,
O there he is, yes, yes, 'tis Kriss,
Right welcome shall you be,
O there he is, yes, yes, 'tis, Kriss,
'Tis Kriss with the Christmas tree,
The Christmas tree, the Christmas tree,
The Christmas tree, the Christmas tree.

Now this is no overwrought, fancy picture. It is a scene that will be witnessed in hundreds of churches in city and country, and judging from some reports that reached us last year through the OBSERVER, will not be wanting even in some Lutheran churches.

Not that we have learned it from our ancestors, or from our German brethren. In Germany and in the German churches of this country, Christmas is a sacred day. It commemorates the birth of Christ, God's unspeakable *gift*. Through him all good gifts came to men. The mummery of Santa Claus has no place in the ritual of the Lutheran church, excepting where some of our congregations have borrowed the folly from their neighbors. . . .

### Reformed Church Attitudes

Possibly through the influence of Harbaugh the Reformed Church— which for some reason seems to have been in general more congenial to the folk-elements in "Gay Dutch" life than the Lutherans—paid more attention to Christmas. At least it seems so as one reads through the Reformed periodicals.

Throughout the 1870's, '80's, and '90's of the last century, the December and January pages of the *Reformed Church Messenger* are full of Christmas items, which, like so "many little Christmas chimes" reverberated through the columns week after week (*Reformed Church Messenger,*

February 2, 1870). The Christmas decorations are described in detail—as they were at Harvest Home earlier in the Fall—the two occasions when the farm and the forest came to church. References to "Holy Christmas," "the joyous Christmas festival," and the "bright holiday season" appear in profusion. Glowing accounts by grateful pastors detail the many "donation visits" that brought him and his family a practical Christmas gift, in one instance "schnitz" and "metzel soups" from the congregation (*Reformed Church Messenger,* January 26, 1870).

That there was a negative strain in the Reformed acceptance of Christmas, and that it occasionally, as among the Lutherans, came to the surface among the clergy, is seen in the writings of George Russell. In speaking of Christmas giving he writes, "Only when Christmas gifts refer with thankful devotion, to the Gift of Christ to sinners, can they have any true and proper significance. Let the Christian, as the child of God, have his joy. But evil subverts the good. The wicked caricature, mocking the goodness of God, turns the religious devotion intended in the true Christmas-gift, to a worldly mimicry and devil service. There is something shocking in the representations of the gift bestowing *Krist-Kindlein,* or Christ-Child, as the 'belsnickel' or the evil spirit counterfeiting the gifts of God." . . .

The Lancaster *Daily Examiner* of Dec. 25, 1984, carries an article on metzel soup, copied from the Harrisburg *Independent.*

There was a time when in the towns and cities of Berks, Dauphin, Lancaster, Lebanon and York counties, every man of family raised a pair or more hogs. Forty years ago a pig sty at the end of the lot of every residence of the then borough of Harrisburg was more common than grape vines are now on such premises. Two or three weeks before Christmas, or earlier, the owners of these hogs had them slaughtered, sausage and pudding made, the hams, shoulders, and sides pickled and then smoked, which furnished the meat of many families for the next summer. Then the old custom of exchanging pudding and sausage was in vogue. When a man slaughtered his hogs, he always sent a portion of his spare ribs, pudding and sausage to his neighbors. It was an act of courtesy which no neighbor could omit without losing his status as a gentleman. If a man omitted what was called the *metzel soup,* when he slaughtered his hogs, his neighbors would have tabooed him, and his good fellowship would have ceased. The *metzel soup* is an old German custom—*metzel* meaning, to make fine by chopping, hence the gift of pudding and sausage is called the *metzel soup*. This old custom has passed out of practice, as have many others of the quaint and generous practices of the Pennsylvania Dutch of the Christmas days' indulgences.

Henry L. Fischer, of York, described a metzel soup in his *Olden Times* (York, 1888, page 465): "The germ metzel-soup is the Anglicized form of the German, Metzelsuppe. Metzeln, means to kill and cut to pieces, animals for meat—preeminently, for sausage. In the olden time, a time-honored custom, (doubtless brought by our German ancestors from the fatherland,) prevailed, of sending to each near neighbor, at butchering time, a taste of the delicious sausage and puddings which were made in such great abundance on butchering occasions, which occurred, as they still do among our country-folk, at least twice during each winter; this 'taste' usually consisted of a good sized dish—holding eight or ten pounds —heaping full, and was regarded as the pledge of continuing friendship between the families immediately concerned; for, if the metzelsoup was either omitted or not reciprocated, there was surely something wrong; and the preacher in charge, who always took a deep interest in keeping up the good custom, was sure to hear of the matter; and he generally succeeded in effecting a reconciliation over a love feast of fat things. This metzelsoup-custom became general among our rural folk of *all* nationalities, but is now gradually falling into desuetude together with many others."

Alice Morse Earle in her *Home Life in Colonial Days* (New York, 1898, page 419) describes the metzel soup: "In rural Pennsylvania a charming and friendly custom prevailed among country folk of all nationalities—the 'metzel-soup,' the 'taste' of sausage-making. This is the anglicized form of *Metzelsuppe; metzel* means to kill and cut in pieces—especially for sausage meat.

"When each farmer butchered and made sausage, a great dish heaped with eight or ten pounds of the new sausages was sent to each intimate friend. The recipient would in turn send metzel-soup when his family killed and made sausage.

"If the metzel-soup were not returned, the minister promptly learned of it and set to work to effect a reconciliation between the two offended parties. The custom is dying out, and in many towns is wholly vanished."

In the interval 1909/1911 the reminiscences of W. W. Davis and Abram Setley appeared in the New Holland *Clarion:* ". . . But one thing had to be done before the holidays. Every family kept hogs, and the poor animals had to be sacrificed. How keep Christmas without sausage and spareribs?

"One unwritten law was observed. The first family that butchered was expected to send a 'metsal-soup' to the neighbors, and when the neighbors butchered they, of course, returned the compliments. In that way for about two weeks we had a taste of all kinds of fresh meat.

"Then we made 'ponhaus,' another delicacy that Taft, I suppose, knows nothing about. A solid breakfast food, beats corn flakes all hollow!"

"Don't forget the Poor."

"Don't forget the poor"—this was one of the newspaper themes each recurring Christmas season in the time of the Open-hearth Christmases in Pennsylvania. And we have seen the rural folk didn't forget. They sent metzel soups. The theme of giving to the poor found expression, also, in one of the earliest bits of Christmas Hymn appended to *The Two Wealthy Farmers* (Philadelphia, 1800), page 35:

> Come ye rich, survey the stable
> Where your infant saviour lies;
> From your full o'erflowing table
> Send the hungry good supplies.

But by the mid-nineteenth century this call "Don't forget the poor" became less and less frequent. A new way of life had come over the land, over all parts of it. And with its coming, the metzel soup season began to be forgotten, too, more and more. By the end of the century the custom was a mere memory. . . .

### Some Christmas Folk Belief

For the past ten years we have been engaged full time in gathering data on the folk-culture of Southeastern Pennsylvania. Roughly, half of this time has been spent in libraries, the other half in field-work, collecting the area's folklore. The material in this chapter, as the reader will soon realize, is primarily the fruit of field-collecting. Folk-beliefs are rarely come upon in printed sources, newspapers and periodicals.

Perhaps the best-known of all folk-beliefs in Pennsylvania is that cattle in the barn can be heard to talk on Christmas Eve, between eleven and twelve o'clock. An interesting literary allusion to this belief appears in Henry L. Fisher's *Olden Times* (York, 1888), page 212:

> I used to love and sit and watch
> The cobbler's cut and tailor's stitch;
> To hear the learned arguments;

> Between those learned disputants,
> Concerning elf, and ghost, and witch,
> And whether they were black, or white,
> Or, oxen talked on Christmas-night.

The old-timers will tell you that special gifts are required to understand what the cattle are saying. A person born on Christmas Eve, between eleven and midnight, is said to possess this gift.

Quite common is the folktale of the farmer who ventures out in the barn late on Christmas Eve. While there, he overhears one horse say to another: "Before many a day is past, we'll be driving our master to the cemetery." The farmer becomes struck with great fear, rushes back in the house, stumbles and breaks a leg. And after suffering for a couple of weeks death intervenes.

The choicest bit of lore along this line comes from Schuylkill County. An old-timer tells of hearing that anyone can acquire the gift of understanding animal talk Christmas Eve. One has merely to follow a certain set of rules: sit down by lamplight at exactly eight o'clock on Christmas Eve and start reading the Bible from Genesis, in the very beginning, and continue reading three solid hours, without so much as looking up. Then at the stroke of eleven close the Holy Book, go and cut yourself a piece of bread (it must be from a rye loaf and a round one at that), sprinkle a goodly amount of salt on it and eat it dry—without butter, that is. Having followed these instructions to the letter, you will be able to comprehend the tongue of all the beasts in the barn.

The dew which falls from heaven on the anniversary of the coming of the Christ Child is supposed to have beneficial effects. We personally know instances in Berks County where the mother of a family places a piece of bread (oftentimes the number is three) outside on Christmas Eve, away from cats and other animals. There it lies during Christmas night so that dew will fall on it. In the morning, the mother takes this piece of bread, breaks off a bit and gives a piece to each member of the household to eat—all before breakfast is taken. Doing this, it is believed will prevent fevers all year long until another Christmas rolls around.

Likewise, the farmers used to go out in the barn Christmas Eve, where they set about throwing some hay down in the barnyard. There it lay all night long. In the morning, wet with Christmas dew, this hay was then fed to every horse and cow in the stables. Our own grandfather, so we are told, used to follow this practice on his Niss Hollow farm in Carbon County. The farmers believed if they did this none of their valuable farm animals would die between then and the following Christmas season.

In Lehigh County farmers used to hold to the belief that bees crawled about on the outside of the hive Christmas night, no matter how cold the weather, no matter whether it was mild or snowing.

A bit of general lore, of literary provenance probably, is the saying that on Christmas night water in wells is changed into wine for a brief moment. We came upon this lore in the Pittsburgh *Post* of Dec. 25, 1858: "It was thought that during Christmas night all water was for a short time changed into wine, and that bread baked on this eve would never become mouldy. The fruit trees were 'wassailed' to insure a good crop, and a great variety of similar simple, emblematic customs were observed."

In the field of the occult, there is John George Homan's famous formula from his "Long Lost Friend," giving instructions on how to go about making a divining rod that works: "To make a wand for searching for iron, ore or water: On the first night of Christmas, between eleven and twelve o'clock, break off from any tree a young twig of one year's growth, in the three highest names (Father, Son and Holy Ghost); at the same time facing toward sunrise. Whenever you apply this wand in searching for anything, apply it three times. The twig must be forked, and each end of the fork must be held in one hand, so that the third and thickest part of it stands up, but do not hold it too tightly. Strike the ground with the thickest end, and that which you desire will appear immediately, if there is ought in the ground where you strike. The words to be spoken when the wand is thus applied are as follows: 'Archangel Gabriel, I conjure thee in the name of God, the Almighty, to tell me, is there any water here or not? Do tell me!' If you are searching for iron or ore, you have to say the same, only mention the name of what you are searching for."

To catch a thief, go out to a crossroads over which a corpse has been taken in all four directions. You must do this Christmas Eve between eleven and twelve. Walk a circle and within it build a fire and melt a dime into a silver bullet. With this bullet the thief will be shot dead ere long.

Very widely known is the lore that a silver bullet, cast on a crossroads Christmas Eve at the right hour will, when loaded in a firepiece and fired, hit one's enemy wherever he may be. This bit of occult lore was tried by a Jonestown native during the Civil War; he tried, the Lebanon *Courier* of Jan. 2, 1862, reports to cast a magic bullet to end the life of Jeff Davis: "On Christmas eve, an individual who has great faith in supernatural agencies, undertook to cast a bullet that should kill Jeff Davis, at a cross-road, in the neighborhood of Jonestown. He made all his preparations, fixed his furnace, drew the magic circle, and was moving along 'all right,' when an explosion took place in his furnace as if powder had been concealed there; frightful creatures with horns and ghostly adornments gathered around his circle, spouting fire at him, and the whole scene seemed as if Pandemonium was on an earthly jubilee. The knees of our patriotic friend began to quake, his blood chilled, and not being able to withstand the terrors longer, he broke and ran for town, pursued for some distance by the fiery demons he seemed to have evoked. He arrived in Jonestown speechless and almost helpless, no doubt willing that Jeff should live rather than that he should undergo another such ordeal to get a bullet to kill him."

Christmas Eve, it is widely believed, is the time for looking into the future. Several years ago an elderly woman in northern Berks County told the author of a method she used, when a young girl, to find out whom she would one day marry. She said she set a pail of water out in the yard one Christmas night when the temperature was below freezing. She went to bed early; just before midnight she got up and dressed, took a lantern, lit it and went out in the yard to study the configuration in the ice that had formed in the pail. She said one was supposed to be able to figure out the tool, the trade in other words, of the man one was going to marry.

An open grave Christmas day means an open grave throughout the year in the neighborhood cemetery, it was believed; also, it was said a green Christmas portended a full graveyard for the coming year.

On Christmas Eve any young lady, they said, had but to spread a handkerchief that had never been wet in the garden and leave it there until the mystic hour, when her future husband would bring her the handkerchief the very minute she stepped into the garden.

Any young man who washed his shirt in the evening and hung it up in the kitchen could, it was said, see his future bride turn the shirt on the line, if the young man waited in the kitchen between eleven and twelve o'clock on Christmas Eve.

No new tasks, it was believed, should be undertaken between Christmas and New Year's. A Bernville Grandfather tells me when he was a hired hand on a near-by farm they were not allowed to take any manure out of the stable at this season of the year. If you did not obey, some of your cattle would be dragged out of the stable the next year on account of death, it was said.

Women were not supposed to sew or spin. Cloth spun between Christmas and New Year's, the old-timers believed, would not wear well.

And one was not to take a bath at this time, nor was one to change his underwear. If one did, it was thought, he would become full of boils.

Best-known item of all our folklore is the Pennsylvania weather lore concerning the Christmas season: if the ground is white on Christmas, it will be green on Easter; or if green on Christmas, then white on Easter.

One used to hear, too, if the ground thawed between Christmas and

New Year's, it would also every month of the year. Put more concretely: If between Christmas and New Year the geese waddle in mud they will do so every single month of the following year.

And finally, the number of snowfalls, it was believed, could be foretold for the winter. This was indicated by the number of days from the first snowfall of the season until Christmas. . . .

## BELSNICKEL AND CHRIST-KINDEL

*(The figure of the Belsnickel raises many questions with regard to origin and significance. He or she seems to be a combination of various European sources, attached in some instances to the mystery of the native American—the Indian either as medicine person, or shaman with his quiver, arrows, and bells. His importance to the spirituality of the Dutch suggests a unique bit of folk wisdom that has been lost to us. The Belsnickel was an exorcist, a shamanistic figure whose role was that of preparing and purifying. He was the rascal side of Christmas, come to remind us of our own evil and sin, in order that we might be prepared for the birth of the Christ-child. Perhaps in this context, the doctrine of the Incarnation in Christian theology and story must also include Herod. There is perhaps no time awareness of the benevolent birth without a visitation of evil—at least without a visitor who helps us to see and repent. Although the accounts of folk beliefs and practices with regard to the Belsnickel are sometimes confusing, they reveal an interesting spiritual formulation. Here is a fascinating set of topics for further study and interpretation. I hope you enjoy the story of the Belsnickel and your reflection on the character of the spirituality involved.*

*The first selection Dr. Shoemaker found in an old manuscript in the Berks County Historical Society. It is part of the Christmas recollections of an old umbrella man—an itinerant mender of umbrellas.)*

It is about forty years now that I began going around over here in Pennsylvania patching and fixing umbrellas. From that time to this day I always made for some place in Berks County when it was near Christmas and New Year's. But, my, how things have changed about Christmas since I first came here to you people. I know when sugar was high up in price, about thirty years back, that there were very few children that got more for Christmas presents than a little candy toy and two or three cookies.

They sometimes got a few *snitz,* which the young children liked to eat between meals, for they were then not thrown around as much as now. *Snitz* was from two to three dollars a bushel. The children of poor people got nothing from their parents. Those old Belsnickel parties used to go to the rich people and get things and then carry them to the poor children. I went Belsnickling several times when I was young. We went to every house in half a township where poor children were. When we had given what we could get from people who could afford it better, we went to some of the big farm houses for fun. Cider and wine and apples we had all we could get down. We got a little cake but not much. About the only Christmas cake there was around in those days was *Leb-kucha.*

When we were done visiting the poor children and scared many of them before we did give them the things, we made our headquarters on one farm. We had fiddles and other music. Nearly always there was music and dancing till daytime, and sometimes till almost dinner time. Young ladies did come to the farmhouse the evening before. Then when we was come back from Belsnickling they joined in the frolic.

One Christmas fun twenty-five years ago that you don't hear much of nowadays was watching the Christ rose. They did say that time a certain variety of rose bush would blossom every year the night before Christmas. Well, those parties that did watch the roses was doing it to have luck. It was said that anybody who did see the Christ rose would be very much lucky all his life. Young girls and fellows went together to see the rose on the coldest night. They stood sometimes deep in the snow with their feet. If a boy and a girl saw the Christ rose while out together it was said they would sure get married. But when the Christ rose would not come out when a young couple so did watch it, it was believed that they indeed would never come together. I know yet the time that most every garden had a Christ rose stalk. Almost all people believed much in it. Some planted the rose stalk so in the garden that it could be easily watched from a window. But year after year they did less believe in the old Christ rose belief. The rose stalks did grow less, and now there are very few of them any more. When you speak of Christ roses to the young people now they do not know at all what you mean. . . .

It is to the Episcopalians that we owe the custom of Mumming on Christmas Eve in early Philadelphia, a custom which they brought with them from England.

Christmas Mummers were the counterpart of the Belsnickel, brought to Pennsylvania by settlers from German-speaking Europe: Germany, Switzerland, and from what is French Alsace today. Though both were masked, they differed radically in purpose. The Mummers were groups of folk performers, each one impersonating a specific character. They presented their bit of theatre as they went from house to house. Their motive in presenting the Christmas Eve performances was the expected hand-out: good things to eat, or lacking this, a remuneration in small coin.

The rural Belsnickel, as often as not, made his rounds of the neighborhood alone. Supplied with cookies and nuts, chestnuts usually, and with whip in hand, he went from house to house, rewarding children who were well-behaved and frightening and punishing with slashes from his whip those little boys and girls who did not obey the orders of their parents.

When the British Isle Christmas Eve tradition of Mumming and the Continental tradition of Belsnickling met in Pennsylvania, a new tradition evolved, one that continued in practice in Pennsylvania inland cities to the opening decades of the present century. Christmas Eve masqueraders—whether they were of English background or not—from the latter eighteenth century on took the name of Belsnickels or Belsh-nickels. The word "Mummers" itself became restricted in Pennsylvania usage eventually solely to Philadelphia, where it no longer referred to Christmas masqueraders but New Year's masqueraders. . . .

In the acculturation process *urban* Belsnickels, under the influence of the British Isle Christmas Eve mumming tradition, became members of a performing group—NOT theatrical, but musical—who went about the community, visiting private homes and public places to entertain, expecting in return to be rewarded with Christmas delicacies or small coin. (It is important to observe that the *rural* Belsnickels generally continued true to their original European purpose as punishers of naughty children, though they, under city influence, too, finally expected to be treated by the families they visited.)

*(Professor Shoemaker includes a selection from Benjamin Bausman's "An Old-Time Christmas in a Country Home," which appeared in the January 1871 issue of the* Guardian, *a monthly magazine founded by Henry Harbaugh in 1850.)*

Belsnickel may either mean a fur-clad Nicholas, or a flogging Nicholas. In the wintry Christmas nights, he is usually robed in furs, and carries his whip with him.

Our Belsnickel is, most likely, some well-known neighbor friend. Under his ugly mask (Schnarraffel-gesicht) and an outlandish dress, such as no child ever saw mortal wear before, no one can tell who he is. We children tremble as in a presence of an unearthly being. Really, the Nickel tries to be pleasant, jabbers in some unknown tongue, and takes a few chestnuts and candies out of his vast bundle on his back, and throws them on the floor for the larger boys. One after another shyly picks up a gift. Among these older boys is a self-willed fellow, who sometimes behaves rudely. Whenever he picks up something, Nickel thwacks a long whip across his back—across his only. Whereupon the little ones scream and hold on to their mamma with a firm grip; and the older ones laugh aloud. The guilty boy puts his hand where the whip has made an impression. Again the unknown being puts his large working hand into the bag and scatters gifts, and again cracks his whip on the bad boy. How does this ugly man know who has been naughty?

Ere the little ones are tucked in bed, mother must repeat to them the story of Bethlehem. Then they kneel at her lap and pray to the dear Christ-Child. Half-frightened they put their ears to the key-hole of the parlor door, to listen whether it is at work already at the baskets. Then they scamper off to their low beds, like lambs leaping into the fold. With their heads under the cover, they discuss the frightful visitor with the long whip, and the blessed Christ-Child, that carries no whip, and fall asleep over their talk. Visions of Paradise, where all good children will have baskets of cakes and candies, that will never be empty, cheer their dreams. Many a time during the night a little head is raised above the cover for a moment, to listen for the blessed visitor in the adjoining room; and quickly plunges into the invisible underworld again. "Can you hear it?" whispers a little neighbor.

Hours before dawn the little folks call the parents. They must see their baskets—shoeless, in their slips, they hopefully follow their mother to the full baskets—full of just the things they had been wishing for. Such a heaven on earth—a foretaste of the bliss above comes only to unsuspecting childhood. . . .

The roots of the contemporary celebration of Christmas in the United States stretch back no farther than the first half of the nineteenth century. Largely devoid of folk roots, our Christmas is basically literature-inspired. In large part it is the accomplishment of three men, all three literary figures. The trio are Washington Irving, Clement Z. Moore, both from New York State, and a third author, an anonymous Pennsylvanian, the editor of *Kriss Kringle's Christmas Tree,* published initially in Philadelphia in 1845.

The purpose of this chapter is to show how the eighteenth-century

Pennsylvania gift-bringer, *Christ-kindel* or Christ Child, in the first half of the nineteenth century became Kriss Kringle, an old and bearded twin of Santa Claus.

What was the eighteenth-century folk-concept of Protestant Dutch Pennsylvania in regards the Christ Child? The author has been able to find but one major literary clue. It is a brief newspaper account in the Lancaster *Examiner* of Dec. 30, 1887. A newspaper reporter, covering a Christmas Festival at Washington Borough, writes about what one Rev. A. W. Kauffman related to his audience, both adults and children, concerning his Christmas experience sixty-five years prior, when he was a seven-year-old hired "lad" on a Lancaster County farm. The reporter wrote: "He started out by saying that at that age he lived with an old farmer who on Christmas eve [about 1822] told him to set his basket as the Christ-kindel would come that night. He did as he was bade, but instead of a large plate or beautiful basket, he was given a larger straw bread basket. He was also informed that he must put hay in the basket for Christ-kindel's mule; for says he, 'Boys and girls, Christ-kindel was not as high toned as your Santa Claus now. Instead of a fine team of reindeer and fine sleigh and bells, he came on a mule—an old gray one at that. Now,' continued the Rev. Mr. Kauffman, 'boys and girls, what do you think I got in my basket?' There being no response he went on to relate, or rather enumerate the contents of his well-filled basket, viz.: 'Walnuts, snits, choostets and starched gingerbread.' "

We shall now proceed to develop the two major facets of what we assume to have been the eighteenth century Christ-kindel folk-concept in Pennsylvania:

a) a gift-bringer, who comes by night aback a mule or ass.
b) setting a basket to receive the presents brought by the gift-bringer. (The hay in the basket is intended for the Christ Child's beast of burden.)

There is one bit of Christmas folklore in the Dutch Country which corroborates the mule as the Christ Child's beast of burden. The author's grandfather was a farmer in Carbon County. Each Christmas Eve, before retiring, he would go out to the barn and throw a pile of hay out in the barnyard. There it lay during the course of the night so that the Christmas dew might fall on it. In the morning he would feed this hay, heavy with dew, to his cattle in the conviction that by so doing, his livestock would prosper another twelve months. The folk mind gave this custom an interesting significance. Said the simple folk, "The hay is for the mule on which the Christ Child comes riding on Christmas Eve."

We shall now proceed to show how the eighteenth-century Christ-kindel became "old and bearded" Kriss Kringle by the 1840's. This was accomplished in two steps, one linguistic and the other literary, the former indigenous to Pennsylvania, the latter definitely not.

Pennsylvanians, originally Dutch in tongue, soon became bilingual. And once bilingual, intermarriage began to take place between the Pennsylvania Dutch and their "English" neighbors. The acculturation process —giving and taking between cultures—started to operate. Nineteenth-century scholars called what was going on "the brewing of the melting pot."

In the anglicization process dialect Christ-kindel became Krist-kingle or Kriss-kingle. And Kriss-kingle, by virtue of a philological law known as "progressive assimilation" was altered to Kriss Kringle. This change was effected, however, not without considerable "cussing" and name-calling. The educated Pennsylvania Dutchman saw RED whenever any writer "mutilated" Christ-kindel to Kriss Kringle. He could partly stomach Kriss-kingle but *not* Kriss Kringle. We now present the evidence:

### From the Pottsville Miner's Journal of Jan. 9, 1847

Letter to the editor: In conclusion, let me say to you, that I have lately seen a very frequent reference to the *Krist Kringle* and his frequent visits. Now my dear Sir, I beg leave to say to you that I am really astonished that a gentleman who possesses so much knowledge of German as I know you do, did not once discover that Krist Kringel is an unwarrantable change of the word *Christkindlein,* which is one of the beautiful compounds in which the German language abounds, meaning the "Little Child Jesus."

### From the Reading Gazette of Jan. 22, 1848

Kriss Kringle. The original word, which some Philadelphia book-publishers have corrupted into 'Kriss Kringle,' is *Christ-Kindlein,* or as it is commonly abbreviated, Christ-Kindle. It means, literally, the Infant Christ; but by long usage it has become a familiar household word among Germans and their descendants, and is applied, particularly to children, to any gift made upon Christmas day. It would be as well, perhaps, for our big-city neighbors, to correct the orthography of the word, even though they may continue to pervert its meaning. . . .

### From the Pennsylvania Dutchman of January, 1873

"Kriss Kringle. This is neither Dutch nor German, but a perversion by uneducated newspaper editors. The German is *Christ-kindlein* (the Christ Child), and the Pennsylvania Dutch is Krisht Kintly, which is too good to be slaughtered by anything so harsh and uncivilized as a 'Kriss Kringle.' "

*From the Philadelphia Weekly Press of Dec. 26, 1874*
A German correspondent writes: "Why is it that your native-born Americans spell this word in a way to make it not only lose its lovely sense, but even to make it entirely senseless? 'Kriss-Kringle' you spell it, and if nobody checks you in this obnoxious orthography, a stupid, senseless word will receive the privilege of augmenting the English vocabulary, when, by a very little care, it could be enriched with a beautiful, friendly, and sensible expression. 'Christ-Kindel' means the little child Christ; L'Enfant Jesus, as the French say."

*From the Philadelphia Lutheran of Dec. 22, 1881*
Do not suffer this lovely picture [Christ Child] to be hidden by the hideous caricature of a Kriss-Kringle, that odious corruption of the German expression *Christkindchen,* or *Christkindle;* and do not substitute for the Babe of Bethlehem, the figure of a Santa Claus.

*From the Philadelphia Lutheran Observer of Dec. 21, 1883*
From an article The Heathenism of Christmas by Germanicus: Thus it was natural for them to combine the customs of the foreigners, the Dutch and the Germans; and Santa Claus and Kriss Kringle, as in their barbarous ignorance of the language they called the Christ-Child became hopelessly intermingled in the American mind.

*From the Philadelphia Lutheran of Dec. 23, 1897*
The Germans taught their children that the Christ-child (Christkindchen, and in dialect, Christ-Kindle), brought the Christmas gifts, and the English speaking people corrupted the name into the horrible "Kriss-Kringle," who is actually represented as the veritable Santa Claus. Santa Claus is the Dutch patron saint of Christmas, and "Kriss Kringle" is supposed to be the "Pennsylvania Dutch" form of the same jolly old saint. What a horrible perversion of the beautiful name "Christ-child."

*An Editor Answers Back*
The only retort we have been able to locate to the furore we have just presented was made by a Pittsburgh newspaperman, in the Pittsburgh *Post* of Dec. 25, 1868. (Perhaps he felt far enough away from the Dutch Country not to fear the area's barbs.) He wrote: "Kriss Kringle has come by this time, and has not missed many homes in this city. Some persons who are very stupid, say, we ought to say Krist Kinkle, and some who are very wise, say, we should say Christkindle, but we are used to plain, merry old Kriss Kringle, and shan't give him up."

### Christ-kindel—A Gift

In the Pennsylvania Dutch dialect the word "Grishtkindel," besides designating the Christmas gift-bringer, also means the Christmas gift. In contemporary usage a *Grisht-kindel* to many speakers of Dutch means only the gift any more, no longer the gift-bringer. An article on Kriss Kringle in the Lancaster *Weekly Examiner* of Dec. 28, 1870, makes reference to the latter usage: "Among the 'Pennsylvania Dutch' where we passed our boyhood, 'Christ-Kindly' was applied to any gift made during the Christmas Holidays; therefore a *Christ Kindly* among those people meant the same as a 'Christmas Gift,' or Christmas presents, among the English." . . .

### Term Kriss Kringle becomes established

The earliest printed use we have been able to find for the term "Christ-kindle" is from the York *Gazette* of Dec. 23, 1823. In a humorous entry the Society of Bachelors of York announce their intention of "fixing a Krischtkintle Bauhm" which is to say a "Christ-kindle tree." From this time up to 1840 we have been able to located *but* three additional instances of its use. John F. Watson in his 1830 *Annals of Philadelphia* writes: "Every father in his turn remembers the excitements of his youth in Belsh-nichel and Christ-kinkle nights." A reporter in the Germantown *Telegraph* of Dec. 24, 1834, speaking of the anticipation of the child at Christmas, remarked: "How his eye sparkles, and his cheek flushes as he listens to the promises which his glorious friend Chryskingle is to realize." The third instance is from *The Gentleman's Magazine* of December, 1837: "It [Christmas] is a day when 'wee responsibilities' rejoice in 'Christkingle's' visit."

With one fell swoop in 1842 and 1845 two Christmas books, published in Philadelphia, CREATED Kriss Kringle as a competitor to Washington Irving's creation, Santa Claus. The two volumes are: (1) Kriss Kringle's Book, Philadelphia: Thomas, Cowperthwait, & Co., 1842 and (2) Kriss Kringle's Christmas Tree. A holiday [sic] present for boys and girls. Philadelphia: E. Ferrett & Co., 101 Chestnut Street, 1845.

The editor or editors who created these two Kriss Kringle books did not utilize any phase of the Pennsylvania Dutch Christ-kindel folk-concept we have described. Kriss Kringle was only another name for Santa Claus, the jolly old man who drove through the sky on Christmas Eve with sleigh and eight reindeer and who came down the chimney, a pack of gifts and goodies on his back. . . .

The rural Belsnickel, who customarily made his rounds alone, went from farmhouse to farmhouse rewarding good children and frightening and punishing the disobedient. When the two traditions, Mumming and Belsnickling—met in Pennsylvania a new tradition evolved, one that continued in practice in inland cities of the Commonwealth until the opening decades of the twentieth century: Urban Belsnickling.

By Urban Belsnickling we mean a group of masked youth who banded together on Christmas Eve and went from house to house entertaining on musical instruments and singing, all with the intent of being rewarded in return with Christmas goodies or small coins.

Throughout the nineteenth century, up to the discontinuance of the custom in the first two decades of the present century, two Belsnickling traditions existed side by side in Pennsylvania: the rural and the urban. The Rural Belsnickel made his rounds usually alone, a bag of nuts and cookies in one hand and a switch in the other, to reward or to punish little children, depending on their behavior in the weeks immediately preceding Christmas; if they were well-behaved the Belsnickel threw good things to eat on the floor for them to pick up and eat, or on the other hand if there was an ill-behaved youngster, boy or girl, a sharp switch of the whip was applied before the child was permitted to pick up the gifts.

Eventually, however, the Urban Belsnickel also influenced the traditional rural one. Rural Belsnickels, too, began expecting a hand-out.

The Belsnickel tradition was carried wherever the Pennsylvanians migrated, into many parts of this country and Canada. Belsnickling, for instance, was practiced up until very recently in such distant places as North Carolina, Virginia and Nova Scotia.

The earliest reference we have been able to locate to the Pennsylvania Belsnickel is from the York *Gazette* of Dec. 23, 1823: " 'Belsnickles' are warned to keep within the limits of the Hall."

Storekeepers in Dutchland used to sell more masks at Christmas time than at Halloween. The Allentown *Daily News* of Dec. 23, 1871, commenting on Christmas provisions in a local store, wrote: "Piles of candies, heaps of cakes and congregations of grinning masks are there to delight the youngsters."

In the accounts that follow the reader will learn of our two Pennsylvania Christmas Eve traditions: Rural and Urban Belsnickling.

*From the Philadelphia United State Gazette of Dec. 24, 1825*
Mr. Grigg, in Fourth street, has food for the mind of the young, as well as the old, at his usual low prices, so that when "the stocking is hung up," as of course it will be in all well regulated families, it is probable that the *bellsnicker* [sic], will fit it in part, with more lasting *sweets* than those which the confectioner serves out—the latter, however, should by no means be omitted.

*From the Pottstown LaFayette Aurora of Dec. 21, 1826*

Bellsnickel. This is a mischievous hobgoblin that makes his presence known to people once a year by his cunning tricks of fairyism. Christmas is the time for his sporting revelry, and he then gives full scope to his permitted privileges in every shape that his roving imagination can suggest. Pottstown has had a full share of his presence this season if I am to judge from the wreck of lumber that is strewed through our streets and blockading the doors generally every morning, which indicates the work of a mighty marauder. A few mornings since a little before sunrise, as I was winding my way past your office, I beheld a complete bridge built across the street, principally composed of old barrels, hogsheads, grocery boxes, wheelbarrows, harrows, plows, wagon and cart wheels. It is reported that he nearly demolished a poor woman's house in one of the back streets a few nights ago. He performs these tricks *incog,* or otherwise he would be arrested long since by the public authorities, who are on the alert; but it will take a swift foot and a strong arm to apprehend him while he is in full power of his bellsnickelship, as he then can evade mortal ken. He has the appearance of a man of 50, and is about 4 feet high, red round face, curly black hair, with a long beard hanging perpendicular from his chin, and his upper lip finely graced with a pair of horned mustachios, of which a Turk would be proud; he is remarkably thick being made in a puncheon style, and is constantly laughing, which occasions his chunky frame to be in a perpetual shake; he carries a great budget on his back, filled with all the dainties common to the season—he cracks his nuts amongst the people as well as his jokes without their perceiving him. His antique clothing cannot pass unnoticed, as a description of its comical fashion may excite some ambition amongst the dandies, who are always on the look-out for something flashy and neat, beyond what an honest, industrious, plain mechanic wears, to correspondent their mode of dress with his, whose costume is entirely novel to the present generation; besides the French and English fashions are completely exhausted and have become obsolete; therefore, a description of his grotesque raiment I presume will be acceptable.

This genus of the night winds and storms is, when at a distance, entirely a nondescript; but when he approaches his uncouth magnitude diminishes, and you can accurately survey his puncheon frame from top to toe. His cap, a queer one indeed, is made out of a black bearskin, fringed round or rather stuck round with porcupine quills painted a fiery red, and having two folds at each side, with which he at pleasure covers his neck and part of his funny face, giving sufficient scope for his keen eye to penetrate on both sides when he is on his exploits of night-errantry. His outer garment, like Joseph's of old, is of many colors, made in the Adamitish mode, hanging straight down from his shoulders to his heels, with a tightening belt attached to the waist—the buttons seem to be manufactured entirely in an ancient style—out of the shells of hickory nuts, with an eye of whalebone ingeniously fixed in each,—when he runs, the tail of his long coat flies out behind, which gives an opportunity to behold his little short red plush breeches, with brass kneebuckles attached to the extremities, the size of a full moon. His stockings are composed of green buckram, finely polished. His moccasins are the same as those worn by the Chippawa nation. He carries a bow with a sheaf of arrows thrown across his miscellaneous budget; thus equipt, he sallies forth in the dark of night, with a few tinkling bells attached to his bearskin cap and the tail of his long coat, and makes as much noise as mischief through our town, while the peaceable inhabitants are quietly reposing under the influence of Morpheus.

### *From the Philadelphia Pennsylvania Gazette of Dec. 29, 1827*

Christmas Eve is an important era, especially to the young urchins, and has its appropriate ceremonies, of which hanging up the stocking is not the least momentous. "Bellschniggle," "Christkindle" or "St. Nicholas," punctually perform their rounds, and bestow rewards and punishments as occasion may require.

Our readers are perhaps aware this Mr. Bellschniggle is a visible personage—Ebony in appearance, but Topaz in spirit. He is the precursor of the jolly old elf "Christkindle," or "St. Nicholas," and makes his personal appearance, dressed in skins or old clothes, his face black, a bell, a whip, and a pocket full of cakes or nuts; and either the cakes or the whip are bestowed upon those around, as may seem meet to his sable majesty. It is not sooner dark than the Bellschniggle's bell is heard flitting from house to house, accompanied by the screams and laughter of those to whom he is paying his respects. With the history of this deity we are not acquainted, but his ceremonious visit is punctually performed in all the German towns every Christmas Eve. Christkindle, or St. Nicholas, is never seen. He slips down the chimney, at the fairy hour of midnight, and deposits his presents quietly in the prepared stocking.

We need not remark that Bellschniggle is nothing more than an individual dressed for the occasion. . . .

### *From John F. Watson's 1830 Annals of Philadelphia*

The "Belsh Nichel" and St. Nicholas has been a time of Christmas amusement from time immemorial among us; brought in, it is supposed, among the sportive frolics of the Germans. It is the same also observed in New York, under the Dutch name of St. Claes. "Belsh Nichel," in high

German, expresses "Nicholas in his fur" or sheep-skin clothing. He is always supposed to bring good things at night to good children and a rod for those who are bad. Every father in his turn remembers the excitements of his youth in Belsh-nichel and Christ-kinkle nights. . . .

*From an article by P. E. Gibbons on the Pennsylvania Dutch in the Atlantic Monthly for October, 1869, p. 484*

I was sitting alone, one Christmas time, when the door opened and there entered some half-dozen youths or men, who frightened me so that I slipped out at the door. They being thus alone, and not intending further harm, at once left. These, I suppose, were Christmas mummers, though I heard them called "Bell-schnickel."

At another time, as I was sitting with my little boy, Aunt Sally came in smiling and mysterious, and took her place by the stove. Immediately after, there entered a man in disguise, who very much alarmed my little Dan.

The stranger threw down nuts and cakes, and, when some one offered to pick them up, struck at him with a rod. This was the real Bell-schnickel, personated by the farmer. I presume that he ought to throw down his store of nice things for the good children, and strike the bad ones with his whip. Pelznickel is the bearded Nicholas, who punishes bad ones; whereas Krisskringle is the Christkindlein, who rewards good children.

*From the Reading Daily Times of Dec. 25, 1875*

Reminiscences of one E. B. W. of Brooklyn, N. Y., a native of Reading: Another old custom prevailed in your city which was amusing. There used to be on Christmas Eve a weird-looking hobgoblin, that went round where there were children, particularly, dressed most fantastically, all sorts of colors of ribbons, flowers, laces, regardless of taste, or style, and withal frightful enough to scare the infantile portion into convulsions. A bell announced her coming, followed by a loud tap at the door with the knuckles, accompanied with the question, "Are there any children living here?" "Yes; walk in, take a seat." "Yes, thank you, I am tired of going round after the little folks." In the meantime all the juveniles of very small growth had huddled round their mother, characteristic of course when danger was apprehended, they waiting to see what kind of antics this "Bellsnickle" was going to perform. Bellsnickles! I am of the opinion that the lexicographer has not furnished us with any such word; it may be found in Germany, very probably, among some of their old dusty tomes. But I digress.

I left the children at their mother's side, and when this nondescript personage had recruited, she flourished a whip she had concealed under her cloak, and hobbled round the room, and then commenced her long string of interrogatories: "Do you obey your parents, attend church, repeat your catechism, say your prayers when you go to bed, go to school, and do every thing which constitutes good and dutiful children?" "Yes, marm!" very meekly responded all of them with a unanimous voice. So they were all thoroughly canvassed and their general behavior found to be satisfactory, notwithstanding the old Adam was hidden away from some future time. . . .

# THE MORAVIAN CHRISTMAS

*In eastern Pennsylvania, the city of Bethlehem shares a distinction with smaller cities like Nazareth and Lititz as the regional home of one of America's most colorful religious traditions, the Unitas Fratrum, more commonly known as the Moravians. Although this movement began with a profound commitment to transcend religious differences, it became strongly communitarian; and for a time in the early 1800s, its communities were closed to all but the brothers and sisters. The colorful Christmas Eve vigils and the brass choirs of Christmas are a continuing testimony to a heritage that retained certain Catholic substance derived from old Bohemia and the liturgical life of German Lutheranism.*

*The Moravians came to America under the direction of Count Nicholas von Zinzendorf. They were committed to missionary work among the native Americans, and to an ecumenical agenda that hoped to unite Lutherans, Reformed, and other German-Americans like the Schwenckfelders. Their strong community life nurtured the musical arts and gave encouragement to folk traditions that were rooted in northern and eastern Germany.*

*Professor Shoemaker provides us with insight into the folk Christmas of Pennsylvania's Moravians.*

"Relating to early Celebrations of Christmas in Bethlehem, Pennsylvania," published in volume 6 of the Proceedings of the Pennsylvania German Folklore Society, page 14. . . .

### THE OLD HOUSE OF BETHLEHEM

(The Reading *Gazette* of Jan. 6, 1849, carried an article "The Old House in Bethlehem." Lifted from the New York *Mirror,* it presented the reminiscences of an alumna of the Bethlehem Female Seminary, founded in 1785. The author, who remains anonymous, presents us a very revealing, as well as a most human picture of Christmas in Moravian Bethlehem circa 1800.)

For a month before Christmas, we commenced saving our pocket-money; a dollar a month was the allowance. Happy they were whose friends remembered them in time to send a remittance. I must premise by saying that we of the Old House, being the younger portion of the school, were in three divisions, inhabiting separate rooms during the day, and separated by connected dormitories during the night. The two younger rooms, containing from twenty to thirty girls a piece, enjoyed the full romance of "Santa Claus," "Chryskinkle," or whomsoever the tutelar saint may be. On the morning of Christmas-eve, we of the younger rooms were gathered round the closet in the wall, wherein were deposited our little money-boxes, to receive a portion of their contents. Away we flew to the "Sister's House," to make our purchases. A dollar went a great way in those days. Behold us returning across the corner of the green, hands and aprons full!

Let me see what you have there? Gingerbread, wafers, doughnuts, a bunch of small wax-candles, exquisitely moulded wax figures of a cat, deer, sheep, and, *apropos* to the time, a cradle, with its little occupant imbedded in moss; bundles of candy, dried fruits, and branches of fragrant box! We gather round dear Sister Caroline Shubb, and to her confide our treasures. . . .

At early twilight the bell tolls, the large centre-door of the Old House is thrown open, hand in hand the youngest girls in the school lead the way. Two sisters have charge of each room. As the sisters of the youngest room pass ours, the second follows in the same order, and so on to the third, fourth, fifth, sixth; the three latter occupying what was called the "New House," a building on the opposite extremity of the play-ground, but within the enclosures of the school. The young ladies in the three last rooms were from fifteen to twenty years of age. Two-and-two, in our simple caps and pink ribbons, we walk beneath the dark arched passage to the church. Two rows of long, low-backed benches occupy the centre of the building. We enter at a door on one side of the pulpit, the youngest children leading the way, and, taking their seats at the end of the first bench nearest the middle aisle, the sisters of the room at the other end, the second room is seated on the next bench, and so on to the end. Two hundred fair girls are here assembled, themselves the unconscious centre of attraction to all eyes, flirtation and coquetry out of the question.

On the opposite side of the middle aisle are seated the male part of the congregation; on a bench the whole length of the church, on either side, are seated the strangers. On the female side this bench is occupied by what were called the "great-girls," that is, girls of an age between childhood and womanhood; they were distinguished by having their caps tied with the same flat-bow of ribbon, but of a bright cherry color. The married women tied their caps with blue, and widows with white ribbon; not a bonnet was seen. On a platform, raised one or two steps from the floor, and extending from door to door, were placed two benches, one on either side of the pulpit, and on these sat the oldest men and the oldest women in the village.

I forget the order of the evening service, but the music was ravishing; instrumental music of every description, together with vocal. After the benediction had been pronounced, women bearing trays, on which were small white mugs of delicious coffee, passed through the church, distributing to every individual; they were followed by others, bearing large baskets filled with small loaf-cakes [streislers] by name; these, in like manner were distributed. The ceremony was called the "Love Feast." The mugs being retaken, the sisters again appeared, each one bearing a separate tray, filled with small wax-candles, inserted in a small square of wood painted green. Each person in the church took one—all were burning.

And now commenced the return. The congregation stood in silence to witness the procession of children, the youngest again leading, with their tapers burning. It was not through a darkened archway that we now passed—a glorious illumination of wax-candles, brilliant eyes, and joyous faces cheered the hearts of all beholders, and as the graceful forms of the older girls vanished from sight, a "Merry Christmas," and "God bless you," were the aspiration of every heart.

At the earliest dawn, the morning-bell roused us from our blissful dream. Descending the entries leading to our respective rooms, we stood in the dim twilight on either side of the closed door; at a given signal, the Christmas Hymn arose, triumphantly proclaiming, "Glory to God in the highest, and on earth peace and good-will to men." The door is opened, our eyes are dazzled with sudden brilliancy. Hundreds of wax-tapers, arranged in lines of light, mark out the portion of the long table allotted to each girl—within these bright enclosures our purchases of the previous day are fancifully disposed. Beneath the tiny box-tree reposes, on a diminutive bed of moss, the speckled deer; in an opposite corner, a little, old-fashioned shepherd tends his patient flock; a portly Dutch doll watches over the safety of the Lilliputian cradle. Bundles of tapers are in readiness to continue the illumination through the day; for, until the appearance of to-morrow's sun, our shutters remain unopened. Walls of gingerbread impart a substantial look to each little domain, while raisins, almonds, sugar-plums, and an endless variety of cake, promise full employment to every happy proprietor. Our kindhearted sisters have decorated the walls with wreaths of evergreen and bright winter-berries. The delicious Christmas breakfast, who can forget the triangular pieces of Moravian sugar-cake, a feast for an epicure.

Happy days! happy days! The orphan found kind friends in the dear
Old House—where are ye now? . . .

### Moravian Christmas Putz

Among Moravians the word *Putz* means a creche or a landscape
which is erected in churches and homes during the Christmas holidays. It
is the German word "Putz" which means ornamentation or decoration.
(A facetious etymology, of recent vintage, derives the word from the English verb "to put": because in building a Putz one *puts* a piece here and
one *puts* one there.)

The principal student of the Moravian Christmas Putz was the late
Elizabeth Myers of Bethlehem. In her book, *A Century of Moravian Sisters,* Mrs. Myers ably describes the Moravian custom:

> The "putz" is so distinctive of a Moravian Christmas that it
> merits a special word. It was, and is, an elaborate miniature
> landscape built under and around the Christmas tree, and telling
> the Christmas story, from the appearance of the angelic choir to
> the shepherds where they were tending their sheep, to the
> manger with its Holy Family, and the adoration of the Magi!
> This was brilliantly lighted with the beeswax candles in tin
> holders, in greater or lesser degree. Much ingenuity was shown
> and beautiful effects obtained. The modern putz is the same
> thing, greatly elaborated with electric lighting effects, painted
> backgrounds and even victrolas hidden under the moss and
> playing the Christmas songs.
>
> Everyone was glad to show the results of their labor, so
> "putz parties" became popular. They called it "going to see the
> putzes" and probably this first brought the boys and girls to-
> gether. Before the town "opened up" in 1844, the sexes did not
> mingle at all in this way, but after that the bars were let down
> somewhat, and although very strict rules were made the boys did
> go out with the girls. They would help drive the cows home, and
> on Sunday go to see the wax works together, and walk down
> Bartow's path along the canal, for wild flowers. But the putzes
> provided the entering wedge.
>
> One of the chief decorations of the putz was the shepherd
> scene, and plenty of white sheep were always placed upon the
> green moss, on a miniature hillside or in a tiny meadow. These
> sheep were also made in the Sisters' House, by one Benigna
> Ettwein, familiarly known as Benel. Kindly, big-hearted Benel,
> whose fate it is to bring a laugh whenever her name is men-

tioned! But a laugh may be a very eloquent epitaph and so it is for her. Benel's sheep were wonderful to behold! They were shaped out of clay, then cotton was wrapped around them, four matches were stuck in to represent legs, and a splash of Chinese vermilion was daubed on the end where the nose belonged. She also made chickens out of tow and glued chicken feathers on them, and both chickens and sheep appeared on the putzes of her friends.

Building putzes in Moravian communities is a custom that reaches back into the eighteenth century. Mrs. Myers, writing in the Bethlehem *Globe-Times* of Dec. 19, 1923, says: "The earliest family putz of which we have definite knowledge, though doubtless there were earlier ones, was that of Peter Fetter, in 1782. In that year Mr. Fetter carved a cow from a piece of wood for the Nativity set on his putz. The cow is still in existence, having been used on the putzes of successive generations in the Fetter family ever since."

One more bit of evidence regarding the antiquity of the putz is to be found in the *Moravian* for December, 1867: "How far back they date we are not prepared to say. They were in the full tide of their glory when we were a boy, twenty-five years ago, when we were sufficiently advanced to lend a helping hand, and *then* the great *Putz*-makers were men well advanced in years, so that it is fair to presume that *Putz* making is amongst the ancient institutions of this venerable town. The taste and ingenuity displayed in these decorations was often very considerable. We use the word 'decoration' for the want of a better, though it does not convey a correct idea of the *Putz,* which is not a festooning of the rooms with garlands and wreaths, but a miniature representation of some scene in nature, imaginary or real. As we have said, the art displayed in these mimic scenes was frequently very creditable. Mountains and valleys, tumbling waterfalls and peaceful fields, lakes and villages, in the bright green of summer, or the delicate snow covering of winter, were represented with a faithful minuteness of detail, and in really artistic groupings. Many evenings, until late in the night, were devoted to the making of them. Who will say that it was labor thrown away? Now-a-days, we fear, you could scarcely gather together a dozen men who would be willing to devote themselves to the preparation of one of these grand *Putzes* of the olden time, just because they loved to do this sort of thing, and the time is now to them so precious a thing for business, that they cannot spare it for the purpose of pure and innocent amusement. Are we any the happier or better now? Are boys any more frank and innocent, or the girls any more loveable and modest than they were then? When, even on Christmas Eve, the great *Putz*-seeing evening, they came home at nine o'clock, and were thankful for the privilege of being allowed to go, and to be an hour later than usual.

"Besides these *Putzes* which were made on a grand scale, there were smaller ones in abundance; the humblest home having its little table, covered with a white cloth, and backed by branches of evergreens, from which were suspended glittering stars, wax angels, bright colored candies, &c., in pretty confusion, illuminated by many burning candles. Who, that ever saw or played at them, will forget those bright Christmas scenes? The cave from which issued the monster bear or lion, the looking-glass lake, on which ducks and geese of various sizes sat in motionless propriety, the silver-sanded road, on which was ranged the contents of a Noah's Ark, with the patriarch and his family walking first, and the animals following two by two in solemn procession; the little village with its church and rows of stiff poplar trees; the pleasant minglings of bird and beast and fish, all in perfect peace with one another, as became them at Christmas time; the stable where the 'blessed child' was born; the mill hoisting up its bags and letting them down again, as long as the hidden machinery remained in working order, whilst the miller smoked his pipe, and his dog kept up a very energetic, if somewhat methodical jumping at his feet; all these, and a thousand other recollections, rise before the memory, and force us to the conclusion that *Putzes* are a great institution, and ought not to be allowed to die out. And there are other memories associated with them, some of which are of too sentimental a character to be mentioned. The expeditions in search of moss, the pleasant preparation for the great *Putz,* the mysterious darkened and carefully locked up room, the anxious suspense, the joyous surprise, the happy hearts and smiling faces, the sweet interchange of precious presents between the juveniles, not of the same family or sex, the fortunate and often repeated meetings whilst going the rounds of visiting the many Putzes, which it was necessary to see. We wonder whether the young ones enjoy Christmas as thoroughly and innocently as they used to do when Bethlehem was only a little village, and the outer world was quite shut out." . . .

# IV

## SPIRITUALITY AND HEALING: MEDICINE AND FOLK BELIEFS

In a discussion of the role of healing in Native American cultures, Sam D. Gill points to the fact that the maintenance of health forms a major portion of the world-view and activity of these peoples. What Gill says of the Navajo and the Zuni is equally true of all people at the level in which we are "folk." Health and healing are of a symbolic nature. They are seldom entirely "scientific" in the sense in which that term is frequently used. "Matters of maintaining health" among Native Americans, writes Professor Gill, "at some levels . . . appear to conflict so sharply with the practice of Western scientific medicine [that] these aspects of Native American religions have been greatly misunderstood—or truncated to a consideration of 'primitive psychology' or 'primitive pharmacopoeia.' This matter becomes especially critical when we attempt to understand a Native American religion such as the Navajo, which centers upon *health as the basic component of the symbolic languages of the religious tradition.*"*

It would seem that health is a basic component of the symbolic language of any culture. Certainly the "Western scientific medicine" of which Gill speaks is a highly symbolic affair. It is not all analysis, precision, technical diagnosis, and careful treatment. It is a way of comprehending the world and of deriving a sense of security and well-being from that horizon. The symbolism of western scientific medicine is dominated by the scalpel and the needle, with the implication that health is a matter of "cutting out" or "putting in." The human being is an independent

---

*Sam D. Gill, *Native American Religions* (Belmont, CA: Wadsworth Publishing Company, 1982), 109.

mechanical unit—medicine "fixes" it as one would a car or a computer. The folk are much more aware of health as an affair of placement in a cosmos. The placement is a complex one, with many forces and energies at work. At the level of folk spirituality all people "remember" what traditional societies knew before the advent of modern science—they know that the individual is in some sense a microcosm of the universe. The business of healing and medicine is therefore an intense drama. One must know lines and movement and be able to enter into the story. Health is a matter of knowing the proper story. Disease is disorder in the cosmic drama; the story must be reinstated in the lives of those who experience the disharmony.

In an essay, "The Two Sciences of Medicine," Professor Jacob Needleman writes:

> According to the Hindu scriptures, bodily disease was unknown in the previous cycles of man's existence on earth. . . . It is rather clear, in what we call primitive medicine . . . that disease is very often regarded as a phenomenon of society. Thus, the healing methods for certain specific diseases intimately involved the participation of the tribe, which I think anthropologists wrongly interpret and explain solely in terms of the psychological support offered by the tribe to the sick person.
>
> Because the ancient teachings saw the cosmos as a conscious harmony of energies, the idea that man is subject to all the forces of creation served as a call for self-examination to individual men . . . disease was understood as the result of interference with this constantly shifting harmony of focus. The enemy to be feared was not nature, but man's insensitivity to the force at work in him. Such a sensitivity by which man could move with the whole of moving nature is, however, a property of microcosmic man, perfected man. The hard conclusion is that what the universe cares for in individual man is only for the perfecting of the microcosm. Great nature is the enemy only of the man who is the enemy of his own perfecting.*

Magic and superstition must be re-examined from this point of view. Originally they were often part of the ancient teachings and the drama of healing. It is only when they become disengaged from that context that they are apparent absurdities. Removed from the affirmations of har-

---

* Jacob Needleman, *Consciousness and Tradition* (New York: Crossroad, 1982), 101–02.

mony and the methods for "the perfecting of the microcosm," they may also become malign and sinister.

The Pennsylvania Dutch emerged in American history at a time when the traditional understanding of microcosmic humanity was being shattered by the onslaught of Cartesian philosophy and the pragmatic and contractual notions of knowledge generally associated with modern science. Until very recent times the wisdom and practices of ancient teaching lingered, and found their expression in folk spirituality, where they suffered by association with those elements in society which were thought to live in abyssal ignorance and "primitive" pathos.

We shall see that the Dutch carried elements of folk medicine with them into our own era. For these people the use of magical formulas, incantations, and the application of special healing techniques tended to be an affirmation of life and a recognition that health was linked to the harmony of the cosmos. The Pennsylvania Dutch have come to call their healers "pow-wow doctors," thereby acknowledging an affinity with the Native American world. My paternal grandmother was such a "doctor." I have been told that she treated and was the source of healing for a childhood disease I had contracted as a toddler. She was at the same time a devout German Lutheran. Her German language Common Service Book rests on my shelves today.

The first selection is from John George Hohman's *The Long Hidden Friend or True and Christian Information For Every Man containing Wonderful and Well-Tried Remedies and Magic Arts, As Well For Man As Beast* (Carlisle, PA: *Carlisle American,* 1863). The book was Hohman's adaptation from German sources, including "The Book of Albertus Magnus." It should be noted that it had long been a common practice to publish folk books of an occult nature under the name of Aristotle or Albertus Magnus. Most of this material was apocryphal. It is very likely that Hohman found many of his prescriptions in folk books and pamphlets that had been published in Pennsylvania beginning in the eighteenth century. *The Long Hidden Friend* went through several editions and was frequently issued without reference to the printer because its material was opposed by many of the clergy. The book was widely influential, its practices followed by many people to the present day.

A second set of selections is from *Pennsylvania German Folk Medicine,* Vol. XLV of the Pennsylvania German Folklore Society, edited by Thomas R. Brendle.

# Hohman's Long Hidden Friend

The author has scarcely any preface to write to his little volume; but, on account of the erroneous notions of certain men, I must not omit it entirely. Many say, you are right, to publish and sell the book. The fewest say, not right. Such men I pity indeed, and pray every man, as best he can, to turn away such men from their errors. It is true that he who misuses the name of Jesus vainly, commits a great sin. Does it not stand expressly in the 50th Psalm? "Call upon me in need and I will save thee and thou shalt praise me." This is in the Lutheran Bible. In the Catholic it stands in the 49th Psalm: "Call upon me in the day of trouble and I will save thee and thou shalt praise me." Where is the physician that has been able to cure disease of the heart, gunshots, small-pox, diseases of the womb? or to heal the *cold burn,* (gangrene) when it attacks the limb strong? To cure all these and yet many more private things are contained in this book, and the author can at any time take his oath that he has already effected many cures, and I can call heaven to witness whether any has ever lost eye, or tooth, or limb, by the use of my remedies. Such men reject the command of the Lord—to call upon him in time of need. *If we may not use forms of words (charms) and the highest name, they would not have been revealed to us, and God would not help when we use them.* God cannot indeed be compelled contrary to His own perfect will. One other thing I must mention: Some say, if you use these words; after that the doctor-stuff will be of no use. That is only your doctor's stuff. For if he cannot cure with the words, much less can he without them. I can any time name a Catholic Priest who had his horse cured by such means, and can name the man who did. He lived over in Westmoreland County. I can also name a reformed minister who performed in the art and cured the gout. *If people misuse the book, it is a sin;* but woe to those who, through fear of wrong, will suffer the loss of life, or limb, or eyesight, or who avert it to subserve thine avarice contrary to the spirit of the command in the 50th Psalm: "Call upon me," etc., and woe to those who, at the dictate of any preacher, shall dare to despise the little book. I have my proof of the

150

efficacy of these means, and can furnish them to any who may wish to see them.

Dated at Rosedale, near Reading, in Berks Co., Pennsylvania, 31st July, in the year of our Lord Jesus Christ, 1819.

*John George Hohman,*
Author and Publisher of this Book.

REMARK

Many people in America believe in no hell or heaven. In Germany such people are fewer. I, Hohman, ask, who cures wounds and gangrene? Who stops blood? I answer; and I, Hohman say: The Lord does it. Therefore there is a hell and heaven. I don't think much of such people.

TESTIMONIALS

That I, Hohman, have used these cures out of this book, and that can be shown at any time:

Benjamin Stoudt, a Lutheran Schoolmaster's son, of Reading, suffered great pain on account of a tumor in the eye. In a little more than 24 hours, that eye was as well as the other. He got his help from me and God—year 1817.

Henry Yorger, resident yet of Reading, brought a child to me in 1814, suffering exceedingly from the same cause or the last; in a little more than 24 hours I and the dear Lord had helped him.

John Boyer, son of Jacob Boyer, dwells yet in Reading, had an ulcer on the leg. He suffered much from it. I attended him and in a short time he was healed. This was in the year 1818.

Londlin Gottwalt, of Reading, had severe pains in the arms; was entirely cured in about 24 hours.

Catharine Meek, then of Elsop Township, suffered severe pain in the eyes from a tumor; in a little more than 24 hours the eye was cured.

Mr. Silver, of Reading, was with me when he worked in the distillery of my neighbor. He suffered great pain in the eyes, as the above. I healed him in a little less than 24 hours.

Anna Schaeider, in Elsop Township, had severe pain in a finger. In a little more than 24 hours I had helped her.

Michael Hartman, Jr., dwells in Elsop Township, has a child which had a very sore mouth. I administered for it. In a little more than 24 hours I had helped it.

John Zingeman, a Ruscomb-mower, has a child which was badly burnt. My wife came in, late in the year—it was 1812. The proud flesh had already set in. She attended it, and in a short time the proud flesh was subdued, and the child was soon cured. At the same time my wife cured his wife of a severe case of Erysipelas in a sore leg.

Susanna Gomber had severe pains in the head. I soon had her well. Also, David Beech's wife, the same.

John Junkin's daughter and his son's wife both had severe pains in the head, and the woman had besides a wonderful Erysipelas on the back. I cured the headache of both, and the Erysipelas in 7 or 9 hours was gone. Her back broke out and healed completely. The woman had already lain in bed with it several days. Junkin's family lives in Mackemixen; Beech and Gomber in and about Reading—year 1819.

Arnold's daughter was burned with coffee. The handle of the pot broke while she was pouring out, and the coffee went on her arm and burned her quite badly. I was present and saw it. I took the fire out; the arm was not disabled but healed in a very short time. Mr. Arnold dwells near Solomon. His first name is John.

Should any one of the above-mentioned witnesses, who have received help through me or my wife and God, call me a liar and say they have not been helped by us, when they have acknowledged it to us themselves already, I would compel them, if it is possible, which I believe it is mostly, to acknowledge it before a Magistrate. The above-mentioned Arnold's daughter had her limb burned about the year 1815.

Jacob Stoufer, in Heckock, Bucks County, had a little child which had convulsions every hour. I sold him a book in which *the 25 letters were written.* At the persuasion of his neighbor, Henry Fronkenfield, he used the 25 letters. Immediately the child was freed from the convulsions and became sound. The above-mentioned letters are in this book also.

A Recipe for Rheumatism has been sold from $1 to $2; and it was not once stated in it how it was to be used, and was worthless.

John Algaire, of Reading, had a very sore finger. I treated him for the Erysipelas and the sore finger. The next morning the Erysipelas was gone, and the finger had begun to heal. Year 1819.

*This book is partly taken from one published by a Gipsy and partly from private papers,* brought into the world with much labor by me, the author, John George Hohman, at different times. I would not have permitted it to be printed; my wife also was against it; but my sympathy for my neighbors was too great, seeing how many had already been cured of grievous diseases. How hard many a woman has suffered from affections of the womb! I ask then, friend, is it not a little praise for me, that I have permitted such a book to be printed? Am I not, in God's name, deserving of some reward? Where is there a doctor who can cure the above-mentioned sickness? I am besides a poor man and am entitled to turn an honest penny by such a book.

The Lord bless our beginning and end in this little book, and stand by us that we may not misuse it, and thereby commit grievous sins! *The word "misuse" means to use the remedy or charm, when it is not necessary.* God bless it! Amen. The word *Amen* means an added desire that he may grant a petition.

HOHMAN.

MEANS AND ARTS

*1. A good remedy for Disease of the Womb. It must be used Three Times.*

Place the upper joint of the thumb—the one next the hand—on the bare skin, over the pit of the stomach, on the point of the bone which projects there, and repeat this:—

Uterus, womb, lay thyself down in the right place.
Else thee or me will they carry on the third day to the grave.†

*3. A Sure Means to Staunch Blood. It is helpful, though the person is far absent, if the one who uses this means for him, pronounces his name right.*

Jesus Christus, precious Blood!
Which soothes the pains and stops the Blood.
Help thee (name) God the Father,
God the son and God the Holy Ghost. Amen.

*6. A Remedy against Worms—in Man or Beast.*

Mary, the holy, went over the land,
She had three worms in her hand;
One was white, another black and the third was red.

---

† The sign of the cross.

Stroke the person (or animal) you would benefit. At each repetition strike him on the back; viz; the first time once; the second time, twice; the third time, thrice; and set a time for the worms, but not less than three minutes.

### 7. For Slander or Witchcraft.

Art thou slandered, or thy head, flesh, limb, send it back home to the false tongues, thus:
Take off the shirt, and put it on wrong side out, put the two thumbs at the pit of the stomach, and carry them around under the ribs as far as to the hips. Do this three times, carefully and devoutly.

### 8. Good Remedy for a Fever.

Good morning, dear Thursday; take away from (n) the 77 Cover Fever! Ah, Thou Dear Lord Jesus Christus, take it from him! This is to be used first on Thursday, once; on Friday, twice; on Saturday, thrice; and each morning thrice. You must, at the same time always say the Creed, and speak with no one till sunrise. The patient also, must speak with no one, eat no swine's flesh, and drink no milk for 9 days, and during the 9 days, not pass over running water.

### 9. Remedy for the Colic (the Gripes).

I warn you, you gripes! There is One in the Judgment: he speaks: Right or wrong. Therefore, beware, ye gripes.

### 11. To make a Wand to seek Iron, Ore, Water and the like.

The first Christmas-night, between 11 and 12 o'clock, break a young branch, of one year's growth, towards the sunrising, in three highest names. When you use the rod to seek something, use it three times; i.e.— take the wand—it must be forked—take one part in each hand, so that the thick part stands *up;* if the third part strikes toward the earth, that is the place where the thing is which you seek. You are at the same time to repeat these words: Thou, Archangel Gabriel, I beseech thee, in the name of God, the Almighty, is *water* here or not? Say. Or *iron* or *ore,* etc.; whichever you seek.

12. *A very good Remedy for irregular action (stopping or ceasing to beat) and enlargement of the heart.*

Heart-ail and increase, retire from (n's) ribs,
As Jesus, the Lord has retired from his crib.

13. *To make sure to Hit in Shooting.*

Take the heart of a field-mouse, and put a little of it between the ball and the powder, and you will hit what you wish. You must use the three highest names when you begin to load, and you must not finish the words till you finish loading.

23. *A very good Remedy for the Hot and Cold Brand, Burns and Gangrene. (? fluctuating, local inflammation!)*

Sanctus Storius res, call rest,
Came the Mother of Jesus to him for consolation,
She reached him her snow-white hand,
For the Cold and Hot Brand.

Make 3 crosses over the place with the thumbs. All cures with forms of words are repeated 3 times, and always wait a couple of hours, and the third repetition is on the next day.
The single N. signifies the first name, and two N.N. the first or Christian name and the surname of the patient. This holds throughout the book.

27. *A Sovereign Remedy for Bad Wounds and Burns.*

God's Word and Mary's Milk and Jesus' Blood.
Is for all wounds and burn-sores good.

It is safest if you make the three crosses with the hand or the thumb at each of the clauses. The three crosses marked indicate the plans.

28. *A Good Remedy for St. Anthony's Fire (or Erysipelas) as well as for wounds: Also for Aching Limbs on which the Erysipelas appears.*

St. Anthony's Fire and the Dragon's red,
Together over the Brook they fled.

St. Anthony's Fire is done;
The Dragons they are gone.

### 36. *To Stop Blood.*

To-day is the day that the evil fell forth: Blood, thou must stay till the Virgin has given another son birth.*

### 37. *A Good Means to Make One's Steps and Goings Safe.*

Go, Jesus, with N.N.; he is my head; I am his member.

### 42. *A Good Remedy for Falling Sickness, when one has not yet fallen into the Fire or Water.*

Write on a bit of paper backwards. It is all done! This must be hung on early the first Friday of the New Moon. The writing must be put in a red scarlet napkin, and a linen napkin put around this. The linen napkin and the thread must be unbleached, and the thread must have no knot in it. This is written on the paper only once.

### 46. *A Wonderful Paragraph from the Book of Albertus Magnus.*

It is said therein that if you burn a big frog to ashes and put it into water, and besmear with it any part on which hairs grow, no more will grow there.

### 49. *For the Headache.*

Form bone and flesh, as Christ in Paradise, who alone can help; and this I say to thee (N) for penitence.
Say this thrice, at intervals of about 3 minutes, and the headache will soon leave. But if it is caused by strong drink, it is not so likely to go away. You must then say it every minute.

### 50. *To Cure Wounds and Pains.*

Wound, thou must not (inflame) heat.
Wound, thou must not sweat.

---

* Which means never, of course.

Wound, thou must not water.
So conjure I thee by the Holy Virgin.

*59. To Overcome and end Battles and Quarrels—To Divine whether a Sick Person will Recover or Die—Also for Dimness or Glare of the Eyes.*

This root grows at the time that swallows and eagles make their nests. If one wears it about him, together with the heart of a mole, he will overcome in battle and end all quarrels. If it is laid on the head of a sick person, then if he weeps, he is about to get well again; if he sings with cheerful voice, he is about to die.

When it is in blossom, bruise it and steep it in a vessel of water over the fire, and skim it well; when it is thoroughly done, strain it through a towel and preserve it. This is a good wash for weak or dazzling eyes.

*62. To Consecrate a Divining Rod.*

When one makes a divining rod, or luck rod, he breaks it as before said and says while making it and before he uses it: Luck-rod, retain thy strength, retain thy virtue, whereto God hath ordained thee.

*63. To Drive Away the Worm.*

Worm, I conjure thee by the living God that thou avoid this blood and this flesh, as God, the Lord, will avoid the judge who pronounces unjust judgment, it being in his power to pronounce right judgment.

*64. For Consumption.*

I command thee out of the bone into the flesh; out of the flesh into the skin; out of the skin into the wide world.

*65. For a Burn.*

There went three holy men over the land,
They blessed the heat and they helped the burn
They blessed it that it consumed him.

*66. For a Snake Bite.*

God enacted everything, and everything was good,
But thou alone, viper, art accursed,

Accursed shalt thou be and thy poison.
tzing, tzing, tzing.

67. *For a Bad Dog.*

Hound, hold your mouth to the ground.
Me God made, thee he suffers, hound.

You must do this toward the place where the dog is. You must make the three crosses at the dog, and before he sees you, but you must say the words first of all.

69. *A Very Good Cure for the Botts.*

Stroke the horse three times and lead it around three times with the head towards the sun and say: The holy one says, Joseph went over a field where he found three little worms; one was black, another was brown, the third was red:

Thou shalt die; go dead.

71. *A Sovereign Remedy for Colic.*

Jerusalem, thou Jewish City,
Which Christ, the Lord, has borne;
Water and blood thou must become,
That is good for N. for Colic and worms.

78. *To Hold a Thief Fixed, that He Cannot Move. It is the Best Charm for this Purpose in the Book.*

O Peter, O Peter! Take from God the power; may I find—what I would bind—with the band, of Jesus' hand—that robbers all, great and small—That none can go no step more, neither backwards nor before—till I then with my eyes perceive, till I then with my tongue releave—till first they count me every stone, twist heaven and earth, and drop of rain—each leaf of tree and blade of grass; this pray I to my foe for Mass.
Say the Creed and the Paternoster. To compel him to stand, say this thrice. If the thief is to be permitted to win, the sun must not shine on him before you loose him. This loosing is done in two forms. The first is: bid him in the name of St. John to go forth. The second is this: with the words with which you (or *those,* if only *one,* or a woman) were stopt, you are loosed.

## 84.  For Stone in the Bladder.

The author of this book, Johann Georg Hohman, am using this remedy and it is helping me. Another man sought help from the doctors a long time in vain; he then found this serviceable, viz: he ate every morning forty-seven peach-stones, and it helped him. If the case is very bad, continue it. I, Hohman, have used it only a few weeks. I began to perceive its good effects immediately, though I had the disease so bad that I was forced to cry aloud when I made water. To the loving Do and my wife I owe a thousand thanks for this relief.

## 103.  To Stop Blood and Cure Wounds in Man or Beast.

On Jesus' grave there grew three roses: the first is goodly, the second all-pervading. Blood stands still, the wounds they heal.

## 104.  For Scurvy of the Gums and Foul Throat.

Job was jogging o'er the land: had his staff in his hand, Blessed him God the Lord and said: Why, O Job, so very sad? Ah Lord, he said, and why not sad? My mouth and throat are very bad.

Said God to Job there in the vale; a fountain flows which thee will heal (n. n.).

The throat and mouth in the triune name; but say the names and say, Amen. Repeat three times, morning and evening, and at the words "thee will heal," breathe in the child's mouth.

## 105.  To Gain a Law Suit.

It is said that if one has a law-suit, and will take of the largest sage, and will write the names of the 12 Apostles on a leaf and put them in his shoe before he goes to the Court House, he will gain his case.

## 112.  For Rheumatism.—Very Good and Sure.

This recipe has been sold as high as $2; it is the best and surest remedy for the Rheumatism. The formula is written on a letter and sewed up in a piece of linen cloth with thread and hung to the neck by a band on the last Friday in the old of the moon. The cloth, band and thread must not have touched the water, and the thread have no knot in it. In folding the letter, 3 ends must be laid together at one side. You say the Lord's prayer and the Creed when you hang it on. The following is the formula:

God the Father, Son and Holy Ghost grant; Amen. Like sought and sought; that God the Lord grant thee by the first man; so God on the Earth may be loved, like sought and sought; that grant thee God the Lord by the 12 Apostles. Like sought; that grant thee God the Lord by the first man, so God may be loved. Like sought and sought, that God the Lord grant thee by the loving, holy Father, so as it is done in the godly holy scriptures. Like sought and sought; that God the Lord grant them by the loving, holy angels, and fatherly, godly Almightiness and heavenly trust and faith, like sought and sought; that grant thee God the Lord by the fiery furnace which is supported by God's blessing. Like sought and confessed. That grant thee God the Lord, by all power and might, by the prophet Jonas who, for 3 days and nights is preserved in the whale's belly. Like sought and confessed. That grant thee God the Lord by all the power and might, out of godly humility to go even to eternity; therefore N be no evils to thy whole body, whether racking gout, or yellow, or white, or red, or black gout or torturing rheumatism, or pains or tortures known by any name, may they do the N no harm in thy whole body, whether head, neck, heart, belly, in thy veins, arms, legs, eyes, tongue; in all thy veins in thy whole body be no evil. This I write for thee N with these words: In the name of the Father and the Son and the Holy Ghost. Amen. God bless thee. Amen.

REMARK.—When one writes for another, where the letter N stands he must write the first name of the patient.

### 116. *A Morning Prayer on Land for Protection from Misfortune.*

I (here pronounce your name) to-day purpose to go out. I will go God's path and way, where God and the Lord Jesus Christ have gone, and the Madonna and child, with her seven rings, with her true things. Oh, my dear Lord, I am thine own; let no dog bit me, no wolf bit me, no murderer kill me; protect me, oh God, this day. I stand in God's hand; there I bind myself; in God's hand am I bound by the sacred fire wound of our Lord God, that no weapon may injure me. Say three Pater Nosters, three Ave Marias, and the creed.

### 117. *A True and Approved Charm. Useful against a Conflagration and Pestilence.*

Welcome, thou fiery guest; seize no further than thou hast. This I reckon to thee, Fire, for a penance, in the name of the Father and the Son and the Holy Ghost.

I pray thee, Fire, by God's power which does and creates all things, that thou stay and go no further, even as Christ stood on the Jordan and was baptized by the holy man John. That I reckon to thee, Fire, as a penance, in the name of the holy Trinity.

I pray thee, Fire, by the power of God, that thou restrain thy flames; even as Mary restrains her virginity before all dames, chaste and pure; wherefore, stay thy rage, Fire. This I reckon to thee for a penance, Fire, in the name of the Almightiest Trinity.

I pray thee, thou wilt allay thy ardor, by Jesus Christ's precious blood, which he shed for us, our sins and misdeeds. That I reckon thee, Fire, for a penance, in the name of the Father and the Son and the Holy Ghost.

Jesus of Nazareth, King of the Jews, help us out of this stress of fire, and protect this land and country from all plague and pestilence.

REMARKS.—This charm was brought from Egypt by a Christian Gipsy King. In the year 1714, the 1st day of June, six gipsys were brought into the Prussian Kingdom, condemned to be hung. A seventh, an old man of 80 years of age, and condemned to be beheaded, was brought in on the 16th of the same month. Fortunately for him, a conflagration broke out; the old gipsy was loosed and brought to the fire to try his art, and to the wonder of all, he subdued the fire in a half a quarter of an hour; for which he was pardoned and set free. This was known in the royal palace of Prussia, and in the general Superintendency of Konigsberg, and has been openly put to the proof.

It was first tested in Konigsberg by Alexander Banman, in 1715.

Whoever has this formula written in the house is safe from the danger of conflagration of thunderstorm; likewise, if a pregnant woman has it about her, magic cannot injure her or her child; it protects likewise against plague and pestilence. When one repeats the form he must go around the fire 3 times. It always helps.

## 118. To Ward off the Disaster of Fire.

Take a black hen from the nest in the morning or evening, cut off the head and lay it on the ground; take out the crop and lay that with the head, taking nothing out of it; get a piece from the chemise of a maiden, who is a pure virgin, in which she has had her monthly courses, take the part she has most stained, a patch the size of a plate; get an egg laid on Maundy Thursday, wrap the three together with wax, put it in a neat little earthen pot and bury it under the threshold as long as a stick remains in the house, with God's help. The fire may rage before and behind the dwelling, it cannot harm thee or thy children. It is with God's power sure and certain. If an unforeseen conflagration arises, it becomes you to get an entire chemise in which a maiden has had her courses, or a sheet in which a woman has given birth, wrap it up and throw it all on the fire without saying a word. It always helps sure.

### 119. Against Witches—for Beasts Write it one Stall—for Human Beings Write it on the Bedsteads.

Trotter head, I pray thee my house and my Court, I pray then my horse-and-cow-stall, I pray thee my bedstead, that thou shed not thy consolations on me; be they on another house till thou goest over all mountains, countest all the sticks in the hedges and goest over all waters. So come the happy day again to my house, in the name of the Father and of the Son and the Holy Ghost. Amen.

### 123. A Charm for Personal Safety.

Cross of Christ and Crown of Christ and Jesus Christ; red blood, be to me at all times and all hours good. God the Father is before me; God the Sun is at my side, God the Holy Ghost is behind me. Who now is stronger than the three Persons, he comes day or night and seizes me. 3 Pater Nosters.

### 124. Another for the Same.

Every step Jesus goes with N. He is my head, I am his member; therefore Jesus goes with N.

### 125. A Certain Remedy Against Fire.

As surged the bitter sufferings and death of our dear Lord Jesus Christ. Fire and wind and heated glow, what thou hast in thy elemented power, I bid thee, bid the Lord Jesus Christ, who commanded the wind, and the sea, and they obeyed Him, by these mighty words which Jesus spake, I bid, command and proclaim to thee, Fire, that thou likewise flee, and they elemented power, thou flame and glow. As flowed the rose-red blood of our dear Lord Jesus Christ. Thou Fire and wind and heated glow, bid thee, as God has bidden the fire by his holy angel, who the fiery glow in the fiery furnace, when the three holy children, Shadrach and his fellows, Meshach and Abed-Nego, by God's command given to his holy angel, that they should remain unhurt, and it also happened; that thou likewise, Fire-flame and heated glow, that thou lay thyself, as the Almighty God has spoken when he created the four elements, together heaven and earth.

Fiat, fiat, fiat! i.e. in the name of the Father and of the Son and of the Holy Ghost. Amen.

### 126. For a Man or Beast Perverted by Evil Influences.

Three false tongues have pierced thee, three holy tongues have be-friended thee. The first is God the Father, the second is God the Son, the third is God the Holy Ghost. They give thee thy blood and flesh, thy joy and courage. Flesh and blood is in thee grown, born and lost. Has a man over-ridden thee so bless thee God and the holy Cyprian. Has a wife over-slaughed thee, so bless thee God and the body of Mary. Has a knight troubled thee, so bless thee by God and the Kingdom of Heaven. Has a maid or a servant run away from thee; so bless thee God and the Heavenly stars. Heaven is above thee; the earth-realm under thee, thou art in the midst. I bless thee before thou art destroyed. Our dear Lord Jesus in his bitter sufferings and death underwent every thing which the false tongues of the Jews uttered against him, in malice. See how the Son of God trembled when he was oppressed. Then said our Lord Christ: If I have not the rider (oppresses) no one will have him. Who helps me to mourn and carry my cross, him will I defend from the rider, in the name of the Father and of the Son and of the Holy Ghost. Amen.

### 127. For a Sprite and other Kind of Witchcraft.

I.

N.I.R.

I.

Sanctus     Spiritus

I.

N.I.R.

I.

Let this all be preserved, here for time, there eternal. Amen.
The character which pertains to it is called:
God bless thee, here for time, there eternal. Amen.

### 128. For Misfortune and Danger in the House.

Sanct. Mattheus, Sanct. Marcus, Sanct. Lucas, Sanct. Johannis.

### 129. Protection of the House and Court from Sickness and Robbery.

Ito, Alo Massa Dandi Bando, III. Amen.

I.R.N.R.I.

Our Lord Jesus Christ went into the hall, there the Jews specially sought him. So also must my days be with those who revile me with their evil tongues falsely, and smite, and for praise of God must I bear the suffering, be silent, be dumb, faint, ashamed, ever and always. God thereby bestows praise. Help me I.I.I. ever and eternally. Amen.

*130. Against the Influence of the Gipsy Art.*

Like as the prophet, Jonas, as a type of Christ, was 3 days and 3 nights in the whale's belly, so also may the Almighty God, of his fatherly goodness keep and protect me against all evil. I.I.I.

*131. To be Used in the Crisis of Distress and Death.*

I know that my Redeemer liveth and that he will raise me up in the latter day upon the earth.

*132. For a Tumor.*

There went three virgins, to view a tumor and sickness. The first said: it is rough. The second said: it is not. The third said: if it is not, come our Lord Jesus Christ. Said in the name of the holy Trinity.

*133. For Adversity and Divers Conflicts.*

Strength, Hero, Joy, Prince. I.I.I.

*134. To Help a Cow that has Lost her Milk.*

Give to a cow 3 spoonsful of the first milk, and say to it: If any one asks thee what thou hast done with the milk, say, the milkmaid has taken it, and I have poured it out, in the Father, etc. Amen. Add a prayer.

*135. Another.*

I. Cross of Jesus Christ milk pour;
I. Cross of Jesus Christ water pour;
I. Cross of Jesus Christ to have pour.

These words must be written on 3 bits of paper, then take milk from the sick cow, and the 3 bits of paper and some scrapings from the skull of a poor sinner, put them in a furnace and boil them well; and so will you exorcise the witch. Or you can mix the bits of paper in the meal and put it in the feeding trough, and say the formula 3 times, and after that give it to the cow. Thus you will not see the witch but it will help the cow.

### 136. For a Fever.

Make a prayer early in the morning, then turn the shirt around the left sleeve and say: Shirt, turn thee around, and thou Fever, turn; at the same time name the name of the patient. Say this for a penance in the name of the Father, etc. Amen. Say these words 3 days in succession.

### 137. To Curse a Thief to Make Him Stand.

This saw must be said on Thursday, early in the morning, before sunrise, under the open sky.

So grant God the Father, Son and Holy Ghost. Amen. Full three and thirty angels by one another stand. They come with Mary to comfort her. Then said the dear, holy Daniel: Sad, dear lady, I see thieves, go which wish thy precious child to steal; that can I not from thee conceal. Then said our dear lady to St. Peter: Bind, St. Peter, bind. Then said St. Peter: I have bound with a band, with Christ his own hand, as my thieves are bound with Christ's own hands, if they would steal anything of mine, in the house, in the chest, in the meadow and acre, in wood or field, in tree, and plant, and garden, or wherever they would steal anything of mine. Our dear lady then said: Steal who will, but if he steal, he shall stand as a bock, and stand as a block; and count all the stones that on the earth lie, and count all the stars as they stand in the sky. So gave I thee praise and demanded of thee for every spirit, that every thief may know a master, by St. Daniel, to bring the goods of earth, to one's burden, to one's hearth; and thy face must not be towards the place, that my eyes may not see thee and my fleshly tongue may not praise thee. This demand I of thee holy Virgin Mary. Mother of God, by the power and might, when he created heaven and earth, by the angelic host and by all God's holy ones, in the name of God the Father, God the Son, and God the Holy Ghost. Amen. When you would lift the bann, bid him go in the name of St. John.

### 138. Another Similar.

Ye thieves, I conjure you to obey, even to the cross, and stand with me, and go not from my sight, in the name of the holy Trinity, I command you by the power of God and the humanity of Jesus Christ, that ye go not from my sight, as Jesus the Lord stood in Jordan, when St. John baptized him. After this, I command you, horse and man, that you stand to go not from my sight, as Christ the Lord stood when they nailed him to the cross, and he destroyed the power of the old-father of hell. Ye thieves, I bind you with bonds, as Christ the Lord has bound Hell, so are ye bound; with the words with which they are fixed, they are also loosed.

### 139. Another, very Swift.

Thou rider and footman, comest here well under thy care. Thou are sprinkled with the blood of Jesus Christ, with the five wounds; thou hast thy gun, flint and pistol bound, sabre and knife are cursed and bound, in the name of God the Father, Son and Holy Ghost. Amen. To be said thrice.

### 140. To Release the Same.

Yes rider and footman, as I have bound you in the curse till this time, so now ride forth in the name of Jesus Christ, by the word of God and the shield of Christ; so ride ye now all forth.

### 141. To Cause the Thief to Return Stolen Goods.

Early in the morning, before sunrise, go to a birch-tree, take with you three nails out of a hearse or three horse-shoe nails that have never been used; hold up the nails toward the rising sun and say: Oh Thief, I bind thee by the first nail which I make to pierce thee in the brow and brain, that thou return the stolen goods to their former place; to the man and place whence thou stealest them, else it shall be as sad to thee as it was to the disciple Judas when he betrayed Jesus. The second nail which I make to pierce thy lungs and liver, that thou return the stolen goods to their former place; to the man and the place whence thou hast stolen them, else it shall be as sad to thee as it was to Pilate in the pains of hell. The third nail which I make to pierce thy foot, thou thief, that thou must return the stolen goods to their former place, whence thou hast stolen them. Oh thief, I bind thee and bring thee by the sacred three nails which pierced Christ through his hands and feet, that thou must return the stolen goods to their former place, whence thou hast stolen them.

### 142. A General Prayer.

Jesus, I am about to undertake (such a thing). Jesus, thou wilt go with me. Jesus, shut my heart in thy heart, to thee I commend my body and soul. The Lord was crucified. And my understanding, oh God, that wicked foes may not overcome me, in the name of the Father, and the Son, and the Holy Ghost. Amen.

### 144. For a Burn.

Our dear Lord Jesus went over the land; there he saw a burning brand; there lay St. Lawrence, all in a roast; he came to him in help and trust; he lifted up his holy hand, and blessed he him and blessed the hand; and lifted away the fire that fed; that it never deeper nor wider spread. Let the burn be blessed in the name of the Father, and of the Son, and of the Holy Ghost. Amen.

### 145. Another for a Burn.

Yield brand away, and never press oh; cold or warm, let burning alone. God protect thee, blood and flesh, marrow and bone, and all thy vines, be thou great or small, they shall be for the fire hand cold or warm, unhurt and protected in the name of God the Father, Son and Holy Ghost. Amen.

### 146. To Administer to a Beast for Witchery and Devilwork.

```
S  A  T  O  R
A  R  E  P  O
T  E  N  E  T
O  P  E  R  A
R  O  T  A  S
```

### 147. To Dress and Heal Wounds.

Say thus: I dress the wounds in three names, whether they be from fire, water, decay or swelling or any other evil, in the name of the holy Trinity. This must be said thrice. Put a thread three times around the wound, lay it under the right corner against the sun and say: I lay thee here, N., that thou mayest take on thyself the lymple, swelling, and one and all, whatever can injure the wound. Amen. Say a Pater Noster, and a God grant it.

### 148. To Relieve a Fresh Wound of Pain.

Our dear Lord Jesus Christ has many sores and wounds, and yet they are not bound up. They endure not long, or do they mortify nor generate matter. Jonas was blind, I, said the heavenly child, as true the five sacred wounds were pierced. They fester not nor become corrupt. I take therefrom water and blood; that is good for all wounds and hurts. Holy is the man who can heal all hurts and wounds. Amen.

*149. For Worms in the Body.*

Peter and Jesus went out into the field; they ploughed three furrows; they ploughed up three worms. One is white, one is black, and the third is red. The worms are all dead, in the name. . . . Say these words thrice.

*150. For all Evils.*

Lord Jesus, thy wounds red; stand we before thee dead.

*151. To Maintain the Right Before the Court and Council.*

Jesus Mazarenus, Rex Judeorum.
First draw this character by you in the figure and then say: I.N.N. went before the house of the judge; there appeared 3 dead men at the window; one had no tongue; the second had no lungs; the third was sick, blind and dumb. When you go before the judge or officer, and they are not favorable to you, and you have a just cause, say the above.

*152. To Staunch Blood.*

As soon as you are wounded, say: Blessed wounds, blessed hours; blessed is the day that Jesus was born, in the name. . . . Amen.

*153. Another, for the Same.*

Write on a slip of paper the four chief rivers of the world, which flowed out of Paradise, namely, Pison, Gihon, Hidekel, and Euphrates. Open to the 1st Book of Moses, C. 20, V. 11, 12, 13, and you will see them. It helps.

*156. A Separate Form to Protect Oneself Against Man or Beast.*

When it is necessary to defend yourself, use this formula: In God's name I attack. My Redeemer will stand by me. On the holy help of God, I go at it full fierce. God with us alone. Jesus, health and blessing.

*157. Protection of the House and Court.*

Under thy shelter I be, from storms and all enemies free. I.I.I. The 3 I's signify Jesus three times.

*158. Precaution Against Firearms.*

Wear these words by you and one cannot hit you: Annanias, Azarias, and Misael, praise the Lord, for he has redeemed us from hell, and has saved us from death, and has redeemed us from the fiery furnace and has kept us in the midst of the fire; therefore shall he the Lord permit no fire to touch us.

I.
N.I.R.
I.

*159. To Fix all Foes, Robbers and Murderers.*

God greet you, ye brothers, hold on, ye thieves, robbers, murderers and soldiers, in humility though we have drunk the rose-red blood of Jesus, your rifles and guns, and rendered powerless by the holy blood-drops of Jesus Christ; all sabres and all swords are also bound with the sacred five wounds of Jesus. There stand 3 roses on God's heart; the 1st is lawful, the 2d is mighty, the 3d is his own godly will. Ye thieves must herewith thereunder stay and hold still as long as I will. In the name of God the Father, Son and Holy Ghost; be ye staid and conjured.

*160. A Safeguard Against All Weapons.*

Jesus, God and Man, protect me from every kind of firearms, weapons, long and short, sword of every kind of metal and, hold thy fire, as Mary retained her virginity before and after her parturition. Christ bound every weapon as he bound himself in humanity full of humility. Jesus stops every gun and sword, as Mary, spouse of the mother of God; therefore protect the three holy blood-drops which Jesus sweat on the Mt of Olives: Jesus Christ protects me from the death-stroke and burning fire. Jesus permits me not to die, much less to be damned, without partaking of the holy supper. That helps me God the Father, Son and Holy Ghost. Amen.

## 161. *Shooting Weapons and Representation.*

Jesus went over the red sea and looked on the land; therefore must all rifle-muskets, flints and pistols become useless, and all false tongues dumb. The blessing which God made when he created man, that goes over me always; the blessing which God made when he commanded in the dream Joseph and Mary to flee into Egypt with James, that goes over me always, be dear and precious the holy cross in my right hand. I go through the freedom of the land, where no one will be robbed, or killed, or murdered, so shall no one be able to cause any suffering to me, moreover, no dog shall bite me, no beast shall tear me. In all things preserve my flesh and blood, from sins and false tongues which reach from earth to heaven, by the power of the four evangelists, in the name of the Father, and of the Son, and of the Holy Ghost. Amen.

## 162. *Another.*

I.N.N. conjure thee, gun, sabre and knife, may all weapons by the spear which went into the side of the Lord, that water and blood flowed out, that ye be not permitted to hurt me, the servant of God in the    . I conjure thee by St. Stephen, whom the Jews stoned, that they be not able to trouble me, a servant of God, in the name. . . . Amen.

## 163. *Safeguards from Shots, Cuts, and Stabs.*

In the name I.I.I. Amen. I.N.N. Jesus Christ is the true Saviour. Jesus Christ rules and reigns, breaks down and overcomes all foes, visible and invisible. Jesus is with me always, ever and eternally, in all paths and ways, on water and on land, in mount and vale, in cot and court, in the whole world where I am, where I stand, go, ride, run, journey; whether I sleep or wake, eat or drink, there art thou, O Lord Jesus Christ, at all times, early and late, all hours and moments; whether I go out or in. The sacred five wounds red, oh Lord Jesus Christ, they are at all times good for my sins, private or public; that the sword may not cut me, destroy me, nor injure me, help me N.N. Jesus Christ with his shield and defence; protect me N.N. at all times from daily sins, worldly harm, injustice, contempt, pestilence and other sickness, from anguish, torture and pain, from all wicked enemies, from false tongues and old scandal-mongers; that no shot may injure my body, help me N.N. and no band of thieves, nor gypsies, street-robbers, murderers, sorcery, or other kind of devil-spirits may enter my house or court, nor break in; that the dear lady Mary may protect every thing, and also all the children, by the help of God in heaven, in the eternal joy and sovereignty of God the Father, quicken me, the wisdom of God the Son enlighten me, the virtue and grace of God the Holy Ghost strengthen me from this hour to all eternity. Amen.

### 164. *Prayer Against the Sword and Weapons.*

The blessing which came from heaven when Jesus Christ was born, come upon me N.N. The blessing which God the Lord made when he created the first man come upon me; the blessing which followed when Christ was seized, bound, scourged, mockingly crowned and smitten, when on the cross he gave up the Ghost, come upon me; the blessing which the priest gave to the tender, sacred body of our dear Lord Jesus Christ come upon me. The steadfastness of the holy Mary and all the holy ones of God, the holy three kings, Caspar, Melchoir, and Balthasar, be with me; the holy four evangelists, Mathew, Mark, Luke, and John, be with me; the earthangels, St. Michael, St. Gabriel, St. Raphael, and St. Ariel, be with me; the holy twelve Apostles of the Patriarchs and the whole heavenly host be with me; the innumerable company of the holy ones be with me. Amen.

### 165. *That no Wicked Man may Defraud me, Bewitch or Effect me with Magic, and that I may be always Blessed.*

As the cup and the wine and the consecrated bread, when our dear Lord Jesus Christ, on Maundy Thursday prayed for his loving disciples; and that me at all times, day nor night, no dog may bite me, no wild beast tear, no tree fall on me, no water drown, no gun shoot me, no weapon or iron or steel cut me, no fire burn, and from false judgment, no false tongue swear against me, no rogue vex me, from all vile friends, from magic and witchcraft, from all these, the Lord Jesus Christ protect me. Amen.

### 166. *Another.*

The holy Trinity protect me; be with and remain with me, N.N., on water and land, by flood or field, in city or hamlet, in the whole world, wherever I am. The Lord Jesus Christ protect me from all my foes, private and public; also protect me the eternal Godhead and the bitter passion of Jesus Christ. The rose-red blood which he poured out on the holy cross, help me, I.I. Jesus was crucified, tortured and dead. These are true words; so must also all words be by his power, which are herein written, and spoken and prayed by me. So help me that I may not be sinned, bound or overcome by any man. May all swords and weapons be before me, useless and powerless. Gun, withhold thy fire in the almighty hand of God. So let all gun shots be prohibited. As they bound the right hand of the Lord Jesus Christ to the cross. Like as the Sun was obedient to his Heavenly Father, so also may the eternal Godhead bless and protect me by his rose-red blood, by the holy five wounds which were opened on the tree of the holy Cross; therefore may I be blessed and defended, as the cup and the wine and the true bread which Jesus blessed for his twelve disciples on the Maundy Thursday Evening. I.I.I.

*167. Another.*

God's grace and mercy go with me, N.N. Now I purpose to ride out or go out. I would gird, I would bind myself round with a safe ring, if God the heavenly Father will, and may he protect me, flesh and blood, veins and members, the present day and night as I have it before me; may my enemies, however many they may be, all be confounded, and become as a snow-white dead man. May no one shoot, cut or throw me, nor overcome me with gun or steel in his hand, of any kind of metal, as all ugly weapons are called. But may my gun go off like the thunder of heaven, and my sword hew like the sword of a host. Our dear lady went upon to a very high mountain; she looked down into a very dark valley, and saw her dear child standing among the Jews, harsh, so harsh, that He, seized so harsh, that He, bound so hard, that,—protect me the dear Lord Jesus Christ from everything which is hurtful to me, N.N. Amen.

*168. Another for the Same.*

Then I cried out on this present day and night, that thou wouldst not permit any of my foes or company of thieves to come near me, they bring to me then his rose-red blood into my bosom. But they do not bring that which was laid on the holy altar. For God the Lord Jesus Christ is gone with his precious body to heaven. Oh Lord, that is to me good for the present day and night. Amen.

*174. To Cause the Return of Stolen Goods.*

Observe carefully whether the thief went out at the door or elsewhere; then cut three splinters in the three highest names, then go with the splinters to a wagon, but unwashed, take off a wheel, put the splinters in the hub, in the highest names, then whirl the wheel and say: Thief, thief, thief! turn back again with the stolen things. Thou wilt be constrained by the might of God; God the Father calls thee back; the Son of God turn thee about, that thou must go. . . .

### 178. *A Charm to Constrain a Man from Growing too Large.*

I.N.N. make to breathe on thee; I make to take away from thee three drops of blood; one from thy heart, one from thy liver, the third from thy vital strength; therewith I take away thy strength and manhood.

Hbbi Mofsy danti Lantien. I.I.I.

### 184. *The Talisman.*

It is said: that whoever goes a hunting and carries this in his pouch, cannot fail to shoot and bring home something worth having.

An aged hermit once found an old lame hunter in the forest of Thuringia, lying by the way and weeping. The hermit asked him why he was so sad. Oh, man of God! said he, I am a poor unfortunate man; I must deliver to my lord yearly so many stags, roebucks, hares and snipes, as a young healthy hunter could hardly scare up, else he hunts me out of his service. Now, I am old and lame, the forest is poorly supplied, I can no longer meet the demand, I know not how it will go with me. Here he was not able to speak another word for sadness. Thereupon, the hermit took a little piece of paper and wrote on it the following formula: There, old man, stick that in thy hunting pouch as often as thou goest out to the forest, it cannot fail that thou wilt shoot and bring home something worth having. But beware that you never shoot more than is necessary, and that you teach the deep meaning of the words to no one till he promises not to make a misuse of it. The hermit now went on his way, and after a while the hunter also arose, and went into the thicket without thinking of anything. Scarcely had he gone a hundred steps before he shot a Roebuck, a finer one than he had seen for a long time. After this he was always successful in the hunt every day and was considered the best woodman in the whole land.

At nemo in sese tantat, desendere nemo.

* * *

At precedenti spectatur mantica tergo.
Do your best and it suffices.

### 186. *A Warding off of Balls.*

May the heavenly and holy sackbuts warm and ward off from me all balls and misfortune,—off from me instantly. I take refuge under the tree of life which bears twelve manner of fruit. I stand under the sacred altar of the christian church. I commend myself to the holy Trinity. I.N.N. entrench myself behind the sacred body of Jesus Christ. I commend myself to the wounds of Jesus Christ, that I may not be seized by the hand of any man, nor bound, nor cut, nor shot, nor stabbed, nor thrown down, nor slain, and especially may not be wounded; to this help me N.N.

Whosoever carries this little book with him is safe from all his foes, visible or invisible, and so also he who carries this little book with him can never be killed without the entire sacred body of Jesus Christ, nor be drowned in water, nor burned in fire, and no unjust judgment can be pronounced against him. Thereto help me. N.N.

### 187. *Unlucky days in Each Month.*

| | |
|---|---|
| January, 1, 2, 3, 4, 6, 11, 12. | July, 17, 21. |
| February, 1, 17, 18. | August, 20, 21. |
| March, 14, 16. | September, 10, 18. |
| April, 10, 17, 18. | October, 6. |
| May, 7, 8. | November, 6, 10. |
| June, 17. | December, 6, 11, 15. |

Whoever is born on one of these days is unlucky and suffers poverty. Also, whoever is sick on one of the aforesaid days, seldom recovers his health; and whoever betrothes himself or marries, comes into great poverty and misery. One must not go abroad, set out on a journey, begin a business, or enter a law-suit on these days.

N.B. On the annunciation day of Mary, Simon and Judas, and the Apostle St. Andrew, one must be bled. The signs of the zodiac, as they are indicated in the Almanac, are to be observed in the course of the month.

If a cow calves in the sign of the virgin, the calf will not live a year; if in the sign of the Scorpion, it will die still earlier, and you must not wean it in this sign, nor in the goat nor waterman.

Only this one formula has been taken from a hundred year calendar, brought from Germany, and many believe it.

HOHMAN.

In Conclusion the following Morning Prayer, to be said in Journeying. It Protects from Ill Luck.

Oh Jesus of Nazareth, King of the Jews, ye King of the whole world, protect me N.N. this day and night, protect me always by the holy five wounds, that I may not be seized nor bound. Protect me the holy Trinity, that no sword, nor shot, nor ball, nor lead may enter my body; may they be mild as the blood-sweat and tears of Jesus Christ, in the name of the Father and of the Son and of the Holy Ghost. Amen.

# PENNSYLVANIA GERMAN FOLK MEDICINE

*(The following material is from Thomas R. Brendle's* Pennsylvania German Folk Medicine, *providing further evidence of the* Weltanschauung *and spiritual direction of the folk, who continued to live and worship as members of the Reformed, Lutheran, and Evangelical churches of Pennsylvania.)*

## THE ORIGIN OF DISEASES

Many years have elapsed since medical science began to supplant folk beliefs of disease and folk ways of diagnosis and cure in the lives of the Pennsylvania Germans; none the less, folk beliefs still linger on. We find three distinct currents of medical belief and practice running through the history of our people: (1) the stream of progressive, scientific medicine, represented by the properly trained physician; (2) the traditional household and family medicine represented by the layman who is his own physician; (3) the mystic, supernatural, and sympathetic cures represented by the *braucher.* Of these three only the latter two belong to folk medicine and properly form the field of our investigations. *The last mentioned stream constitutes the remnant of ancient, primitive, mystic medicine which originated in religious cults; the second stream represents the household remedies which grew out of the mystical and magical;* the first stream represents the scientific medicine that in some part developed out of the household remedies.

The fact that these three ways of looking upon and treating diseases existed side by side and to a certain extent still exist side by side testifies to the power of folk beliefs, and also to the tenaciousness of the folk mind.

New methods are slow in reaching the layman; he more or less distrusts their efficacy and is reluctant to adopt them; more than all else he feels that the traditional remedy which he has tried or which his parents have tried before him or which his neighbors have tried, all with seemingly good results, will continue to cure despite the fact that it has been discarded by scientific medicine. And where medical science fails or errs, there the ordinary man is prone to find an excuse for the remembrance

175

and resurrection of some almost forgotten remedy, be it ever so fantastic or curious. He justifies himself by saying: *D'r dokter wees net alles*—the doctor knows much but not all. That is, there are some mysterious things beyond the physician's knowledge or help, which can be fought only through a more potent mystic or occult force; or, the knowledge which comes from experience is superior to that which comes from books.

There are other factors which help to prolong the life of folk beliefs and the use of simple and traditional remedies among our people. The early German immigrants turned to agriculture and handwork. They often lived far from physician and apothecary shop. In case of sudden illness or accident they were compelled to use any help that was at hand and even to think up remedies. Necessity is the mother of invention in folk medicine.

The ordinary man treasures that which he at some time or other found helpful; he recommends it to his friends; he firmly implants a knowledge of it in the minds of his children and children's children. The advice of a loved parent or trusted friends is held as precious as gold.

Just as there are accretions to the Pennsylvania German dialect from the English language which surrounds it on all sides, so there are steady additions to folk medicine from the dominant scientific medicine with which it continually comes in contact. This scientific content increases its adaptiveness and efficacy for the common ills of man and prolongs its life.

Medical science is continually changing. The theory and practice of today give way to a different theory and practice tomorrow; we may, likewise, say the medical practice of today becomes the folk-lore of tomorrow. This would not be an unfounded statement, for we find in our folk medicine the flotsam and jetsam of schools of medicine that once wielded a profound influence but are now almost forgotten.

*Back of all medical practice lie the conceptions of disease; back of all folk medicine lie the folk conceptions of disease; and as long as common folk retain their own peculiar conceptions of what disease is and of its cause, so long will they retain their own peculiar ways for warding it off or of curing it.*

Our people look upon those ailments for which there is an apparent cause differently from those for which there is no visible occasion: the former they ascribe to a sequence of natural events, the latter to supernatural agencies. Their conceptions of the origin of disease in the main are the following:

## (A) DISEASES ARE ACTS OF GOD

In the long past ages our pagan ancestors believed in a multitude of gods, or perhaps, it would be more correct to say that they *attributed will and passion to the acts of nature. They, however, also believed in a higher force or power beneath which not only man but nature and the gods themselves had to bow.* This destiny of fate did not enter into their active religion, was not worshipped or prayed to, did not even have a name. It was useless to attempt to propitiate it. *In the course of time, under the influence of Christianity, this immutable power became identified in some measure with the Christian God.* Even to this day, however, although dimly and nebulously, this view of fate persists; and there is something in it which prevents its complete harmonization with the Christian idea of God and which betrays its pagan origin.

The mental processes of our people are sometimes very simple, though in the final analysis deeply philosophical. They reason that what is was to be and trace all things back to the omnipotent and omniscient ruler of the universe. The things that be are ordained of God. *They know nothing of their heathenish forefathers; for them the will of God is destiny and destiny is the will of God; diseases are a part of destiny.* This way of looking at things lead to a more or less fatalistic view of life and indeed we have a deep strain of Christian fatalism. At the open grave of a loved one, or at the bedside of the sick, expressions like these are often heard: "The Lord has willed it, and it is well"; "One must patiently bear his misfortunes for that is all that one can do"; "What happens is to happen and that's all there's to it"; "When one's time is here to die, he will die and that's that."

Afflictions that come from God are believed to have a purpose. They are sent as *a trial, as a punishment, or as a part of a preordained order* of things. The direct hand of God is particularly seen in the *schteech*—stroke of apoplexy (a stroke of lightning is called a *gwidded-schteech*), in inexplicable mental ailments, in the death dealing stroke of lightning, which is frequently spoken of as occurring in cases of great blasphemy as in drunken parodies on the administration of the sacraments. A violation of God's law will be punished by God, if not in this life, then in the next; *Gott losst sich net schpodde—God will not be mocked.*

A man's days on earth are numbered; when his allotted time is ended he will die. But *mingled with the belief is the view that if he had done this or that, things would be different.* We are not consistent in our theology, but we do not trouble ourselves about our contradictory interpretations of events; sufficient unto the day is the philosophy thereof.


### (B) DISEASES ARE INHERITED

Diseases, such as cancer, tuberculosis, palsy, epilepsy, are still commonly believed to be inherited: *'Sis garebt*—it is inherited; *'Sis im blud*—it is in the blood. Of a cancerous person we have heard it said: "His father and his grandfather had cancer; he has bad blood."

The red cheeks—the hectic flush—of the child of a tubercular parent are regarded as ominous: "She has the red cheeks of her mother and she will go the way of her mother." *Es hot zurick gachlaje*—it has struck back, is said of tuberculosis when, after skipping a generation, it recurs in the family.

Physical characteristics and infirmities come from the parents: "He is hard of hearing as his father was before him"; "My mother had grey hair at the age of thirty and I shall be like her"; "My father was rheumatic in the same way as I am."

Birthmarks and deformities are due to prenatal influences, to sudden fright, or to undue attention given by the expectant mother to some physical deformity in another. Sometimes children are inflicted with the physical characteristics which the mother derided in other children—this as a punishment to the mother.

Mental peculiarities are also inherited: "*Die B—familie sin all e'wen-ich dumm*—all the members of the B-family line are a little stupid, or *schtarr keppich, dickkeppich*—stubborn, or *eefeldich*—simple minded; feeble-minded children are sometimes ascribed to excessive emotionalism (weeping, anger, melancholiness) on the part of the mother during her pregnancy.


### (D) DISEASES ARE EVIL SPIRITS OR ARE CAUSED
### BY EVIL SUPERNATURAL POWERS

Now and then we come across traces of the belief that diseases are demons, or caused by demons, or that a person is possessed by evil spirits; as a folk belief it has all but died out.

Our pagan ancestors believed that sicknesses were caused by malignant demons—some of them the spirits of dead ancestors. The dread of these demons led to the offering of atoning and propitiatory sacrifices. In Christianity this disease giving power was in great part attributed to Satan, the hereditary arch enemy of the human race, who not only was able to attack the soul but also the body.*

The devil exercises his power, sometimes directly, at other times through his associate demons or through his tools: sorcerers, witches (Hexen, Unholden), etc.

Those of our people who still believe in the satanic origin of disease hold that the primary object of Satan is to torment the human race, *far die leid gwele*—to torment the people. A witch who has given herself into the power of the devil is compelled to continually torment people, *en hex mus immer ebber gwele*—a witch must always be tormenting someone. The free hand which Satan seems to enjoy in the matter is permitted to him by God as a punishment for sinners and as a trial for the righteousness. The diseases coming from Satan are nothing more than demons.

These occult diseases or disease causing entities were not only thought of as elfish spirits or as devils of a more demonic form and character but were often conceived of as devouring worms. We still meet traces of this belief: *warm am finger*—worm at the finger, *ringwarm*—ring worm, *hann warm*—the worm causing insanity by gnawing at the brain, *zehr warm*—the worm which causes mirasmus by gnawing in the spinal cord; or, as another animal, as in the case of a cancer—*krebs,* which was literally taken to mean an evil gnawing crab.

Our proverbs shed interesting light upon the way our forefathers looked on marriage. They did not like to see great dissimilarity in the ages of man and wife. It is the natural thing for young to marry young—*gleich gesellt sich gern.* It is better this way: *liewer iwwer en wieg schtarze wie iwwer en dodes falle*—a cradle may bring cares but a corpse more so; *liewer iwwer en weig gschtolpert wie iwwer en aldi gschtieje*—a cradle may be in the way but an old woman more so.

Marriage is for life and no matter what the hardships should be dissolved only by death—*wie m'r d'r schtuhl macht so sitzt m'r.* A second marriage is different from the first, *die erscht frah aus d'r lieb, die zwet schenkt uns Gott, die dritt kummt vum deiwel*—the first wife through love,

---

* Adam and Eve, Job, Jesus—Mt IV. Paul—2 Cor 12: 7, the Canaanitish woman—Mt 15; Mary "possessed"—Lk 11. Such biblical instances as these did much to perpetuate the belief that diseases are due to the devil.

Several years ago the writer officiated at the funeral of an old man who had been ill a long time and suffered most painfully. After the funeral a young relative of the deceased remarked that the man suffered such a fearful death "because the devil had gotten hold of him."

the second a gift from God, the third from the devil; another, *die erscht frah vum himmel, die zwet vun d'r hell*—the first wife from heaven, the second from hell. Not all proverbs are so cynical; there is a very common one which says that the woman who cuts thick slices of bread will be a good stepmother—*du mascht en gudi schtiefmutter, du duschts brod dick schneide.* As a matter of fact remarriages are almost always happy and successful unions, and only very infrequently do they interfere with the integrity of the home.

Since the creation of Eve out of a rib from Adam the body of a man has one rib less that the body of a woman; since Adam was created out of the dust no person is able to wash himself clean. This latter belief has reference to the peelings of the skin which come from too much washing and which are looked upon as "dirt."

General debility—*alderschweche* comes with old age. When mental debility accompanies physical debility in old age one is in his second childhood—*sei zwetti kindheit.* The number of years which one lives are allotted by God. When one has lived his allotted time death will overtake him, whether natural or accidental. The years over and above three score and ten are a gift of God—*schenkt was Gott.* A person of great age is said to be *schtee alt.* Many spots on the finger nails presage long life.

Practically all our folk calendars carry standing astrological directions for bleeding and cupping—a page or half page of directions accompanied by a woodcut picture of man's anatomy surrounded by the signs of the zodiac. This bloodletting chart appeared in the calendar published by Saur,* who had gotten it, at least in part, from European sources. The chart as it appears in subsequent calendars differs little from the Saur chart, which in translation is as follows:

### BLOODLETTING AND CUPPING

Each one may determine for himself as easily as he may be told whether or not to cup, and when the time is appropriate for such act, namely, when there is a stretching, itching, and biting in the skin, from which commonly the well known itch comes. For cupping the room must be warm, for if the skin is bare, and in addition holes cut into it, cold may set in, and the likelihood is that conditions may become worse as easily as better; if there is

---

* Christopher Saur, early Pennsylvania Dutch publisher. (REW)

no improvement after the first treatment, one may repeat a second or third time.

Letting of blood is beneficial in cases of fullbloodedness, numbness, spitting of blood, and choking rheum. At such times one should have regard neither for the zodiacal sign or for the time or hour. Those who are used to blood letting and naturally build up much blood, may let blood most opportunely in the waning moon, when day and night are equal, or in May when the roses bloom. No blood should be let in cases where there is a scarcity of blood, malignant fevers, or swooning, nor for bloated persons, weak old people, nor in many cases of pregnancy, cases of long continued illness, or to any extent when light red blood flows.

As to the signs of the zodiac: The ram is good; the bull, bad; the twins, middling; the cancer, middling; the lion, bad; the virgin, middling; the balance, good; the scorpion, bad; the archer, middling; the goat, good; the water-bearer, bad; the fishes, middling.

The ram rules the head; in this sign it is good to let blood but not at the head.

The bull rules the neck and the throat.
The twins rule the shoulders, arms, and hands.
The cancer rules the lungs, spleen, and stomach.
The lion rules the heart and the back.
The virgin rules the stomach and the bowels.
The balance rules the kidneys and the bladder.
The scorpion rules the genitals.
The archer rules the hips.
The goat rules the knees.
The fishes rule the feet.
The planet Jupiter rules the left ear, heart, liver, and ribs.
Mars rules the whole head and the gall.
The sun rules the face, especially the eyes, also the teeth, heart, sides, and the shanks.
Venus rules the kidneys and the genitals of both sexes.
Mercury rules the memory, mind, tongue, and the skin.
The moon rules the genitals of both sexes, brain, throat, stomach, belly, intestines; and together with Jupiter the liver; and together with the sun the face and the eyes.

This is to be remembered, that he who would let blood, be it on the arm, hand, or foot, must have without fail the whole limb warm; should it be cold as often happens when people come in spring or fall from a distance to the bloodletter, or when it is cool in the morning, the blood will flow little or not at all, since the cold has made the blood torpid, and though one puts the feet or hands in warm water, nevertheless the warmth does not ascend in the body above the height of the water. If one has come a long distance on foot and is of a weak nature he may easily faint during the operation, nevertheless a swoon should not interfere with blood letting.

We would naturally look for charms to ease the pain and to bring about the successful mending of the sprains and fractures, and the prevention of blood poisoning from the inflammation. There are such.

The play on words which is a characteristic feature of a charm or *brauch* formula is frequently hard to retain in translation:

Christ hung on the cross in pain,
And thy leg has got a sprain.
As his hanging hurt him not,
So thy sprain will not hurt thee.
In the name of the Father, Son,
And Holy Ghost, Amen, Amen.

The instructions which accompany this formula are: "For sprains, stroke with the hand three times over the sore part of the body, and each time say these words."

Another formula with the same directions from the same imprint reads:

Christus maketh walk the lame,
The dead he raiseth up again.
So thy lameness cured be,
Sunk into the deepest sea.
Jesus only heals the ailing,
To him alone give thanks unfailing.

Common people do away with traditional remedies only with great reluctance, as witness the following:

> For sore swollen legs, take rue and nightshade, pound fine and press out the juice and apply to the wound; and take of the juice and put in salt water and wash the legs. Lay the pressed cut leaves upon the wound, and give the patient water to drink in which fir tops ("Dannengipfel") have been well cooked. This will heal all old hurts without exception, be they what they may. Before the amputation of a limb is undertaken this remedy should be used, as I experienced in the case of a poor woman, whose leg the other doctors were just ready to amputate, and she turned to me and I cured her with the help of God and this remedy, and she may be living to this hour.

### SKIN ERUPTIONS, PIMPLES, ITCHES, ETC.

*Ausfahres, ausbreches, ausfahring:* eruptions on the skin.

*Hitzpocke, nachtbrand, nachbrand, summerpocke, Nacht Brand:* prickly heat; the eruption in chicken pox; cold sores (Herpes) on the face.

*Grind, koppgrind, millichgrind, millichgretz, millichgruscht, erbgrind, Flechte:* scabby heads; eczema; tetter. *Salzfluss:* salt rheum.

*Wibbelsucht, wiebel, wiwwel sucht, Kriebelsucht, Nesselsucht:* nettlerash, urticaria.

*Zetter, tetter, Zitterach:* tetter; herpes; eczema, etc. *Drucke detter, schibbe:* dandruff.

*Heibs:* hives.

*Finne, pfinne, gsichtbloder, hautfinne:* pimples (acne). *Hunspocke:* large pimples of a more or less bluish cast.

*Gretz:* itch. *Grundgretz, heckegretz, arschgretz, buschgretz, hembieregretz, hucklebieregretz, blackbieregretz:* itchy swellings resembling mosquito bites caused by minute ticks.

The water which falls from heaven has healing powers, whether in the form of rain, dew, hail, or snow. It is especially beneficial if it falls during a holy season or on holy places—as during Easter, and on God's acre, the cemetery.

To remove freckles one was to wash the face with water gathered from tombstones, and come away without looking behind; on the first day of May with water that was found in a stump; with May dew and dry the hands on that part of the body to which the freckles are to be transferred; on the morning of the first day of May, before the sun is up, with the dew from the grass, but now word may be spoken aloud before or during the procedure; smear with frog spawn.

These remedies contain an occult element. The month of May, *d'r rollich Moi*—the roll-May, comes after Walpurgis night, when the spirits are abroad. The remedies may originally have been preventative measures, which in course of time became curative.

Where women take upon themselves a greater or less portion of the outdoor work, their countenances become hardened and roughened by exposure to wind and weather. To such a clear white skin is a thing of beauty. Clear skin could be gotten by washing with whey, buttermilk, with the rag used in washing milk cans and butter churns, wine, May dew, water from the cooling cask of a smithy; "if persons have freckles, let them take the dew which lies upon the wheat and mix it with rose water and lily oil and wash."

Baptismal water was looked upon as good for freckles. Here the idea of holy water again recurs. The power of purification of baptismal water is so great that if a mother drinks of the water with which her child was baptized she will be divorced. "Holy water" could be gotten by gathering March snow or rain water and inserting it in pieces of paper on which scriptural texts were written.

> To remove warts or scars the person so affected must look at the moon and repeat the words: "*Was ich raib, mem ab; was ich sen, nem tsu*—what I rub, decrease; what I see, increase." This must be done three nights in succession, beginning with the full moon, so that the last trial comes on the night of the full moon.

The increase-decrease *brauch* formula mentioned above was also used for wens: Look directly over the growth towards the moon, and say: "Whatsoever increases, increases; whatsoever decreases, decreases." This is to be said three times in one breath. The cure seemingly is due to the scriptural passage John 3, 20: "He must increase, and I must decrease."

Otherwise a wen was to be removed by striking a severe blow on it with a small Bible, hymnal, or prayer book and rubbing briskly; with a hammer used by an undertaker to nail coffins together; by passing it across the head of a criminal just hanged; by drawing a snake head and tail nine times across a wen and each time saying, "Amen"; bottling a snake and leaving it under the eaves of the house (probably a sequence of the preceding); bathing a wen three times with May dew taken from grass in a graveyard after the burial of a youth.

Wounds were healed with "wound wood," which could heal all wounds. Our old people remember the name and nothing more. The "wound wood" must have been widely known for the remedies which mention it pay more attention to its cutting than to its use, seemingly taking for granted that the latter was common knowledge.

> To cut wound wood. Go out and hunt a small ash tree. On Good Friday, before sunrise, take a sharp hatchet or axe and cut off a branch or the whole tree with three strokes—it is to be noted that if the tree does not fall after three strokes the wood is useless. After cutting the wood rightly let it lie until the sun is risen and shines upon it, then cut the wood up into small pieces and you have the true wound wood. Preserve it well. If you should hack, stab, cut, or pinch yourself, so that the flow of blood is not easily stilled, lay the wood upon the wound so that the wood becomes warm and the wound will heal without festering. If your horse has a swelling lay the wood upon the swelling make three crosses upon it.

A goiter is frequently called *gropp am hals.* There are those who say that it is due, especially in the case of young persons, to lifting or carrying overly heavy loads.

Commonly, however, its coming, like that of warts and freckles, is seen to lie in no outward circumstance, but to be shrouded in mystery. For such an affliction sympathy medicine holds the only cure:

> A goiter was to be rubbed with the hand of a corpse; three times with the hand of a corpse; with an afterbirth; with a bone from a carcass; a toad was held against the swelling until dead.

In the folk mind similar stimuli bring similar reactions. What is good for the mysterious wart and the equally mysterious wen, is also good for the mysterious goiter:

> Look at the waning moon, pass your hand over the diseased parts and say, "What I see must increase; what I feel must decrease."

For swollen glands fat was applied.

A tumor was to be moistened with spittle from an empty stomach; a string which had been tied around the finger of a corpse was to be tied around a tumor, removed and placed in the coffin, and as the string decayed the tumor would disappear. Stroke a tumor with the hand of a corpse and the tumor will disappear with the rotting of the body.

During the pronouncing of the benediction in church the tumor is to be stroked and the words spoken: "That is sin which I see, what I stroke shall cease to be."

There are more *brauch* formulae for erysipelas than for any other affliction, seemingly showing that *brauche* was widely practiced in this instance. Even at the present time persons are met who steadfastly claim that there is no cure save *brauche* for erysipelas—*Wann sie nett zum brauchdoktor geht schtirbt sie*—if she doesn't go to the *braucher* she will die.

A sympathetic cure was to kill and cut open a dog, and have the sufferer place his feet in the cavity upon the entrails. The *braucher* or person essaying the role of *braucher* would throw shovelfuls of live coals over the patient, at the same time whispering the healing words; pass a shovelful of live coals over the patient who faced the west, from east to west three times; wave a firebrand or lighted tallow candles over the patient; pass a blazing white oak splinter three times around the body; throw a shovelful of live coals over the body; strike sparks over the body with flint and steel.

When we turn to the examination of the words used we find that erysipelas was regarded as a demonic personification. One formula used was:

Wild fire, I chase thee; wild fire be gone,
In the name of the Father, the Son, etc.

To prevent fevers rye blossoms were eaten; the first three rye heads seen in the spring in the name of the Trinity; the first three hail-stones of the year—a protection not only against fevers but against all sickness throughout the year; hardboiled eggs, shells and all, on Good Friday.

In these remedies there is an occult element, viz., the number three, hail stones from heaven, a holy day, which is present in many of the old remedies for fevers:

To still heat in small children, take three worms out of the earth, and in the morning cut three chips from three sweeps ("Born-stielen oder Schwingel") with which one draws out the water.

Tie in a rag and hang at neck of child. Do this three days in succession but every day with fresh rain worms and new chips. In this way the child will lose all unnatural heat.

A *brauch* remedy:

The stork has no tongue, the wolf has no lung, the turtle dove has no gall, thereby I let my 77 kinds of fever fall, in the name of God the Father, etc. Thereupon splash water up stream in flowing water. Speak this three times and repeat three days in succession, every day early in the morning before sunrise, but it must be done unbeshrewed.

For ague, take one quart of ale, put into it nine pieces of burdock root and nine pieces of plantain root, and after dark bury the vessel under the eaves of the house. Take up the next morning and drink. The eaves of the house, unlit by the light of the sun, were places, where in ancient belief, the protective house spirits dwelt. The eaves are the boundaries of the house; thus far and no farther can the evil spirits come. The belief goes back to the time when some protective symbol was mounted on the roof of the house.

We still have these protective symbols. It is a frequent sight to see the carcass of a hawk, crow, or owl, hanging or nailed to the side of a farm building. The reason given for this custom is that the other birds of prey will be frightened away by the sight, and this undoubtedly is the present day motive for the custom. Our Teutonic ancestors, however, nailed birds, wings of birds, or carved figures of birds on their barns and sheds to frighten away pestilence and disease.

Ague was to be cured by tying it to a tree. An early printed remedy, which was used, is accompanied by an explanatory paragraph:

Cold Fever (Ague). It has already been said that the external cures in great measure rest on a sympathetic foundation. Do we, in passing by, wish to know what this sympathy truly is? . . . There are under the sun very many secrets, that rightly used, work wonders, but he, himself, who knows the secrets cannot say even if his life depends on it, how, why, or through what these wonders work. One must be as unbelieving as Thomas if

he seeks to deny sympathy remedies whose good accomplish-
ments have been proven on many hundred occasions.

The following remedy, to be used to drive away ague, is also
of such nature:

Set on a small piece of paper one after another in proportion the following Latin characters:

```
A   B   R   A   C   A   D   A   B   R   A
  A   B   R   A   C   A   D   A   B   R
  A   B   R   A   C   A   D   A   B
    A   B   R   A   C   A   D   A
    A   B   R   A   C   A   D
      A   B   R   A   C   A
      A   B   R   A   C
        A   B   R   A
        A   B   R
          A   B
          A
```

Wrap this paper in common plantain leaves and lay it on
the stomach at once when the fever comes on and let it lie for six
hours. Also lay some of the leaves behind the ears and in the
crotch. Here, it is not my purpose to decide if it is the herb or the
charm that has most to do with driving away the fever but to
testify that the remedy has unquestionably helped many and
that in the above characters there is neither blasphemy nor the
invocation of evil spirits or anything else, unbecoming, sinful, or
unworthy of a Christian and his holy religion. It is also necessary
to note that the patient, in the eight days following the disappearance of the fever, shall guard himself against milk, fish, and
salted foods.

A simple remedy for headache was to wring out a cloth saturated in
vinegar and bind around the throbbing forehead. A person born on Sunday can cure headaches by placing both hands on the forehead so that the
finger tips touch in the middle of the forehead and then drawing the
hands, the one to the right, and the other to the left, across the forehead
and temples, down back of the ears, and out into space. This is to be done

three times. The efficacy of the cure is heightened by the repetition of *brauch* words.

A white headed person is a *weisskopp;* black headed, a *schwatzkopp;* red headed, a *rotkopp.* The parting of the hair on the head is called *scheededl. Warwel* is a cow lick and indicates cleverness or stubbornness. A red headed person is hot headed—*hitzkeppich.* Red hair, maybe on account of its rarity, was looked upon with suspicion. Red hair, in some European countries, is the sign of a witch. A proverb in the Pfalz is, "Rode Hoor und Erleholz wachsen uff kem gude Boddem," signifying that under the red hair there is evil. We have the same proverb, "Rote hoor un allhecke wasche uff ken gute flecke"—red hair and alder bushes are not found in good ground.

As cutting grass causes it to become thicker, so cutting hair causes it to become thicker. Hair should be cut in the zodiacal sign of the shaggy Leo; in the waxing moon; on the first Friday after the new moon; on the first Friday of the new moon to prevent it falling out. It should never be cut in the waning moon as that will cause baldness. The waning moon is propitious for all things that are to decrease, fall down, or stay down. This is the significance of the symbolical representation of the waning moon cut in the doors of outbuildings.

Apoplexy is supposed to be fatal, either at the first or third attack. Of a mild attack our people say, "apoplexy struck him, but only slightly." An unexpected fatal attack of apoplexy is still regarded as the direct work of God. One stricken will recover, if he gapes—*maul uff macht.* Full blooded, red cheeked persons were regarded as in danger of apoplexy. In their cases, formerly, bleeding was resorted to as a preventative and as a cure. An attack was frequently preceded by a dull dizzy feeling in the head, by *schwindel.*

In the past apoplexy and epilepsy were regarded as kindred diseases, and the treatment was similar:

For apoplexy, on St. John's day, in the morning before sunrise, unbeshrewed, go to a red beech sapling and dig under the roots and you will find coals. (The coals "under the roots" are partly decayed roots which have become separated from the stalk.) Take them up and preserve them. If one has met with apoplexy so that he cannot hear or talk, see, or walk, pulverize one of the coals and give to him in oil of lavender or in wine. Repeat several times, for the coals have great power and help every time.

For epilepsy, on St. John's day, in the morning before sunrise, unbeshrewed, dig under the roots of the red wormwood, and you will find coals. Crumble one and give to the patient in water and hang another at his neck.

Or, for apoplexy:

Give immediately six or seven drops of the blood of a turtle dove, in linden flower, May flower, or black cherry water.

For epilepsy:

Take a turtle dove, cut off its neck, and give its blood to the afflicted person to drink.

The *braucher* would essay a cure by drawing his hands down the body over the dode—dead limbs—three times and at the end of each movement slightly raise the hands and drop them as if letting a weight fall to the ground.

In the past both apoplexy and epilepsy, the latter even to this day, were regarded as the work of evil spirits. The dove particularly on account of its religious symbolism in Christianity, was looked upon as a protection against evil and the blood of the dove infused into the human body drove out the evil, and gave new life. Blood is life and life is blood.

This belief of evil influences is less evident in the case of apoplexy than in that of epilepsy.

The sign of the cross has great curative powers. For some afflictions it is made on the body with spittle. In epilepsy, according to the York manuscript, it was to be cut out on the body:

As soon as the sickness befalls, one must cut off three small locks on the right side of the crown, then on the left side of the crown, then in the front on the forehead, then back in the neck so that a X is formed. Thereafter cut off all the nails on the right hand and the left foot, then on the left hand and the right foot. Place all the hair and the nails in a quill and preserve until the patient has another seizure and then take the quill with the contents.

Not only is the symbol of the cross beneficial, but the very word "cross" indicates remedial powers:

> Keep a crossbill bird in the house and lightning will not strike the house. And let a child that is subject to epilepsy drink out of the dish out of which the bird drinks and it will be helped immediately.

The following *brauch* formula was used for sore mouth:

> Job lay upon the dung,
> As our dear Lord Jesus came along.
> "Job, why dost thou mourn?"
> "Why should I not weeping and mourning be
> When my lips and tongue would rot for me?"
> Take three straws out of the dung,
> Draw them through your mouth along,
> And your lips and tongue will again be strong.

> The sick one lies upon the dung and then takes three straws out of the manure and draws them through the mouth and says the words above and draws each one through three times until the above words have been spoken. Then he ties them together and hangs them in the chimney.

Scurvy was supposed to be gotten by eating fruit into which a chicken had pecked. A mouth wash was made as follows: "Take barley flour, milk, honey, and salt; boil well in wine. When using boil a little part and take as warm as bearable into the mouth."

In our *brauch* formulae scurvy (?) and quinsy are frequently associated:

> If thou with scurvy or quinsy be
> I'll blow my breath thrice into thee.
> X X X.

An interesting variation is the following:

> John Han, hast thou a sore mouth,
> Hast thou scurvy or quinsy?
> I blow my breath into thy mouth.
> God, the Father, etc.

The commonest brauch is:

Scurvy and foul mouth
I call you as dead as the dead in his grave.

*Brauche* was resorted to not only in the case of a sty but also for a cataract:

For dim and cloudy eyes, go before sunrise to a flowing stream, and wash the eyes with the left hand five times, and each time say the following words and then cast a handful of salt into the water and go backwards seven steps and then go forward to the house, three days in succession.

As this salt ceases to be,
So my eyes shall clearer see;
Christ is our help from every harm,
Herewith begins this holy charm.

To folk etymology, the name *wekschisser* means that a sty is due to defecation along the roadside. It is to be washed with one's own urine applied by hand.

The favorite treatment for a sty was *brauche* for which there were various formulae. The following may serve as examples:

Sty, thou corruptest N.N.'s blood
Therefore I take away thy goods.
God help thee N.N.

Another, heard at Egypt:

N.N. *Ich taufe dene schuss bladder an des Gottes Eli.*
N.N.I. I baptize your sty with God's eye.

The baptismal name and not the married name (in case of a married woman) is to be used. The patient is to stand under the eaves of the house, facing the rising sun. After the above has been spoken, the operator is to blow three times into the patient's eye.

Consumption was, and still is, widely regarded as a disease that is inherited. *Sis in blut*—it's in the blood. The inheritance of the disease from a consumptive parent is seen in the red cheeks of the child—*sie hot die rode backe von ihre mutter un sie geht d'r same weg*—she has her mother's red cheeks and she will have her mother's death. Where the disease skips one generation just to appear in a subsequent one we say *es hot zurick gschlaje*—it struck back. A consumptive person *guckt aus wie dar tod*—looks like death, or *wie dar lewendich tod*—or like the living death. For such a one there is no remedy—*ken graut gewachse*—no herb grows. Where death results from suffocation due to the collection of phlegm it is ascribed to *schtickfluss*.

Consumption is known as *auszehring;* in its early stage as *lungenzindung*. Our people distinguish *halsauszehring*—throat consumption; *lungeauszehring*—lung consumption; *schnellauszehring*—galloping consumption. Phlegm is *schleim* or *ausschpaues*. To spit is *schpautze* in Lebanon County, *schpaue* in Montgomery County.

There are no sympathetic cures for consumption apart from some *brauch* formulae. This is strange in view of the fact that our people see a sympathetic relation between nature and the disease; consumptives die either in spring, when the leaves appear on the trees, or in fall, when they drop from the trees.

A very old remedy, old because of its use of milk, consists of the Indian onion boiled in sweet milk. The liquor was drunk. The Indian onion was put in whisky with antimonium, a spoonful taken every morning (M4). Pipsissewa was put in whisky with rock candy.

To know whether a person, ill for a long time, would recover or not, horseradish was grated fine and a spoonful given to the sick one. If vomiting ensued, recovery would follow; if not, death.

### MARASMUS, ATROPHY

*Abnemmes, kinner auszehring, abnemmedes, abnehmes,* "waste away," "go back," "take off": marasmus.

*Schweining, schwinne, die schwinne, schwinde, Schweine, Schwinen, Schweinung, Schwind, Schwindung, Schwinden:* atrophy, muscular atrophy, shrinking of the flesh in any part of the body; marasmus, consumption; sweeny of horses.

*Abnemmes* is a well known term in common use for marasmis (sic) conditions of children. "Waste away," "go back," and "take off," are attempts to give the word an English equivalent.

*Schweining,* with many different pronunciations, was a common affliction judging from the numerous recipes for its cure. In medieval times the folk used the term for general wasting away conditions of the body such as consumption, marasmus and atrophies of different organs and parts of the body. In the past among our own people the term had much the same significance. Today it is usually applied to muscular atrophy.*

*Schwinnsucht,* elsewhere included in this work, was more specifically and usually used for long drawn out febrile conditions attendant upon pulmonary consumption.

The evidences of *abnemmes* are loss of appetite, emaciation, and feebleness. The causes of *abnemmes* are: food that is not nutritious; a change in food; to occult influences; to the presence of a worm in the spine that absorbs the vitality.**

To kill the worm a plaster of ground glass and pine sap—*bindhortz,* was laid over the back; the child's back was smeared with honey over night and the next morning scraped with the back of a razor—this was to be done three times; honey was smeared along the spinal column and the child was placed with its back to a fire or hot stove so that the worms would be drawn out to the honey and then after some time had elapsed the back of the child was closely shaved with a razor, by which action the heads of the worms were cut off.

Long ago—1784—an ailment was known as the *zehrwurm*—the devouring worm, for which a written *brauch* is as follows:

> "Oh God, shall the moth and the worms eat me. Nay they shall not eat me." In His name one must take the bone of a human being and scrape it and add as much white lead and a little olive oil, mix together and smear. If it does not disappear take a little alum ... (The hawk moth is known as *menschefresser*—man eater, even at the present time in Lehigh County; a large green caterpillar is called by the same name.)

The sympathy cures contain the common idea of "transference": the child is fed with a stolen spoon; out of the same dish from which the cat is feeding—the cat will die; the child is fed three times from a new saucer

---

* *Schwinden,* the atrophy of the limbs—the shortening of the extremities following outer or inner illnesses, be they rheumatism or bone illnesses (necrosis). At other places also *Flechten* and other skin eruptions of the limbs are called Schwinden.—Brenner-Schaeffer.

** "N.B.—Here it is well to note that where the *Abnehmen des Leibes* is caused by a love potion which persons, who have forgotten God and honor, have used that the poor fellow shall drink only mare's milk sweetened with a sugar. This will surely help."

from which the cat is also to be fed; a sage leaf of fine contour, as perfect as possible is drawn over the tongue in the mouth, in one side and out at the other.

A sympathy remedy, frequently met in the imprints and written remedies is the following:

> Boil an egg hard in the urine of the patient, pierce with a wooden prick and bury in an ant hill.
>
> Take an egg, pour over it some of the patient's urine, so that the egg is covered to the height of the width of two fingers, boil well and thereafter make holes in it all around with a small piece of wood to the depth of the yolk; then boil in the remaining urine until it has all disappeared; finally bury the egg in an ant hill. And when the entire egg has been buried (wonderful to relate) the half dried up person will again take on flesh and become, as it were, rejuvenated.

In the *brauch* formulae colic and puerperal hysterics are frequently joined together:

> Colic, birth-mother (mother womb),
> I adjure thee, through the holy Gospel,
> Draw not up, draw not down, draw not to the side,
> On the name X X X. For colic
>
> For womb ache and colic,
> Birth-mother, I adjure thee,
> That you subside for me,
> And no more become turbulent in me,
> Until the mother of God bares another son X X X.
>
> O Jerusalem, thou Jewish town,
> Thou, who the Christ didst crucify,
> Who spake that fresh water and fresh blood,
> Were for bowel and colic good.
> Strike the side three times with the hand X X X.

In earlier ages, and in folk meaning in some measure up to today, a *warm* (Wurm, Worm) was any footless or earth creeping animal from the tiniest true worm, or creeping reptile or insect, to the fabulous dragon

(Drache, Lindwurm). The term as used in folk medical nomenclature generally was intended to designate parasitic intestinal worms, but was also commonly applied to conditions such as a whitlow or felon, more rarely to the sebaceous squeezed out contents of "black or pin head" postules on the faces of children and to any worm-like or coiled morbid accumulation such as hemorrhoids, etc. Some people believed that worms were the cause of certain ailments giving a sharp gnawing or boring pain, of diseases that caused erosion such as caries of the bones and various ulcerated sores, of certain symptoms leading to insanity, or to various atrophied or marasmic conditions. The worm was definitely related if not identical with certain evil or demoniacal spirits such as the Elben, Alp, Trud; the dragon (Drache) was itself a supernatural entity.

The *metesser* in ancient days were regarded as devouring elves (Elben) or goblins; or they were bewitched worms, small worms or maggots or sebaceous material in the pores of the skin in children that undermined their sanity or that caused marasmus. More definitely the name was attributed to coiled snake-like sebaceous material squeezed from the so called "black head" pimples. Vaguely and uncertainly this connection is still believed. Finally, the name *mitesser* is now also used for the intestinal tapeworm.

The Herzwurm was the supposed cause of heartburn, stomach cramps, ulcerated navel, etc., a remnant of the old custom of sometimes calling the stomach region "Herz."

The haarwurm has a louse or mite in the hair or beard but more often a more or less fabulous worm in the intestines, lung, or liver supposed to cause a dry atrophy or consumption of the entire body. This worm was supposed to occur in the form of a hair, *es wor en hoor in sei maje*—a hair was in his stomach.

> To heal a rupture, take a chicken egg and when the sun has set in the evening, let the father take the egg and press the pointed end in the child's navel three times. Then let him raise a hearthstone upon which the fire was built, and make a hole in the ground where the stone rested. Put the egg therein with the pointed end upward and lay the stone again in place.
>
> On Good Friday, before sunrise, go to a healthy apple tree, cut a peg out of the wood of the tree, bore a hole in the tree on the morning side and knock in the plug with three strokes, and in the striking say, I knock in this plug that Mr. or Mrs. ("dem oder der") N.N.'s rupture will grow herein X X X.

*Awachse* used in its ordinary sense means to "grow together" and is occasionally so applied to such neighboring body parts as have been joined by morbid growth or to healing fractures of bone.

As usually used among the Pennsylvania Germans, however, it is the name for a quite mysterious but common ailment in early childhood. The name is also known in their ancestral home regions of Germany. Quite a few old *brauch* charms for its cure are in existence, and in these as well as in the minds of our people, the name is usually associated with the term *haerzgespaerr* (or *hazschpann*). The latter is not exactly synonymous but covers supplementary symptoms usually found with or following *awachse.*

No two medical authorities, either in this country or in Germany, seem to be able to agree as to the exact disease the people have in mind when using these terms. In attempting to give it an English equivalent the people themselves call it "liver grown"; possibly from "Lebertran," a dialectal German folk term sometimes used in Franconia. It is conceivable that there might be rare cases of the liver attaching itself through some morbid growth to the neighboring and outer parts, but since the ailment under discussion is known to almost everyone among our people, it is idle to think of any such explanation. It must also be confessed that in using this name the people have very definite and well known (even if little understood) symptoms in mind. The muscular or fleshy part of the lower chest region (more usually on the same side as the liver), in the region of the short ribs, contracts as if by adhesions of some sort to some inner part, leaving the ribs sharply defined and giving them the appearance of being ridged or swollen; the abdomen itself consequently is or appears to be raised. Quite often the symptoms known as *hazschpann* (and *herzgeschpaerr*) accompany or follow this condition; that is, there is a cramped, restricted feeling in the lower chest and upper abdominal regions and the breathing becomes labored or asthmatic.

The *haerzgschpaer* symptoms probably were bronchial colds or more often pleurisy. It is a question also if such constricted conditions of the ribs as described were not in themselves enough to produce difficult breathing. Furthermore it is quite probable that pleurisy alone, more especially when complicated with adhesions to the chest wall or diaphragm, was responsible for many cases.

It must be remembered that the word *Herz* (heart) in folk use was often stretched in meaning to include the outer heart region, the breast, liver and abdominal region. The *hazschpann* symptoms were often attributed to a demoniacal incubus.

*Agewachse* is thought to happen when a child is taken out of doors on a windy day; kept out in the open air a long time; is shaken up while conveyed from place to place. Its coming is sudden and its presence is made known by the loud and persistent crying of the infant. One is able to discover whether a child is livergrown by pressing the hands on the abdomen below the short ribs. If the pressure causes pain one may feel certain that the child is *agewachse.*

A remedy was to make the patient creep three times around the leg of the dining-table. In case this failed the child was induced to creep through a horse collar brought from the barn for the purpose. If this brought no relief the mother or aunt anointed the sufferer's chest with melted lard in a peculiar manner, making special pressure along the lower ribs with the thumbs, and if this failed to ease the child's labored breathing, a professional powwower was called in, who, in addition to the hot lard, "used words in the name of the Trinity."

The cures are sympathetic: pass the child underneath a bramble bush that has struck root at the tip—*iss agewachse;* crawl forwards or backwards three times around the leg of the dining room table, stopping where you began; crawl through a warm horse collar; crawl through the legs of a chair; put the child through horse collar for "livergrown" or "spells"; pass the child three times through a horse collar; "pass the child beneath a table to an assistant."

Seemingly the idea of "creeping through" is to transfer the affliction to that through which one creeps. That, however, is not the only belief back of the procedure. In sympathy medicine something usually is done to the subject to which the affliction has been transferred: it is burned, buried, dried up, nailed up, thrown away, etc. But here nothing is done to the table, the chair, or the horse collar.

There is reason then to suppose that originally the cure was a symbolic performance rather than a sympathetic one. The child whose internal organs have gotten out of joint is reborn so that it may be as it was at birth. The idea is apparent in the cure of passing the child through the legs—*bee* of the table to an assistant.

The sympathy idea naturally became bound up with it, especially when the cure was used for other afflictions.

For the cure of *hzehzschpaerr* the leaves of the mother-wort are fried in lard and used as a salve. A leaf of the same plant is taken and laid on the chest of the child and the following words spoken:

Heart pain,
Come from the rib,

As Jesus child
Came from the crib.

For the heart-span in little children.
I speak with the thumb
That the heart span may not torment me
And not stab me
In the name of God the, etc.

One must know the baptismal name.
"Heart injury and adhesion
Pass from the ribs
As the child Jesus
Out of the crib."
This is for heart-span every three hours.

Heart-span and adhesion pass from lung and live,
Pass from kidney and rib
As Jesus out of the crib.
This I do for penance to thee
That it soon away must flee.

And one more written formula:

When a child is grown fast or has heart-span, smear it with your
spittle from the pit of the stomach to the lower belly and then
from the shoulders to the end of the spine—six times in half an
hour, and each time saying the following words:

Adhesion and heart-span go out of my child's rib,
As Christ the Lord went out of his crib.
God the Father, God the Son, God the Holy Ghost.

Two mythological snakes are the *reef schlang*—hoop snake, and the
*hannschlang*. The former taking its tail in its mouth runs as a hoop at
incredible speed; the latter is similar to the former, with this difference
that it has a horn at the end of its tail which causes death to anything
which it strikes. Then there is the *schlangekeenich*—queen of the snakes
(the queen bee is also called *keenich* or *iemekeenich*) at whose whistle all
the snakes rally to waylay and fight the wayfarer.

Snakes crawl up trees to waylay the traveller. This is particularly true of the blacksnake, which drops upon its prey and kills it by constriction. "*Es hot sich schun um mei beh gewickelt ghot*—it had wound itself around my leg, and I had a hard time to kill it." The blacksnake is likewise feared on account of its color; it was often regarded as a favorite personification of evil spirits. A hunter told the writer that he had been out hunting for squirrels and that he had spied a big gray squirrel in the top of an oak tree. "Three times I shot at the squirrel and missed it and then I happened to look at the foot of the tree and there lay a great big blacksnake, whereupon I went home as fast as I could go."

Snakes are able to charm birds. One hears frequently told of birds, crying out piteously and flying closer and closer to the ground in ever lessening circles. Such birds are charmed—*gebannt,* by snakes who are drawing them to the ground for their prey. Human beings are in danger of being *bannt* by snakes if the snake catches the eye.

Burning a snake to death will drive other snakes away; a salamander cannot be burned to death. Snakes will avoid places where old shoes have been burned; where rubbish has been burned; burning old dish cloths will keep garter snakes away from the house. Garter snakes will get into a house that has ivy on its wall.

Snakes detest the odor of onions and will not attack a person who carries an onion with him. Human spittle is fatal to snakes and spitting into a snake's mouth will cause its death.


The following formula was practiced by specialists in Northern Lehigh County:


Gott hot al'les arshaf'fa, und al'les war gut;
Als du al'le shlang, bisht ferflucht',
Ferflucht' solsht du sain und dain gift.
                    X X X
          Tsing.     tsing,     tsing,


Which means:


God created everything, and it was good; except thou alone, snake, art cursed, cursed shalt *thou* be and thy *poison.*
          X Tsing,     X tsing,     X tsing,

The operator recites the above phrase and then, with the extended index finger, makes the sign of the cross three times over the wound, each time pronouncing the word *tsing*.

This old formula, which is frequently met with, arose among a people who supposed the snake's poison to lie in its forked tongue. The rapid movement of the tongue is known as *tsingle*.

Another version of the above:

And God created everything that is in heaven and upon the earth; and everything was good. Nothing did God curse except the snake only. Cursed shalt thou remain. Snake, draw at thy poison! Say this three times.

A different version of the above formula comes from the year 1817:

For snakebite, wet the middle finger with spittle and draw a ring around (the bite) and then place the right hand over the bite and say: "God created everything that is between heaven and earth and it was good, except alone thou snake, cursed art thou, cursed art thou, cursed art thou, swelling I get thee, poison and pain I kill thee"; then stroke three times over it with the hand and blow over it; then make a cross upon it, with the hand, three times in the highest names and then cut an onion in two and bind upon the wound, or take gunpowder and spit three times upon it and apply.

    And God created all things in heaven and on earth and all were good; none, but the snake did God curse; snake, thou shalt remain cursed; swelling I set thee, poison and pain I kill thee; snake draw at thy poison (three times). Amen X X X.

Wasps may be *banned*—charmed, so that they will not sting. The formula used is widely known:

Breathe on the wasp and repeat the following words without taking breath,
    "Wish'bli, wesh'bli, schtech mich nicht
    Bis der Dai'w'l di Sega shricht."

The equivalent of which is

Wasp, wasp, sting me not,
Until the devil recites the creed.

A similar conjuration to charm wasps is this:

"Wespi, wespi, wespi, ich Beschwere Euch bey Gottes kraft das
ihr mich nicht stechen sollet Ihr sollet nicht so wenig dass ein
Falsçher Ketzer in dass Himmel Reuch kommt in XXX."
    Wasp, wasp, wasp, I conjure you by the power of God that
you sting me not as little as a false heretic may get into heaven.
XXX

The dogs belonging to the early settlers were kept primarily as watch-
dogs—*haushund,* and were generally of a mongrel shepherd breed. They
warned their owners of the presence of intruders, Indians, and wild beasts.
    Frequently a *haushund* bore the name *Wasser*—water. There was
hidden power in names and a dog named *Wasser* would protect the house
against the outbreak of fire; neither would he become mad or bewitched.
    Dogs have long memories and always remember, by smell and by
sight, those who at any time tried to harm them. The safest way to meet a
cross dog is to catch his eye and hold it; to put on an air of bravado; to pick
up a stone or stick as he approaches. The vicious dog will always leap for
the throat.
    Dogs have supernatural gifts. They are able to tell a good man from
an evil one. "Our dog is very cross and we are always careful to warn
visitors to remain outside the yard until we have chained him. But when
old Betz K (a supposed witch) came to visit us she came straight through
the gateway into the yard and our dog just looked at her and slunk away."
    The evil spirits' favorite appearance is in the form of a dog. "When
Rev. X was a young man he took his weak-minded stepbrother out for a
ride and came back without him. No one ever discovered what became of
the stepbrother. Years later Rev. X was conducting his first services in the
church at X. Just before he began to preach a big black dog came into the
church and proceeded toward the pulpit. The Rev. cried out to the deacons, "Take him out, I cannot preach." This was told to us in good faith.
The inference is plain.
    Another incident was related to us as follows: "I came home late one
night and as I was walking along, I became aware, all of a sudden, of a big

black dog walking at my side. He went with me to the woodland and then disappeared."

Dogs can recognize evil spirits, no matter what form they assume; they are afraid of them. "We were out for raccoons one night with our four dogs. About midnight the dogs stopped hunting and came to where we were standing. They slunk between our legs. We could not get them to leave us. We did not know what the matter was until we saw a little black animal walking along side of us. Immediately we turned and went home."

Dogs sense the approach of death, and the mournful baying of a dog in the night or at the ringing of a church bell was regarded as an omen of approaching calamity.

Dogs were prized possessions and every householder sought to have one. To prevent a dog, newly obtained, from becoming homesick for his former home, one was to take a piece of bread, warm it in the shoulder pit and give to the dog to eat; or take a spicewood "lorbeer" berry, give half to the dog and eat the other half oneself.

Before the state of Pennsylvania passed laws requiring the licensing of dogs, towns and country sides were full of vagrant dogs. There may have been a considerable number of real instances of madness and the number of persons bitten by mad dogs may have been considerable, but it is quite likely that the number of supposed cases were equally large of not larger. Mad dogs and mad dog bites, however, were real specters haunting the lives of the common people.

A dog given the milk of a woman to drink will never become mad.

The Reading Neuer Hauswirtschafts Calendar of 1798 sums up in a lengthy article what was current folk medicine for mad dog bite:

> If the misfortune of being bitten occurs then one must seek to destroy on the spot the poison which came into the body with the bit of the dog, hinder its entrance into the blood or at least weaken its power. The whole future fortune, life or death of the one bitten, hangs upon quick help at this time.

The treatment of mad dog bite described in 1798 was followed in the main through the succeeding century as we find from a remedy written in 1859:

> Take the root of the yellow poplar ('gullene happel) or American tulip tree; boil in water and bathe the hurt of swelling therewith very often; give the person to drink $\frac{1}{2}$ pint every half hour and take some of the boiled and broken root and apply as a poultice.

The very best remedy is to rub salt into the wound immediately after the bite so that the absorption of poison may be avoided. Dissolve a handful of salt in a measure of water and bind the wound with a linen rag saturated with salt water. The rag should be kept wet at all times. In want of salt urine may be used. Sauerkraut liquor is to be used for the washing out of wounds.

In olden times the outstanding cure for hydrophobia was to cast the afflicted person, unsuspecting, into the water and to dunk him.

A black powder is frequently mentioned as a remedy, seemingly both internal and external, for madness. Its composition was as follows:

On Good Friday before sunrise, unbeshrewed, gather driftwood. Burn to charcoal and pulverize. Then take mummy (mumia), mint (balsamirten), maiden hair (Widerdon), fennel (schwarz-kimmel), allium (Neinhember), aristolochia (Holewurtzel), angelice (Angelica), dandelion (Danielica), saffron (Safrich), and cinnamon (Zimet). Mix all this into a powder and then it is ready for use. It is good for man and beast. It is also good for one who has been bitten by a mad dog, in which case the following herbs are to be added, white hoarhound blessed thistle, rue, cinquefoil, all being powdered.

# BELIEFS AND SUPERSTITIONS
## OF THE PENNSYLVANIA GERMANS

*(The following epigrammatic items are taken from Edwin Miller Fogel's* Beliefs and Superstitions of the Pennsylvania Germans, *Philadelphia: American Germanica Press, 1915. These are not so much beliefs and superstitions as sayings which help to ritualize the lives of the folk. Many are shared by folk of varied ethnic and national heritage. I have removed Fogel's references to the regional prevalence of the sayings.)*

### I. OMENS, FOREBODINGS, AND DEATH

To break a looking glass is a sign of death in the family before the year closes.

A picture falling from the wall is an omen of death.

If a hen crows there will be a funeral.

When a dog howls there will be a funeral.

The continual crowing of cocks indicates a funeral.

If a cricket gets into a house, there will be a death.

If the clock stops suddenly there will be an accident or a death.

If a sick person pulls at the bedclothes he will soon die.

Meeting a crow on the street is the sign of a funeral.

Green Christmas means a fat churchyard.

If, while sowing grain, you miss a strip, you will die within a year.

If a child cries while being baptized, it will die young.

A bird flying into the house is an omen of death or ill luck.

If thirteen sit down to a meal, one of them will die within a year.

Neighing of horses at a funeral indicates another death.

The blossoming of fruit trees in fall is a sign of death.

If the weather is calm on Innocents' Day (Dec. 28), many children will die the following year.

If you are taken sick on Sunday your sickness will be fatal.

Many women will die in confinement if there are thunderstorms on Ascension Day.

Change a sick person from one room to another and he will die.

205

Sneezing at the table is a sign of death.

If you miss a row in planting onions, someone will die.

If cucumbers bear only small fruit, it forbodes a funeral.

If you wash on the Wednesday nearest an Emberday and are taken sick, you will never get well.

The hooting of owls near a house is an omen of death.

If the body of the deceased in church or on cemetery faces its home, there will soon be another funeral.

If there are any funerals between Christmas and New Year, there will be many funerals in that congregation the following year.

If everything is in confusion at a funeral there will soon be another one.

If singing at a funeral is wretched there will soon be another funeral.

A funeral procession must not halt or another death will soon follow.

All jewelry should be taken from the corpse before burial.

An ignis fatuus is the spirit of the deceased who has returned to earth to look after his line fences.

If there are many deaths in a family in rapid succession, the grave of the first of those to die should be opened, to see whether the corpse has not drawn a part of its shroud into its mouth.

Everything planted by a person before his death will gradually die.

A light is frequently burned in the room where the corpse reposes until the day of burial.

If the mirror is not turned to the wall while the corpse is still in the house there will soon be another funeral.

II. WITCHES

Fasten a sprig of St. John's wort (Hypericum perforatum) to the door to keep out witches or flies.

Put the foot of a goose [draw a pentagram] on the stable door to keep the witches out.

Nail a toad's foot over the stable door to drive and keep the witches out of the stable.

To keep away witches, draw toads' feet with chalk on the bedstead or in the room above window or door.

Cut off the ears of a black cat, burn them and feed the ashes to the witch.

### III. THE WEATHER

When it begins to snow in fall, you say: the people along the Blue Mountains are plucking geese.

Aching corns are a sign of rain.

The cry of the whippoorwill presages rain.

The number of snows during winter is indicated by the number of days from the first snow in fall to the next following full moon.

If chickens moult in August, winter will be severe; in October, mild.

If the lower legs of chickens are well covered with feathers, the winter will be severe.

If it is clear on the Visitation of the Virgin there will be no rain for six weeks.

The Virgin crosses the mountains to visit her sister.

If it rains on the Visitation of the Virgin (July 2) there will be a dry spell when she returns (Aug. 15) and vice versa.

The weather for the year is determined (on Christmas night) by taking twelve onions, naming them, one for each month, hollowing them slightly and filling them with salt. The wet months of the year are indicated by the onions in which the salt is melted.

Rains will not be beneficial if it rains on Whitsuntide.

Rain on Whitsunday is followed by seven rainy Sundays.

If it rains on Ascension day, rains will do no good for the rest of the summer.

If it rains on Good Friday, you may look for high winds and little hay.

If it rains on Good Friday, rains all summer long will do no good.

Seven rainy Sundays follow rain on Good Friday.

The crowing of cocks before nine at night indicates a rain.

The crying of peacocks denotes rain.

The cry of peacocks in the evening indicates rain.

As the last Friday of the month, so the following month.

The nut crop will be poor if it rains on John Huss' day.

Tall bitterweed (ambrosia artemisiaefolia), deep snow.

There will be rain on Good Friday, even if only three drops.

When many women are seen on the street, it will rain next day.

When the old women display their nightcaps, you may expect rain. [Spider webs are meant.]

### IV. SPECIAL DAYS AND SEASONS

Cast a bullet on a crossroad on Christmas night between eleven and twelve. Load it into your gun and it will hit your enemy wherever he may be.

Cattle talk between eleven and twelve on Christmas night.

Lightning will strike your barn if you sew on Ascension day.

If you take a drive on Ascension day you will have an accident.

Never till the soil on Ascension day.

Lightning will strike anything on which you worked on Ascension day.

The only thing you may do on Ascension day is go fishing.

By drinking seven kinds of tea on Ascension day you will escape contagious diseases for the rest of the year.

If you eat sausage on New Year's you will be robust all year.

Snakes have their picnic on Pius' day (July 11).

To prevent fevers you should put three kinds of food on the sill outside of the window on Christmas eve, and on Christmas morning you should eat some of each kind of food.

If you sew on Shrove Tuesday you will sew up the hens' cloacae and prevent them from laying eggs.

Sweeping all the rooms on Good Friday and burning the sweepings brings good luck.

If homespun is to wear well there should be no spinning between Christmas and New Year and the spools should be empty before Christmas.

Stables must not be cleaned on Good Friday lest the witches enter.

Your cattle etc. will not thrive if you eat any meat other than fish on Good Friday.

None of your cattle will die throughout the year if on Christmas morning you feed them the hay which was put out of doors the night before to collect the Christmas night dews.

You must not butcher beef on an Ember day but you may cut it up.

Washing on an Ember day is unlucky.

Never cure meat on an Ember day.

Never slaughter any cattle on an Ember day.

As many cattle will die during the year as are slaughtered on any Ember day.

Plants will not bloom unless you wish them a happy New Year.

The designs formed on water which is set out on Christmas night to freeze are omens of the future.

You will rid your house of vermin if you sweep your house on Ash Wednesday and throw the sweepings on some one else's property.

Shrove Tuesday ashes spread on cattle and poultry on Ash Wednesday will keep them clean of lice.

Tea gathered on John Huss (July 6) and Virgin Mary (August 15) is twice as strong as that gathered at any other time.

If you sweep on Good Friday you will have many flies all summer.

To cure fever gather nine species of herbs or any phanogamic plant flowering on Ascension day.

If your wash hangs out on New Year's, you will have to wash daily all year.

If a barn is raised on Ascension day, lightning will strike it.

The Amish do without breakfast on Good Friday.

If you cast a bullet on Christmas or New Year's night, you will see the devil.

Unless you eat some thing green on Maundy Thursday, you will get the itch.

You will not become lousy if you eat something green on Maundy Thursday.

Eat some green vegetables on Maundy Thursday to prevent fever.

On Christmas night water in wells is changed into wine for three minutes.

Your cattle will not thrive if you clean the stables between Christmas and New Year.

You ought not to take a bath or wash or change clothing between Christmas and New Year, for you will have no luck.

**HAPPY NEW YEAR!**

# V

# IMAGES IN ARTS AND CRAFTS

Perhaps the most significant indicators of folk spirituality lie in those forms of culture least amenable to precise analysis. The arts and crafts of the Pennsylvania Dutch have long been an identifying characteristic of the culture. The tourist is familiar with the unique design of the Pennsylvania barn, with its overhang providing shelter for the farm animals and its colorful display of geometric symbols commonly referred to as "hex" signs. Although it is certainly true that a correct rendering of these designs may have been thought to ward off evil and hard luck, their more authentic origin was in the folk memory of biblical texts, ofttimes syncretically related to ancient Nordic, Near Eastern, and cabbalistic imagery. The designs on barns, quilts, blanket chests, and other items of furniture and household utensils were visible prayers. The folk, through story and craftsmanship, had been nurtured on symbols which they used to express their hopes, and which revealed the sources of their sense of ultimate order and meaning.

This is not to say that with the onslaught of secularization the original power of the imagery did not often give way to a sense of decoration. And there are those observers of culture who refer to the German and middle-European propensity for gaudy ornamentation. Even today one notices the yards and gardens filled with colorful pots, figurines, and miniature windmills along the highways and streets of eastern Pennsylvania. However, it is worth risking the hypothesis that this disposition is very likely *derivative* of the cultural storehouse of religious symbolism. Often the color and even some of the imagery remain after the meaning has seemingly disappeared.

Pennsylvania Dutch decorative arts draw upon the folk memory of lilies, doves, swastikas, and peacock/phoenix birds which are part of the millennialist traditions of Christianity as well as the broader heritage of

211

mysticism and theosophy previously discussed. In word and in visual artistry, the images found their way into books, birth and baptismal certificates, as well as onto the more utilitarian furnishings of home and farm. The images expressed their belief in the day of redemption and resurrection, when Christ's peace would be brought to the human family.

In order to do justice to the material of this chapter, an illustrated book would be necessary. However, we must confine our examination of sources to the record and study of those who have devoted themselves to the spiritual heritage of the Pennsylvania Dutch. Our sources are secondary and represent an appreciative awareness of what is essentially a visual body of evidence.

# Pennsylvania German Folk Art

*(John Joseph Stoudt's* Pennsylvania German Folk Art *is itself a classic work of Pennsylvania Dutch culture. It was first published in 1937 [Allentown, PA: Schlecter's, 1948.] under the title* Consider The Lilies, How They Grow. *It is a scholarly work, but it breathes the very spirit of the people whose art it sought to analyze. Certainly the book is not in itself a folk resource according to the usual technical understanding. But it belongs to the folk as well as to the folklorists and the interpreters of folk culture. As a source by means of which we may study the arts of the Dutch and encounter their spirituality it is worthy of our attention. Stoudt believed that this folk art was basically spiritual in concept and expression, that its symbolism and imagery were Christian in orientation even though part of the "collective unconscious" and historically related to various cabbalistic, Persian, Nordic, hermetic, and occult traditions.*

*(Stoudt was a student of Rufus M. Jones and the son of John Baer Stoudt, a pioneer in the study of things Pennsylvania Dutch. These two influences, along with the psychology of Carl Gustav Jung, are present in much of his work, which spans several decades of the mid-twentieth century.)*

Some of the verses [one finds on furniture and utensils] are exceedingly simple, like the English lines on a pie-plate:

Surely no hawk will ever seize this bird
Because the tulips bend over and protect it.

But other verses have a profounder meaning. . . . Consider the words above a ribbon-weaving stool. They suggest the picture of a diligent *Hausfrau* sitting at her hand-loom, busy with this world's affairs, but dreaming of another world where such cares do not annoy. She says that Faithfulness (*Je longer, je lieber;* forget-me-not; faithfulness) must contemplate alone. What is the reason (*Ursach*) when Trust and Faith (*Trey und Glauber*) have grown weak? The *Hausfrau* answers her own questions; she tells us that, though in this world Faith may be weak, yet in the Rose

Valley beyond the grave numberless Roses grow. There also is the field of Lilies, there in that new heaven. There everything will bloom according to its kind; there will be ripe figs; and there the grapes will bear the sweet new wine. There, too, will be Faithfulness. . . .

On the tombstone of Christina Oberling in the churchyard of the Bergstrasse Lutheran Church in Lancaster County there is the following quotation from a hymn by the famous Paul Gerhardt:

> Jesus, I shall enter into
> Thy Kingdom's joys;
> So let Thy Blood be my purple cloak:
> I would clothe myself therein.
> It shall be my head's crown,
> In which I do not wish to depart
>
> From the Father's highest Throne.
>
> And to Thee to whom I am betrothed
> As a well-adorned Bride.
> Dwell by Thy side.
> Christ's Blood and Righteousness
> That is my ornament and cloak of honour.

Here, decked out in the imagery of *The Song of Songs* and *Jesusminne* is expressed a highly developed spiritual experience. But the modern reader will find the language strange, for it is unknown in the secularized world-view of his modern life.

Consider also the verses on a piece of illuminated writing made by Maria Souder in the Franconia School in 1812:

> How one sees in the springtime
> Beautiful flowers in the meadow!
>
> Who has conceived the flowers?
> Who has made them so beautiful?
> Yellow and red and white and blue,
> That I look at them with pleasure?
>
> He who is and can do this,
> And who does not tire thereby,
> Is God in His vitality—
> Who creates these lovely flowers.

Or, consider the English verses on a decorated towel which portrays flowers and birds and urns:

I, SUSANNE LANDIS, made this in my youth.

A blooming paradise of joy
In this wild desert springs,
And every sense finds straight employ
On sweet celestial things.
White lilies all around appear,
And each his story shows:
The Rose of Sharon blossoms here,
The sweetest flour (sic) that blows.
                                        1838.

Now, was Susanna Landis talking about the natural flowers of the field, those many and gaudy botanical specimens which grow in the lush Pennsylvania meadows? What is this "wild desert" in which the blooming paradise springs? What are these white lilies, each one of which tells its own story? What is the deeper question concerning the origin of nature which Maria Souder is asking? And why did the relatives of Christina Oberling put that verse from Paul Gerhardt on her tombstone? . . .

Much of this mystical longing after something not possessed, much of the striving for certitude in a transient existence and much of this clothing of naked faith in mystical images drawn from Scripture found its literary fulfillment in the poetry of Angelus Silesius, or Johannes Scheffler (1624–1677), whose influence upon the iconography of Pennsylvania German folk art was large. . . . The main work, on which his fame rests and which is of interest to us in our study of Pennsylvania German folk art, is his poetry. This falls into two parts: The *Cherubinischer Wandersmann,* a collection of six books of rhymed verse, and *Heiliger-Seelen-Lust oder geislichen Hirten-Lieder derin ihren Jesum verliebten Psyche,* a collection of hymns. It may perhaps be assumed that the former reveals Scheffler the sectarian, while the latter reveals Scheffler the Roman. For the two books show wholly diverse spiritual experiences. The former embodies that mystical apprehension of reality in which creeds are dissolved into metaphor, and the latter speaks the language of ecstatic devotion to the incarnate Saviour. The latter draws its images from that source to which the Christian mystics have so often turned, to the *Song of Songs,* and it has had a close connection with the Pastoral poetry of Germany. The opening lines of many of its songs are borrowed from some of the popular songs of the age; and many have been used in the hymnals of the

German Protestant churches, including several of the Pennsylvania German hymnals.

One of these hymns, *Nun will ich mich scheiden von allen Dingen,* (which is the 346th hymn in the *Kleine Davidische Psalterspiel*) presents in its 13 stanzas an amazing array of images. While the hymn is not as well tailored as some others, it does, nevertheless, present an interesting aspect of the theological use of natural objects as descriptions of God. In fact, the writer asserts finally

> Nothing in heaven or earth can
> Be found or named
> That He Himself is not for me.

Jesus is called the comfort, the refreshing drink, the fountain of life, the sea of desire, the gracious evening star, the morning blessing, the sugar-sweet dew of morning, the morning red, the sun, the moon, silver, gold, pearl, ruby, jewels, blooming garden of roses, a field of many flowers, a field of growing crops, a forest, a meadow, the land of milk and honey, the noble Rose-Lily-Branch, the beauty of May, a garden and an apple tree. Even the field of music is not omitted:

> For me thou art the loveliest music
> My jubilation, joy and triumph,
> My cymbal-tone and joyful song,
>
> I hear Thee rather than trumpets,
> Trombones, cornets, organ, flute;
> Than lyres and pealing bells.

Jesus is said to nourish the heart with sweets which this world cannot supply; he is the believer's "*feste Burg*" or castle. But in the end the poet confesses:

> Now I ask no more for heaven,
>
> For earthly-pleasure and worldly turmoil,
> Thou art for me an entire world,
> Thou art the heaven I have in mind,

The paradise for only me,
Without which nothing pleases me.

The 263rd hymn in the *Psalterspiel,* which is also the 670th hymn in
the large Moravian Hymnal of 1753, has the first line, *Keine Schon-
heit hat die Welt,* and it continues the mood of searching nature for the
Biblically-grounded images which can be applied to Jesus. The poet says:

The world has no beauty
Which does not prevent to my eyes
My lovely Jesus Christ,
Who is the source of all beauty.

The poet sees Jesus Christ in the morning-red, in the light of the day, in
the moonlight at night, in the springtime, in the glorious lily of the garden,
in red roses, even in all the flowers wherever they may be. Jesus is sweeter
than milk and honey; He sings more sweetly than the nightingale; He is
the *ne plus ultra* of all nature. All of these images have their Biblical basis
and in such hymns as this we are not in the world of allegory, but we are
more in the world of nature-mysticism as found in Valentin Weigel and
Jacob Boehme. Hymns like those of Angelus Silesius, found in the Pennsylvania hymnal, the *Psalterspiel,* contain exquisite imagery, frequently
referring to Jesus as: Beautiful, Bridegroom, Shepherd, Lamb, Lily-child,
Fountain, (cooling) Stream, Source, Forest, Plain, Green Fields, Dove,
True Pelican, the Heights, Valley, Guiding Star, Sun, Moon, whole Fir-
mament, Beginning and End, Exultation, Ecstasy, Life and Death,
Heaven, Paradise, and Heart. Each one of these images finds its original
source in Scripture, and the poet has here created a remarkable hymn in
search of the Exalted Christ. In a paraphrase of Silesius' work, provided by
an anonymous folk writer, we find some new insights, like the use of the
pelican image—the pelican which has done great work in that it has
brought life again to the seeker.

One of the greatest of all the Pietist hymnwriters was the well-known
and sainted Paul Gerhardt, another of the writers whose poems had an
influence upon Pennsylvania German folk art. More than any other poet
Gerhardt attained a reputation and influence, not only in German, but
also in English hymnody. One of his hymns is of special interest to us and
it is his famous *Sommerlied* which first appeared in 1653. In this hymn all
the various images of the new being in Christ Jesus are realized with a

poetic unity that cannot be easily surpassed. The poem is not merely lyrical ecstasy about the natural summer; but here the content is spiritual, for the Biblical allusions clearly establish that. . . .

Here in this one hymn by Paul Gerhardt the mystical game of searching for the names of God, begun by Pseudo-Dionysus and continued through medieval mysticism and baroque poetry, came to a high state of growth and development, a living tradition which had its influential effect upon the hymnals used by the Pennsylvania Pietists. . . .

Johann Kelpius was one of the first poets in Colonial Pennsylvania to express the style of his age, and the roots of his religious style go far back to his own native Transylvania. In Eastern Europe there also were flourishing schools of religious poetry; indeed, it can be said with certainty that the soft sentimentality that later marked the Pietistic and sentimental schools of Western poetry appeared very early in Transylvania, perhaps as early as the middle of the seventeenth century. Some of the titles of the Transylvanian collections of religious poetry are interesting: *The Holy Swan-Song* (and "swan-song" here does not mean what it means in modern metaphor) and *Spiritual Musical Flower- and Rose- Forest.* This school of poetry was at its height when Johannes Kelpius was a young man, before he had left his home for the universities of Germany; and it was Kelpius' brother, Martin, who as a schoolmaster and teacher inculcated these ideas in the mystic of the Ridge. And, augmented by the gaudy style then fashionable, these trends found expression in Kelpius' own hymns. But these poems of Kelpius have something more than imagery, for they are mystical and metaphysical poems, poems in which the religious quest of Kelpius' heart and the longings of his own age are apparent. He wrote (in the not-too-capable translation of Dr. Christopher Witt):

Make me as the New Wine! from many noble berries . . .
Make me a new heart in me, and only in Thee living
In sacred Unity. . . .

or,

Me, only Thy Sun-Flower, let after Thee be turning;
And in the pensive night, and Darkness for Thee mourning,
Until Thy form in me, Like Christ's hath full pow'r
Then shall I still in Thee—I, only Thy Sun-Flower.

Kelpius wrote about the mystical death of the self in Love, about the necessarily bitter quality of religious mortification. For his was a tormented heart, a melancholy and pensive spirit, writing about the deep anguish and despair of his heart:

> I long for Love, and yet I dare not think of loving
> Since I unworthy am. . . .

And this is not romantic love.

> To love is my desire, yet am ashamed of loving,
> I, worthy but of hate. . . .

Again:

> Resigned to Thy Will, with content I am filled,
> If I but Love Thee still, though by Thee I am killed. . . .

And he concludes this deeply-conceived poem thus:

> Like as the birth appears by Anguish e'en near dying,
> Like Bitter when made Sweet has cordials in it lying—
> The fading flower past, then first the seed is sought,
> So also through this Death the Soul to God is brought.

This is real mystical dialectic; and Kelpius' goal was to seek in his solitary hermit's den that perfection of Love which has been the goal of so many people and of so many of the earlier settlers in William Penn's lands.

Such mysticism was accompanied in these hermits of the Ridge by an intense apocalypticism. The forty hermits felt that the year 1700 would see the ending of the world and the final triumph of the Lord and His Thousand Years of Peace. As Kelpius himself wrote:

> We wait the dear Sabbatick year
>           of Peace and judgment quitting,
> All Enemies, made then Thy Prize
>           and at Thy feet submitting

When unto Thee, shall ev'ry knee
   in all the world be bowing
And all-in-One united grown
   but in Thy Love be flowing.

Kelpius also wrote about the Virgin Sophia of Boehme, and of the deeply lamenting voice of this hidden Love.

In the year 1709 a Colony of German Mennonites from the mountain regions of Switzerland, under the leadership of Hans Herr and others, settled along the Conestoga in what is now Lancaster County, having purchased 10,000 acres of some of the richest land on this continent. These people were the descendants of the sixteenth century Anabaptists and they had endured the horrible persecutions which had been directed against them, for they had certainly been proceeded against with great tyranny, cast into bonds and tormented with burning, sword, fire and water. Many were undone in a short space of time, but they persevered and they survive today as the colourful Mennonites and Amish of the rich Lancaster region.

The most interesting literary memento which these people brought with them, and which the Amish still use to this day, is their hymnal, *Ausbundt das ist, etiche . . . Christliche Lieder,* the oldest Protestant collection of hymns in continued use. This was the hymnal of the Swiss Anabaptists and German Mennonites, and it is an interesting one. At the basis of this collection there are the 51 ballads of Anabaptist martyrdom of the Swiss Brethren who were imprisoned in the fortress at Passau between the years 1535–1537. These are amazing hymns, some of the finest religious literature, easily capable of sustaining the faith of their children and children's children. But other hymns are also included in this rich collection, some written by men like Sebastian Franck, Felix Mantz, Georg Wagner, Georg Blaurock and Hans Hut. Eleven of the hymns were translated from the Dutch Mennonite Hymnal *Het offer des Heeren,* and some were taken from Michael Weiss' Hymnal of the Bohemian Brethren.

In these hymns the imagery is subdued and the peculiarly Anabaptist notes of martyrdom and faith dominate. But the imagery is not wholly absent. Thus the 64th hymn by H. Walter deals with the new summer which is prophesied in the twenty-fourth chapter of Matthew:

I am heartily joyous
With the lovely summer-time,
When God will well renew
All for Eternity.

But probably the most interesting of all images in the *Ausbundt* is that found in the 71st hymn, written by Hans Buchel:

For He who accepts Thy Word

Is like the pelican bird
    All serpents avoid him.

When he goes away from his nest,
The serpent slithers to his young,
    And puts their life in jeopardy.
But the bird's instinct is good,
Opens his breast and lets his
    blood
       flow, and gives it to them.

With Christ also is the figure
When He maintains His own young
    Against all enemies.
On the Cross's stem He opened His
    breast,
And His own Rose-coloured Blood
    He gave with desire for them.

\* \* \*

From out of the stream of German Pietism there came a man, gifted with all the impetuosities of genius, who left his indelible mark upon Pennsylvania religion, literature and art. That man was Johann Conrad Beissel who . . . at the age of twenty-five, was converted. But "ere the spirit of penitence came upon him his reason became so enlightened that he could easily solve the most intricately involved matters." He turned his attention to mercantile calculations, covering the walls of his back room with cipherings, mastering this without help. Soon afterwards the awakening spirit knocked so loudly at his conscience that his whole being was thrown into the utmost perplexity, and so the foundations were laid for his conversion, which followed soon afterwards, wherein he is said to have attained such super-human faithfulness to God that it may well be regarded as one of the great miracles of the times. This conversion, his followers believed, was direct and unmediated.

    Conrad Beissel apprenticed himself to a baker—the family trade—

and in a few years he set out on his journeyman travels. He departed for Hungary in company of four hundred others, but at Strassburg he left them, and this was his good fortune, for the rest were massacred by the Turks. From Strassburg he went to Mannheim, where he worked in a bakery run by a man named Kantebacker. Here the "drawings" of the Heavenly Virgin (Sophia) grew so strong within him that he bade a goodnight to all earthly women. His biographer suggests that because of this the sex was thereafter attracted to him.

From Mannheim he went to Heidelberg, where he worked for a man named Prior. Here in this University town, still smarting from the French invasion, there were many Pious. At the beginning of his stay he attended orthodox Protestant services, hearing the eloquent Divines Mieg and Kirchmayer, but "without receiving any edification." Here he also met the learned scholar, Haller, a "strong suitor of the Virgin Sophia," and correspondent of Johann Georg Gichtel, the editor of the 1682 edition of Jacob Boehme's works. Haller introduced Beissel to the secret conventicles of the Pious held in the forests outside of the town, and here Beissel made fast friends. . . .

In 1720, in company with four others, he came to America, landing at Boston in the Autumn. He proceeded to Germantown, the settlement of Pastorius, where he studied for a year with Peter Becker, the Baptist leader. In the following year he went to Conestoga, where he erected a solitary hut along the Mill Creek. Here he lived with two of his voyage companions, Stuntz and Von Berben. The following year these men paid a visit to the Labadists in Maryland. A fourth member joined them, Georg Stieffel, another of the voyage-companions. This strange establishment aroused the interest of nearby settlers; it was stern and strict, with little concern for the world. Gradually the others became dissatisfied with Beissel's strictness and they withdrew.

In 1722 an important awakening took place. Missionary journeys, conventicles, prayer-meetings, foot-washings, baptisms, love-feasts—all helped to spread the fame of the *new inspiration* abroad. This was a part of the Great Awakening which was felt all over the American settlements. On the 12 November 1724 a meeting was held at the home of Henry Hain and a group of believers baptized themselves in the Pequea Creek. The bad name of "Quakerland" which Pennsylvania was earning was slowly being forgotten through the efforts of these Pious Palatines. Beissel wrote to a friend back home: "Ere I was aware, that whole region was illumined by that heavenly light, which in times following spread over almost all of the American provinces, and over the races and tongues of people."

From the many thousands thus awakened a new congregation arose, a spiritual church which thought of itself as Rachel, who now, in this sixth or Philadelphian season, was again pregnant of a new child. And a virgin shall be made ready for the Bride of the High Priest in this new and specially blessed land of Pennsylvania. The imagery of *The Song of Songs* was again applied. The winter of sin and death was past. The rain had stopped. The flowers were budding. The birds were singing. Soon—yes, very soon—in the red-blushing dawn of the Conestoga Valley, the Bride-groom would appear in company with the Heavenly Dove which feeds among the lilies!

This was the mood of the times.

The first love-feast (Agape) was held by this new congregation in December 1724. A new location was found on Rudolf Nagle's land. Here these "Spiritual Israelites" made their first encampment. Others soon joined the community, surrendering their love for the world, and the congregation resembled those of the primitive church. Beissel journeyed far and wide to get converts. The Love-Feast of Pentecost, 1726, was the gift of the Spirit to this congregation. Revivals were induced and singing was developed to such a pitch that it "had never been equaled in the Christian Church from the days of Ignatius on, to whom was first made known by revelation the antiphonal mode of singing practiced by the Holy Angels."

Beissel's followers elected him their teacher. This ordination he felt was direct from God. A change in his personality followed. He grew more serious. He sought to be worthy of his trust.

Near the beginning of 1732 he called his congregation together, and with sorrowing heart spoke to them words concerning the Spirit, and then withdrew eight miles to the north, to the place where the Cocalico winds past wooded hills to live alone with his God.

But he was not destined to live alone. Religion is revived by just such acts, and his followers came after him. A new community was formed. And he named it Ephrata.

This was the sixth period, the Philadelphian season. The elect shall indeed be sealed! The four hundred forty thousand shall finally achieve the Enochian life. The purity of the Apostolic Church will be restored. The Sabbatical Church will come into being. Here, in this place that the savages named *Koch-Halekung,* den of serpents, the Mount Zion of the New Jerusalem will be established. And here in this land, in a red dawning of the Pennsylvania sun, the new leader, the new Christ, will come with his heavenly hosts planting His Lily of wonders.

When the news of this establishment in Lancaster reached the towns, men and women of all sects and walks of life came to follow here the Apostolic life. Three Orders were established: Bethania, or Kedar, the men's unmarried brotherhood; the Order of the Rose of Sharon, the unmarried sisterhood; and the Householders, who were married, and who lived on the neighboring farms. A prior and an Abbess were elected. Conrad Beissel had no organic relationship to these groups. He lived alone in his hut, wrote hymns, and directed the worship services, caring for the souls entrusted to his guidance. His *Letters* breathe the spirit of deep concern for his followers. . . .

After a struggle of epic proportions Beissel succeeded in reestablishing his strict idea of spiritual order. This was the means of creating his idea of spiritual therapeutic through art, singing, and labour. He worked out the first new theory of music on the American Continent; he established the writing school where the ornamental Gothic texts were made; he set up one of the finest printing establishments in the Province, where mystical literature was published—all of which were means for the crucifixion of the flesh.

*    *    *

Now, what was the mood, the tone of these settlements?

Project yourself back to the crude Pennsylvania frontier of the 1750's! You see some pious pilgrims coming down a rude path which leads to the Ephrata establishment. They arrive just as the members of the community are proceeding to the *Saal* for worship. The visitors follow the Brethren and Sisters into the low-ceilinged room. Silence reigns. The Spirit seems to move through the whole congregation. The tension increases. Finally one of the visitors, Georg Adam Martin by name, is seized by an inward emotion. His spirit feels the presence of the divine majesty. The veil in which all the nations were enveloped is removed. He sees the pathway to the Holy of Holies. The gracious spirits kiss each other with the spiritual kiss of peace. All is one—a divine, mutual, holy unity and fellowship. Voice, utterance, speech are forgotten. Smell, taste, feeling, hearing—these are no more.

But the spirits are soon called back to the wilderness room. The world is remembered. Its sin is felt. The Sisters begin to sing in their wailing, five part melody. Tears come, for their hymn is *The Streets of Zion are desolate.* The woe, the barrenness of this world's sin is re-called. The visitors are moved. When the Sisters finish, one of the visitors rises and says: "You sang a hymn for us! Now we shall sing one for you."

And then they sang the *Song of the Lilies:*

The heavenly drama, the perfume of lilies,
Awakened anew the Spirit's desire;
The Roses of Sharon, though low on the ground,

Bring heaven to spirits for the covenant bound.
The apple tree's shade bends forward with pleasure
To seek in the field of the lilies its treasure.

The colours of lilies, their figures so fine,
Arouse all the love in this bosom of mine;
The Roses of Sharon that bloom in the field
Are kindred to me 'neath God's holy shield.
So away with your crowns and treasures so rare
With lilies so beautiful you cannot compare.

O heaven! How rich and how happy am I,
For the beauty of lilies you showed to mine eye.
She groweth as straight as the smoke on the plain,
And love-like she clings to me now and again.
I stay with her always, because she so charms,
As long as I breathe she'll rest in my arms.

Thine odour divine, thy heavenly form,
My poor sinful heart did wondrously warm.
My heart how it longs to join in the hymn
That swells from the throngs of Manhanaim.
Oh, might I, low-bowing, without any fear
Pluck off all the roses so plentiful here.

My life I would give it forever to thee,
With heart and with soul; yea, so it should be!
For Thou art the Lily, else nothing can clothe
My poor naked soul in peace to repose.
If Prince I were called, I'd wish nothing more,
Nor care for aught else that I wanted before.

Enraptured I am by this beauty of thine,
I sway like one drunken and vanquished by wine.
The apple tree casteth its shadow so still
Where the lilies abound by God's holy Will.
The carpets of Solomon, ever so fine,
Are nothing compared to these beauties of mine.

Melchisedec's altar, here also it stands,
As Master it guardeth this purest of bands;
As oft as he thinks of them in his abode,

The Manna of Paradise falls to their lot.
The strength of the lilies, like secret-kept fire,
Springs forth with new force in the virginal choir.

Come dearest! O come! and make me thine own,
To rest on thy heart and there have my home.
O give me the juice of the lilies so mild,
The balsam of love and heaven's strong child.
Baal-Hammon, my vineyard brings splendid new wine,
It robbed Thee of life, O Beloved of mine!

Let therefore the Virgin by all be extolled,
As long as of crown and sceptre we're told.
As though she despised the hot and the small,
Through shame she high honour hath brought to them all.
The little ones feed in the dale with the Rose,
For brides and espousal the Lamb did them choose.

The flowers of Sharon are counted no dross,
Because they're betrothed to the Lamb on the Cross;
And follow his footsteps through danger and chance
Drawn closer to Him through the Love of His Name.
Yes they are the virgins Christ chose for His Brides,
He made them His own and set others aside.

> From the *Chronicon Ephratense,* translated from
> the German by J. Max Hark, Lancaster, Pa., 1889.

The poetry and the music of Ephrata—like its art—was wholly unlike that of the ancient church where the same conditions prevailed. It possessed nothing of the rhythm and swing of the religious and secular folk song of the sixteenth and seventeenth centuries. Contemporary visitors at Ephrata attest to the sweetness, beauty, the lilting upon the angelical or celestial quality of the vocal music as it floated through the rooms.

Beissel, in his *Apology for Sacred Song,* argues that it is consistent with Scripture to sing praises to the Lord, but he believed that the degree of spiritual integration had something to do with the quality of the music. Only those with Christ in their throats can sing to Him. . . .

In 1730 two German books, written by Conrad Beissel, appeared from the press of an enterprising young Philadelphia printer, marking his first venture into German publication and, with one exception, they were the first German books printed in America. They were written by Conrad Beissel and printed by Benjamin Franklin: *Ehebuchlein* and *Mystische und Sehr Gehymne Spruche.* In the same year Franklin printed a hymnal bearing the title: *Gottliche Liebes und Lobes Gethone....* In 1732 he printed another Ephrata hymnal: *Vorspiel der Neuen Welt....* And in 1736 there appeared the third of the first trilogy of Ephrata hymnals: *Jacobs Kampff und Ritter Platz....* The mood of these hymnals is found in the following hymn:

> Come all ye dear, trusting souls
> Ye who have bound yourselves to me;
> We want to tell God's praise;
> For the springtime is beginning.
>
> In the Spirit one sees how everything blooms,
> And prepares itself for fruitfulness
>
> Therefore the harvest is not far off.
>
> The cold weather goes to an end.
> The joyous year now stirs.
> Therefore lift up heart, heads and hands,
> For now is revealed and clear
> That which has long been covered and hidden;
> Now the beautiful day is breaking forth,
> Wherein one may joyously sing.
> Promised land, I see thee greening.
> And blooming white in beauteous flower;
> Also bearing fruits for those who serve
> As food for the pure angelical choir.
> I mean the bride who betroths herself
> To the Lamb here in this world.
> Doing only that which pleases Him.

This is the note of Ephrata, of its art, music and poetry—the note that was reiterated again and again in the mood and historical *milieu* of the settlement. It was a mood of expectant apocalypticism, of disgust for a sour world, and the metaphorical presentation of this hope in tangible images and figures of speech was taken from Scripture and from the devotional literature of the immediate past.

> Arise, Zion, Arise! Arise!
> Virgins, do not delay!
> Thy Bridegroom comes
> To embrace thee with friendliness!

After the three hymnals mentioned above had been printed by Benjamin Franklin, there appeared from the newly-founded press of a young Germantown clockmaker another collection of hymns made by Conrad Beissel for use at Ephrata. This was the famous *Weyrauchs-Hugel,* the title of which runs in English as follows:

> Fragrant Hill of Zion, or Mountain of Myrrh, embracing many varieties of incense prepared according to the art of the apothecary, consisting of various love-inspired works of God—redeemed souls, expressed in many varied spiritual and delightful hymns in which, among others, the last call to the supper of the Great God is excellently and variously presented for use of the awakened western church at the time of the setting of the sun, preparing her for the midnight advent of her Bridegroom. Printed by Christopher Saur, 1739, Germantown.

Here, even in the title-page, the mood and the symbolic attitude of the people at Ephrata is evident. The dedication of this work was to "all the Solitary and cooing Turtle-doves in the wildness, as a spiritual harp-play in these divers times of God's visitation." And to the selection of hymns added as an appendix this title was added:

> The withered but now revived and fruit-bearing Rod of Aaron, consisting of an addition of solemn and experienced hymns in which the ways of God in his inner sanctuary are closely presented for the comfort of the orphans and forlorn in Zion. *He that goeth and weepeth, bearing precious seed, shall doubtless come again with rejoicing, bringing his sheaves with him.*

Indeed, the withered rod of Aaron—the churches of the world—has put forth the renewed branch—Ephrata—which now was sprouting and flourishing in this new world, a vitalized shoot of the new age in the new land. Indeed, as another hymn said:

> The lily-twig shows itself again in these days;
> The penetrating rays of the Eternal Sun
> Are again inwardly bedaubing the cold land!
>
> The Lily-number of the Holy Elect is also revealed;
> They stir the harp with rising and falling (scales),
> And give off, like liquors, many love-songs.

Or, consider these four short lines:

> Am I called a flower,
> To God's praise and fame;
> But am I so arranged
> That my smell pleases him?

Or take the highly revealed imagery of the following hymn:

> Thou shalt sing, my Dove;
> Come to my gaping wounds,
> So that no enemy looks at you;
> Here there is certain fragrance.
> Lay Thyself at my breast.
> And partake of sweet vitality.
>
> Hear, ye flowers in the meadows!
> Hear, ye birds up in the air!
> I want to betroth myself in love
> To my Jesus, who calls to me.
> I am His and He is mine.
> For ever shall his love endure.

So, turtle-doves and lilies symbolize the same thing: the lonely dove hiding in its rocky cleft cries to heaven for its mate, the Heavenly Dove; and the Rose in the meadow too:

> Therefore daily do I feel within me
> That Thy pure love-engendering,
> Leads me along the way of the Cross
>
> To true, quiet spiritual fruit.
> That I shoot forth like a rose in the valley,
> Which with humble lowliness extends itself amongst the thorns.

And then there is the wonderful rhythm of this:

> O Jesus, Thou Flower of Virginal virtue,
> Thou Sweetness greater than the love of youth;
> I can do nothing else, I must give Thee my life,
> My praise, honour, Kingdom, possessions and fame.

These hymns were from the first of the great trilogy of Ephrata hymnals, the *Weyrauchs-Hugel,* and they show in full measure how the new life in Christ which was experienced in the Community and the new age that was expected, were expressed in metaphorical and symbolical language. But it was not only from the over-wrought imagination of Conrad Beissel that these images came. Others also had mystical enthusiasm as well as the intellectual curiosity to create them. Johannes Hildebrand, one of the Ephrata Brethren, had written his Doctorate at Giessen under the Pietist Rembach on *The Song of Songs,* and, having thus approached these images from the intellectual point of view, it is not surprising that they appear in Ephrata poetry.

The second of the great trilogy of Ephrata hymnals was printed on the newly-established press of the Brotherhood in Ephrata and bore the title which reads in translation: *The Songs of the Solitary and Deserted Turtle-Dove, namely the Christian Church. . . .* The date of the first edition was 1747, but two other editions were subsequently issued without change of imprint-date on the title-page. In the last of these editions an epilogue is added: "A Scriptural monument and eulogy for the crowning of the priest of the Order of Ephrata, by a Sister Warrior of Jesus Christ who for many years has suffered spiritual Martyrdom." And then these quaint words are added: "The spirit closes with an abundance of Praise and gratitude, and prophetic fragrance of the lilies."

The Foreword of the 1747 edition says:

> In a general sense the hymns contained in this collection may be looked upon as roses which have grown forth from among the piercing thorns of the cross, and consequently are not without some beauty of colour and pleasantness of fragrance. . . But to speak yet further of the compilation of this spiritual work; it is a field of flowers, grown forth of many different colours, and of various fragrance; as they were produced by the Spirit of the Church, out of the mystery of God. In some the spirit of prophecy soared above all mountains of the Cross, bidding defiance to His enemies, setting forth as present the future glory of the Church. In others the spirit trod into the inner court, and exalted his voice in the holiest of all. Again others have the pleasant odour of roses; others, on the contrary, sprung up on the myrrh mountains.

The various internal divisions of this hymnal carry on the metaphorical imagery: The Pleasant Smell of Roses and Lilies; the song of the Solitary Turtle-Dove; the Cooing of the Dove, etc.

The love which overflowed in the Settlement and which was the motivation of this communal society was compared in the first hymn to the lily:

It is the noble lily-twig
Which blooms in God's Kingdom;
Yea, also the field of beautiful flowers
That appears here in the tent of misery.

And then too, the new-born faith of the believer is compared to this flower:

I am a Rose—
Let no one do away with himself
When herewith there is the thornprick
So that he does not retreat.

And then the believer is Aaron's stem:

I am a green twig
Sprouting from a dry branch;
The life-stream from God
Has permeated my spirit.
Now am I planted
And stand in God's garden,
And bear my fruit
Of many and various kinds.

The third of the trilogy of Ephrata hymnals was the *Paradiesisches Wunderspiel* which was published on the Press of the Brotherhood in 1766. This is the largest and most complete of the Ephrata hymnals, containing most of the materials which appeared previously in the others. But the hymns are beginning to lose the intensity of their religious emotion, and the imagery itself is being watered-down and weakened so that it lacks the clarity of the originals. Indeed,

The bloom is over, the blossom has fallen;

And the golden age seems to recede more and more. The rational images of Boehme's writings, the Virgin Sophia and other conceptions, appear and the purely Scriptural images, the history of which we have been tracing, are lost in the work. Indeed, the 425th hymn says:

Zion blooms and greens again,
Sing new wedding-hymns!

But this was an empty hope. The age had passed. The time of the singing of the birds and of the blooming of the flowers was gone. As one of the inhabitants at Ephrata later wrote on a decorated fugitive piece:

Proceed then, my soul, lament and mourn, the beautiful rose and flower garden, which the Mother of Eternity has planted among us, before these times and days, has been despoiled. For the beautiful flowers are fallen off and the roses are withered, even around the lilies there are so many bushes and thorns to hinder plucking one for needed use. Wild animals have broken the hedges or enclosures, and the Mother of Eternity with her trusty gardener is as if disowned, since the wild-animals have no regard for the hedges or hedge-tender. And since this beautiful rose and flower garden has been turned into a wilderness various kinds of hostile birds have built their nests therein, as magpies, owls and the like and hatch their young therein. Even the bird cuckoo has come there, who sucks the eggs of other innocent birds and throws the young of other unsuspecting ones from their nests. For all this the beauteous growth of lilies and roses, and the lovely song of the birds of paradise is lost; the wild animals having no regard for hedge or enclosure, have turned the beautiful rose and flower garden into such a wilderness. [This translation made by Rudolf Hommel, and printed in the *Pennsylvanisch Deitsch Eck* in the Allentown *Morning Call,* August 4, 1945.]

Now, the cuckoo bird does not live in Pennsylvania, it is a European bird; and so this imagery declares its European origin. But the mood and the meaning is clear enough. The roses and lilies have faded. The heavenly garden has lost its blooming. The time of the singing of the birds and of the blooming of the Springtime flowers is past. The dull world of the flesh has intruded, and the life of God is gone.

The radical Pietists and sectarians of Pennsylvania, like their brethren in Europe, were dissatisfied with the Lutheran version of Scriptures. So, in Berleberg, there appeared a new translation of the Bible with commentaries, and this work was sold in Pennsylvania by Christopher Sauer, the printer of Germantown. The editor was Johann Christopher Haug and he was aided by Dr. Horsch, Christopher Seebach, Tobias Eisler and Dr. Georg DeBenneville, the last of whom came to Pennsylvania. It was supported by the generosity of Duke Casmir of Seyn-Wittgenstein-Berleberg and the entire Bible appeared in eight parts between 1726–1742. The Commentaries which were appended to this Bible were not scientific in purpose, for no "human meanings" were desired, but they sought to create the "mystical sense" of Scripture. The various previous versions were compared and the Pietist literature, emphasizing the cultivation of the heart, was searched for commentary. It was this Bible and not the Lutheran which was the version from which the Pietist folk artists in Pennsylvania drew their inspiration, and as a result the mystical-allegorical approach to Scripture, which had had such a wide popularity during the medieval period, was revived. And it can be said that, from the Biblical point of view, the chief influence in the revival of the imagery was this Bible of Berleberg. . . .

In the Archives of the Schwenkfelder Historical Society there is a manuscript dated 1756, which is the *Gesangbuch* of one of the ministers, Hans Christoph Hubner. The fourth hymn in this collection is *Ein schon Lied von den Himlischen Rosen und wohlriechenden Lilien* (A pretty hymn of Heavenly Roses and fine-smelling Lilies). The marginal references added by hand show the Scriptural source for most of the lines. The old method of lining out the hymn was used in the meetings; first the stanza was sung by the assembled congregation, then the preacher would follow, beginning with the second verse, using each stanza as the text for short remarks. In this way the hymn was explained and the references made clear. The hymn given below does not appear either in Koch's *Kirchenlied* or in Wackernagel's *Das Deutsche Kirchenlied*, though it does appear in the first American hymnal of the Schwenkfelder Church, Germantown, 1762.

> There is a flower in the meadow,
> Jesus, my Lord,
> In Him do I have my joy,
> Would gladly be with Him.
> I shall encompass Him within my heart,
> And keep Him there forever;
> Renounce everything on earth;
> Wander the narrow streets;
> All my senses are directed to Him.
>
> The Flower that I do desire,
> Has no equal on the earth;
> Jesus, my God and Lord,
> Above in the Kingdom of Heaven;

Where the Flower rules;
From Him in the sap flows forth;
Glorified in God.
So Solomon was not adorned
In all his glory.
In *The Song of Songs* he sings:
I am a Rose in the meadow.
Wholly surrounded by thorns;
Now placed upon God's throne.

Another hymn is a Song in which Christ is compared to a Flower, and it was written by Triller. It uses, as the first line, a phrase which comes from the folk song. The translation is by Nancy Bickel Frendt.

I know a flowret fine and fair,

To me affording pleasure.
It blossoms out in God's free air,
Above all others treasure.

The branch on which such flowers blow,
From David is derived.
Thence has the blossom's wondrous glow
Its splendid growth contrived.

As great Isaiah clearly hints,
This Twig of Jesse's Root, it
Blooms forth all clad in fairest tints. . . .

For this flower has virtues fair, able to heal the greatest of illnesses. It is more wonderful than gleaming gold or any earthly treasure.

My garden I shall dig with care,
In it shall plant the Flower.
Its odours sweet can strengthen me,
And shall my spirit nourish.

This Wonder-Flower I will guard,
Will cultivate and cherish.
It shall replace all other flowers,
My Being it shall gladden.

On an illuminated New Year's Greeting made by Susanna Hubner, the Schwenkfeldian artist, there is the following hymn, the second and third stanzas here given:

> The flowers now are blooming strong,
> With the smell of pleasure;
> Nearing hope and love
> Grace, Kindness and Blessedness.
> God's fruit is blooming
> Before all peoples;
> Consider now how I mean it,
> The summer is before the door.
>
> The turtle-dove's voice
> Is heard in the green forest.
> Who will go with me from here,
> I hear the nightingale? . . .

Here is the mood of these pioneers in Penn's lands, the mood of the new age and the new spiritual time, the age of the spiritual summer and of roses and lilies. . . .

That the birds of Pennsylvania German folk art are . . . Scriptural birds is clear from two decorated bottles which have on them the designs and also inscriptions. The first one is in the Pennsylvania State Museum and bears this inscription:

> Billing must be permitted
> Two beloved turtle-doves.

And the second bottle is the one which was given to Johann Matthias Stoudt when he left his native Zweibrucken for Pennsylvania; and therefore it can be established that this folk art was brought to America with its meaning. This bottle, still in the Stoudt family, presents the figures of two doves united into one heart, with the inscription:

> Two beloved hearts
> Have one pining.

In the Pennsylvania German hymnals the dove is of course omnipresent. In fact, the title of the finest of the Ephrata hymnals is the *Turtledove* and the following passage is quoted opposite page one in the Ms: "O my dove that art in the clefts of the rocks . . . let me see thy countenance, let me hear thy voice; for sweet is Thy voice, and thy countenance is comely." (ii, 14).

Of all the many images used in Pennsylvania German hymnody, the image of the turtle-dove does not permit easy application to Christ. For the logic of this symbolism is too strict. Christ is instead the lonely heavenly mate of the dove, the one to whom the dove is crying, the one for whom the dove is longing. Christ is the heavenly bird, the phoenix, the bird of paradise, the pelican (Cf. *infra*) or the peacock. But he can hardly be the turtle-dove. It is the symbol of the languishing believer seeking the Saviour:

> Permit me, as a dove,
> To flee into this rocky cleft.

The device of the two doves united into one heart is clearly prefigured in the following lines from the Ephrata *Turteltaube* Ms.:

> Where the dove shows itself artlessly
> In the senses of pure children
> There wisdom's treasure is achieved
> With much blessing and profit.
> Well then now! It has succeeded.
> I forget what I have been.
> I am burdened with nothing else
> Because I am a pair of doves.
> When two are beloved
> And unite themselves into one
> Then one can certify the other's
> Worth and Virginity.
> The pure Spirit, the Dove,
> Has drawn myself to it,
> Has paired itself with me.

Here the New Testament meaning of the Dove is introduced. To continue:

> And moved (itself) by passionate love
> What shall now separate us
> From the united flames
> Which have brought us together
> Through its passion.

There is a cunning use of the dove image in the following verse from the *Homburgisches Gesangbuch* (#784, verse 1):

I, a lonely turtle-dove
Sitting in arid waste,
All languid, weary in thirst and pain,
In chaste love-passion.
I cast my eyes here and there
To see who possibly might
Love my soul.

Here the erotic overtones associated with the dove image are clear.

In Pennsylvania German folk art one often finds a gaudy bird surrounded by flowers. This is the lonely heavenly bird "with dove's eyes" who "feeds among the lilies.". . .

The allegorical representation of Christ as a pelican is based on Psalm 102:6: "I am like a pelican of the wilderness."

In ancient Christian art the pelican in her piety is one of the most widely used and striking symbols of the atonement.

The image appears in a long passage in the 71st hymn of the Amish hymnal, the *Ausbundt,* which is quoted above. It also appears elsewhere as

O Pelican! O pure Swan!
Allow such to stir my thoughts!

\* \* \*

In folk art . . . style is the imprint of a common cultural point of view upon works of art—and by "art" the applied arts are meant for the distinction between artists and craftsmen has not yet arisen.

But the point of view is *commonly held!* This presumes a homogenous culture and the interdependence of all elements of that culture. Verbal expression and plastic or graphic expression agree; for, if they do not, then culture is divided and there is no unity in the forms of thought, no culture.

And that there was a Pennsylvania German culture, that there was in Pennsylvania a commonly-held point of view and unified form of thought, that the many elements which go to make up the Pennsylvania German formed a common point of view, is certainly the greatest surprise of all. When one considers the various origins of the Pennsylvania Germans, is it not remarkable that Swiss Mennonites, Dutch Quakers, Frankfurt Pietists, Silesian Schwenkfelders, Saxon Herrnhutters, Danish

Doompelaars, Palatine Reformed, Wurttemberg Lutherans, Wittgenstein Pietists, Alsace Huguenots—that all these fused into a homogeneous culture with a commonly held point of view—the Pennsylvania German? Is it not unusual to find a culture produced of so many elements and points of view? Genetic and casual arguments are not valid here, for one cannot argue that because most of the Pennsylvania Germans came from the Palatinate their folk art derives from the admittedly similar folk art of the Palatinate. This theory would not explain why Georg Hubner and Susanna Hubner, who were Silesians, used the so-called Palatinate motifs in their decoration. This would not explain the intensity of the art of Ephrata, because no similar intensity is found in the folk art of the Palatinate. Or, those who argue that Pennsylvania German folk art comes from Sweden because the Swedes first settled along the Delaware cannot explain away the fact that Heinrich Otto, Daniel Schuhmacher, Christian Seltzer and a host of others were not Swedes. All methods which seek casual genetic connections must fail because they ignore the cultural *milieu* in which the folk arts have arisen. In fact, the argument can be turned about. Palatine and Swedish folk arts are so like the Pennsylvania German because their cultures are almost alike; the Pietist verbal imagery also appears in the hymnals of Sweden, Transylvania and other regions.

Isolated parts and segments of culture do not transmit themselves from one land to another; but what do transmit themselves are the modes of thought, the points of view of the people who produce the forms of art. People migrate to colonize and they come with little baggage. And if the Pennsylvania Germans *copied* Palatine or Swedish designs, then they were poor copyists, and then too the differences must be explained.

No! Genetic, casual methods are not adequate to explain the sources of Pennsylvania German folk art any more than they are adequate to explain the origin of ideas. Not only are these methods incapable of explaining how Silesians produced Palatine designs, but they cannot explain the variety of styles which exist even within Pennsylvania German folk art itself. For why was the art of Ephrata so different in style and execution from that of the potters and chest-painters, even though the same iconography was used? . . . Why did Palatine architecture not survive in Pennsylvania after the third generation? Yet, why were all the forms of folk art in Pennsylvania so similar in their conception, even though they differed in execution? Why do the pieces with secular motifs fit into the religious frame of reference, exhibiting a unity of conception which even the artificial distinction between the religious and the secular cannot destroy?

And the only explanation which fits the facts is the one which is based upon the unity of all cultural expressions in a common point of view expressing itself through words, designs, shapes, colours, textures, etc.

And the point of view expressed in Pennsylvania German folk art is certainly dominated by one thing—which may or may not be religious—the process of "salvation" or the process of psychological individuation.

The human imagination has been ever stirring—and perhaps ultimately in vain—to express the ineffable abyss at the center of life in form, shape and figure; or, to put it differently, the human soul has been seeking to express the words (*logoi*) of life.

# FOLK ART OF RURAL PENNSYLVANIA

*(It is difficult to provide an adequate basis for an investigation of the spirituality expressed in the artistry and craftsmanship of the Pennsylvania Dutch. One must see it to understand it. Photographs would help. However, it is not our purpose to deal with the historicity of the arts and crafts themselves. Rather, we wish to get to those sources which will help us to comprehend folk spirituality—the extra-ecclesial religiousness of a people. The following material is from Frances Lichten's* Folk Art of Rural Pennsylvania, *New York: Charles Scribners Sons, 1946.)*

Unlike his Quaker neighbors, "who not only had no time for art but no place for it in their scheme of salvation,"* the Pennsylvania German never renounced his love of color and pattern. To please himself and his clients, he was apt to add some decoration on even so humble and commercial an article as a pie plate. It may have been no more than a pattern of fluidly drawn lines in an ochre-yellow which contrasted agreeably with the red-brown background, but the application required several extra operations which one might think his native thrift would have dispensed with. This type of decoration, called "slip decoration," was applied to the flattened disk. . . .

It must not be overlooked that this large, scattered group of country folk had their own dialect, known as "Pennsylvania Dutch," in which they transacted all their affairs, many of them never using a word of English. In the eighteenth century 95 percent of the population in certain towns conversed wholly in German dialect. English was the language of law and of the State, and the Pennsylvania Germans who had dealings with the English-speaking courts were forced of necessity to learn it, but as rugged individualists they wrote it in a manner untrammelled by any rules of spelling, one in which d's and t's, b's and p's were cheerfully interchangeable. Without this knowledge of their orthographic practices, it would be difficult to detect the classic "Dorothea" lurking behind the Pennsylvania German's "Dor-de-a" and "Veronica" would be sunk for-

---

* In the words of Elizabeth Robins Pennell.

ever in the curious "Fronica." Even after the introduction of the public-school system, when country dwellers were forced to study English, they still carried on their transactions with townspeople, compelled to be bilingual, in "Pennsylvania Dutch."

This persistent adherence of the early settlers to their own tongue explains why a dish ornamented with a homely proverb, with a bit of vulgar peasant humor or a verse from the Bible set down in the only speech familiar to a woman, had a more intimate appeal to her than the most elegant of objects imported from far-off, unknown England. The sight of one of the well-known Old-World maxims brought back to her the memory of the sententious shake of the head with which the solemn ones had been uttered, or the good-natured smile which accompanied the hundredth repetition of the familiar joke. The frequency with which the same German sayings appear on the work of the local potters shows how greatly this traditional ceramic literature was cherished in this strange new land. . . .

The double eagle* centered with a heart was a favored device. . . . As a central motif the peacock alternated with the eagle. The tulips with their odd, unbotanical, pinnate leaves vary little on any of the pieces. Georg Hubener seems to have been the only local potter to use double bands of inscriptions, the outer one of which states:

> Mathalena Jung; her dish
> This dish is fashioned out of clay
> And when it breaks the potter's gay
> So take good care of it, we pray.

The inner, excellently lettered band carries an equally familiar legend:

> Anyone can paint a flower
> To give it fragrance only God has power. 1798. . . .

### THE PEACOCK

Readily identified among the various birds used as decorative motifs by the Pennsylvania German potters is the peacock. His crest and tail furnished them with two details easily depicted within the limits set by a line scratched in clay. . . .

---

* Lichten identifies as an eagle what was probably a turtledove (*Turtel Taube*). (REW)

The Tree of Life was a favored motif. Often the remarkably virile design was distinguished by wavy, repetitive lines with unusual arrangement of tulips tangent to the rim of a plate.

In a Sgraffito plate made on January 17, 1794, in Bucks County, Pa., one can see rhythmic, undulating stems supporting tulips and pomegranates crowded together with long scalloped-edged leaves make a bold space-filling device. Violent, not too well placed dashes of green detract a little from the pleasing rhythms. . . .

A Sgraffito Plate (signed R.G. 1812) features a peacock perched on the top of a Tree of Life. The effect is curiously Oriental. The series of concentric arcs, suggesting loops of drapery, is faintly reminiscent of the Adam and Regency periods, the attenuated influence of which by 1812 had probably seeped even into the "interior.". . .

The craft of whittling and carving with a pocket knife is one familiar to most European peasantry, the Swiss above all. With the skill inherent in him and the love of decoration as well, it was natural for the Pennsylvania German also to use his gift in making other articles that were needed in the house. A strong, sharp knife was in every farmer's pocket; with it he shaped all manner of necessary household articles—egg-beaters, ladles and measures, spoon racks, and buttermolds.

The well-tended stock of the Pennsylvania farmer produced quantities of butter, an always marketable product. As butter and pastry were the two plastic substances available on the farm with which to gratify the love of form, the opportunity to transform them by wooden molds into decorative reliefs was not overlooked. Tradition was always behind the practice, though the molds made in this country differ both in shape and detail from their European prototypes. The buttermold is the most commonly encountered household article carved of wood. Every farmer, against the time when he might feel an urge to whittle, had laid away a bit of walnut or a small chuck of pale, smooth, seasoned wood saved from an ancient apple tree. From it the welder of the penknife cut the mold and its handle in one satisfying piece, shaping it skillfully so that it fit the hand comfortably. Into its flat face, with sharp, unerring strokes, he cut in intaglio the invariable tulip, star, heart, and all the motifs so familiar to him. On the wholly hand-whittled molds the variations rung on these few motifs seem unlimited. Later on, when molds were turned out in quantities on a lathe, though still ornamented with hand carving they became a much less individualist expression of the carver's traditional, artistic instincts.

Every farm kitchen had a wooden box to hold salt, hung by the fireplace to keep the contents dry. The back, which was also the support, was usually whittled into a graceful outline. In addition these boxes were sometimes carved, sometimes decorated with designs in color. On other types of wall boxes, used to hold kitchen cutlery and tableware, a little thought was always given to the shaping of the general contour. Even the shapes of the openings by which they were suspended contributed their bit to the decorative whole.

Once the household was well equipped, when the powerful urge for whittling overcame him the farmer occasionally carved objects for pure love of the craft. These carved birds, animals, and figures were often primitively conceived, but when painted in bright colors they provided some of the few ornaments the country folk had.

Weathervanes, though ordinarily the work of the smith, were also carved out of wood and then well protected by paint. Some are quaintly shaped humans, their movable arms whirled around by every passing breeze.

After the general disappearance of the skilled craftsman in the middle of the nineteenth century, the artisan who once earned a simple livelihood by working in wood could no longer find enough work to keep him busy. Some took to the road as itinerants, rambling the eastern section of the State, leaving behind them a trail of crudely carved eagles, roosters, and peafowl—ornaments which they often exchanged for board or for liquid refreshment at the country taverns. . . .

An odd example of this persistent urge, this survival of medieval craft, is seen in the work of Noah Weis, 1842–1907, the lifetime proprietor of a tidy country inn located in a Lehigh County village. As a boy working on his father's farm in Hosensack, in the same county, he showed a definite artistic bent. . . . He tried his hand at anything. To appeal to the secular tastes of his patrons he placed round the walls of the reading room a complete hunting scene. There is the life-sized hunter and his spotted hound-dog, a covey of quail, his old home, and a stage-coach drawn by six horses.

All of these familiar objects were carved as large as possible and with all the realism Weis could achieve. As the folk sculpture current in his day, the cigar-store Indians and merry-go-round figures, were as gaudy as fresh paint could make them, he too colored his carving as realistically as possible. In some of these carvings he achieved a highly personal style, which can only be described as a double-faced bas-relief. Panel after panel of

Bible subjects, translated from engravings in a Bible history, covered the walls of the outbuilding. These huge wooden decorations, executed with only one tool, the pocket-knife, were done with great gusto, even if they lacked the artistic finesse which would have resulted from academic training. For many years Weis found the time to work at his beloved carving only in the very early morning hours, before even the first tavern patrons arrived. . . .

Ctesias, a contemporary of Herodotus, on hearsay alone first described the fabulous unicorn as a wild ass, native to India, colored red, white, and black, with a long horn on its forehead. By medieval times, it had become the symbol for virtue and piety. So skittish was the unicorn that its capture could be effected only by setting a young virgin as a lure. The entranced unicorn, seeing her, put his head in her lap and fell asleep, a tale quite acceptable to a world which knew not the symbolism of Freud. The unicorn was a favorite heraldic figure; on the British coat-of-arms it is the left-hand supporter. That it actually existed, even in this country, was still believed in the eighteenth century. Mittelberger in 1750 reports a conversation with an English fur dealer, returned from the West: "They [Indians] had also met an animal which had a smooth and pointed horn an ell and a half long on its head; said horn pointed straight ahead. This animal was as large as a middle-sized horse, but swifter than a stag in running. The Europeans of Philadelphia had taken the animal for the unicorn."

A striking arrangement of ancient motifs. The lion, heart, doves, urn, peacock, the tulips, and the dominant crown, are spotted about on chests. . . .

From the earliest times, the mermaid myth took hold of the popular fancy. In medieval days, it symbolized the divine and human facets of man's nature. The mermaid was credited with the gift of prophecy; force of bribery were the means used to compel her to reveal the future. . . .

Ever since the ninth century, by Papal decree, a cock has adorned the church steeple. Originally a pagan symbol dedicated to Apollo, the sun-god, for his unfailing services in heralding the rising of the sun, the cock became a Christian symbol after his crowing became associated with the repentance of Peter. The early Pennsylvania German settlers followed European ecclesiastical tradition when building their Lutheran and Reformed churches. No steeple was without its weather-cock.

In France, only the nobility were permitted to sport weathervanes. After the Revolution, when their prerogatives were taken away, the custom was adopted by the bourgeoisie, and even the peasants took on the fad. For the first time, the once proud vane appeared over barns and humble cottages. . . .

To place a blessing or prayer on the door lintel of the new house was an ancient Rhenish and Swiss custom. The new settlers did not depart from the tradition. [A motto frequently seen reads:] "Whether I go out or in, Death stands and waits for me. Better a dry morsel to enjoy than a house full of fresh meat with strife.". . .

The American eagle was a favorite device, sometimes so stylized that the line between it and the dove is not clearly drawn. The shield is ingeniously incorporated in the body of the eagle on several of the motifs. . . .

Pennsylvania German churches and their graveyards often perch on breezy hilltops. . . .

The ancient [tomb]stones are never gruesome; the skull and crossbones, so common in New England, is rare. In its place one finds the same motifs as are employed on other forms of local decoration.

Both the reverse as well as the obverse of [these] tall, thin, slate slabs are [often] elaborately incised in a firm, sure line, preserving to this day the curious intricate design. . . .

The country artisan, in emulation of the stone-cutter's art of his homeland, used the same symbolic heart with its springing tulips or lilies, the heavenly crown, the stars, the whirling swastika, as well as other geometric symbols. . . .

When Pennsylvania German tinsmiths began to turn out coffee-pots, they enriched the surface with their favored motifs, the branching tulips in the usual urns, the peacock, the barn symbols and birds, worked out in repousse dots, called "punched work.". . .

That always ornamental motif, the Tree of Life, supposed to be rooted in Paradise, has been an inspiration to many peoples. It was the frequent choice of ancient potters, of oriental rug makers, and in recent times it flourished just as luxuriously on the very best quilts of Colonial needlewomen.

The details of [a] Pennsylvania German [quilt present] a motif of [very] ancient lineage. . . . Close study [reveals that] they are worked out with the means at hand. Birds perch naturally on the branches, and their many kinds of flowers blossom, their botanical relationships cheerfully ignored. Actual ivy and oak leaves, their forms easily identified, serve as the pattern for the ones cut of cotton, not only for the shape but for the correctly observed veinings, executed in tiny quilting stitches. Small circles, later to be lined up as graceful sprays of berries, were marked around a thimble. . . .

The watermarks used by the first paper-makers in the State followed a tradition of symbolic design. As almost all the paper mills were owned and operated by German colonists and immigrants, it is natural to expect to see familiar motifs used in their watermarks. A search for them is gratifying, for it reveals not only the expected tulip but also the other characteristic devices for which they evinced a preference. . . .

Fractur manuscripts made here were the local flowering of a European tradition transplanted without substantial change to this new country. They were used by the ultraconservative until the universal spread of the printing press wiped out all need for the records illuminated by hand and the last practitioner of the art of the medieval scribes no longer found it worthwhile to practice his ancient craft. In Germany the law demanded that a record of vital statistics be preserved; it followed that trained scriveners were always available to provide the necessary documents. Because of this need, in any plan for the immigration of colonists to Penn's lands, a schoolmaster or minister was always included in the group. These "educated" men, in addition to their ability to read and write, were expected to be proficient in the art of "fractur writing" in order that they might supply the new settlers with the documents custom demanded. In strange new surrounds they kept up the old traditions, and being set free from the limiting artistic conventions of their homeland, in the Pennsylvania German counties they developed fractur writing into something lively, original, and even more decorative.

"*Fractur-schriften,*" as it is called in German, is a decorative calligraphy named after a sixteenth-century German type face called "fraktur," which was itself an imitation of the work of the manuscript writers of the day. It was considerably less rigid in outline than its predecessor, the early German Gothic or black-letter. Another source of inspiration was provided by a type face called "Schwabacher" which featured an even rounder, more cursive letter. With these type faces as a springboard, the Pennsylvania German scribes evolved a personal style of calligraphy which varied from the extremely professional to the extremely naive, the result of a lack of thorough training.

The persistent practice of the European medieval art of manuscript illumination for considerably over a century in a new and different environment would indeed be strange if we did not recall that, when only one copy of a document is needed, the art of "engrossing," as it is called today, still has its place. With all its facileness the printing press has not quite wiped out the last trace of the medieval calligrapher, still relied on when needed to produce an impressive piece of lettering.

It has been pointed out that in the early days in Pennsylvania, the scribe's craft was joined to that of the country schoolmaster or clergyman. This representative of learning was expected to be a very versatile man, and was called on to give advice in many fields. As scribe, he prepared legal papers and wrote letters for the analphabetic; as carpenter he kept the school building in repair. If the settlement lacked a minister or the minister was absent, the schoolmaster took his place. When necessary, he acted as janitor, church clerk, choir leader, and organist. Despite the variety of his occupations his income was pitifully small. To add to it, he and his sons worked for his neighbors on their farms. From the labor of his daughters, who he hired out to spin, he wrung a few extra pence. As there was always a steady demand among his neighbors for handwritten documents certifying important family events, such as births, baptisms, and weddings, the schoolmaster or clergyman further added to his income by specializing in the production of these rustic papers.

School teaching in the eighteenth century was a desultory affair. Children of the rural districts were taught to read in order that the precepts of the Bible and hymn book could be imparted to take root. Writing and ciphering completed this elementary education, which was considered quite adequate for farm children. Since some teachers were hired by the members of a community and others by Lutheran or Reformed congregations, the administering of the curriculum was free of any taint of standardization. . . .

To teach writing and at the same time to demonstrate his skill, the country schoolmaster prepared a beautifully handwritten manuscript called the "*Vorschrift*" which was the individualistic forerunner of the familiar, more formal copybook of the nineteenth century. From it children learned how to form the numerals and the capitals and small letters both in German script and in fractur writing. When they had learned to read, the pious maxim which headed the paper and on which the schoolmaster lavished his greatest flourishes and most elegantly ornamental capitals carried to them its specific injunction to lead a godly life. A *Vorschrift* was often presented to a pupil as a reward of merit and as a token of the instructor's regard. As evidence of this personal intention, the maker frequently signed his name, a naive testimony to his own admiration of the flourishes he was able to produce with his fluent craftsmanship.

A quaint and charming custom of the more kind-hearted among the schoolmasters was to present a drawing of a bird or a flower as a prize for diligence and good conduct. These little gifts were carefully saved from generation to generation. Today they bear witness to the artistic skill of their makers. While the form of the *Vorschrift* was governed by usage and varied but slightly, the greatest variety of decoration and artistic conception in fractur is found in the birth and baptismal certificates, called "*Taufscheine*," which the schoolmasters also executed in order to earn a little extra money. The early *Taufscheine* were entirely hand-drawn and hand-colored, but were somewhat supplanted towards the end of the eighteenth century by the pushing product of the printing press. . . .

The decorations on *Taufscheine* and other related manuscripts cover a wide range of subject matter. Floral motifs, which predominate, are almost invariably pure conventionalizations, with the exception of the tulip, whose stylized form is still close enough to the botanical one to be so identified. The fractur writer picked up his inspirations from many sources. Lions, crowns, and unicorns are obviously taken from the symbols used in heraldry. . . .

Highly decorative birds are one of the favorite motifs. While the greatest number are sheer stylizations, a few are identifiable as parrots, peacocks, eagles, and doves. Pomegranates, plucked from traditional textile designs, disclose their Persian inspiration. Ingenuously drawn angels, worldly human figures, and an occasional mermaid are quaintly delineated. Heart shapes are very common, with symbolic religious connotations. Pictorial representations of actual objects taken from nature or landscapes are infrequently encountered, but geometrical forms are often seen. The use of architectural forms and constructions seem of nineteenth-century inspiration.

Besides producing *Taufscheine,* the fractur writer illuminated family records in Bibles, drew and painted the frontispieces in song-books, made charming bookplates, and lettered the *"Haus-segen"* or house blessing—a prayer invoking the blessing of God on the family and its dwelling.

Each fractur writer seems to have adhered closely to his original choice of motifs, introducing slight variations in arrangements to avoid monotony, but nevertheless retaining his own decorative idiom over a period of many years. . . .

Many persons who were not creative artists nevertheless had a lively urge to draw and paint. At a time when all other amusement was rigidly limited, an indulgence in drawing and painting was sometimes permitted on Sunday afternoons. Beautifully executed religious texts and precepts in fractur were set before young persons as models. These they laboriously copied, deriving both pleasure and, it was hoped, spiritual profit from the quiet task. . . .

As recently as the beginning of the twentieth century, an elderly man carrying an umbrella and a case containing the tools of his craft could be seen trudging the dusty roads of the most Pennsylvania German of the eastern counties, following his graceful craft. Like any other travelling salesman, the old calligrapher made the rounds of his territory annually, calling on his regular clients. Families who were traditionalists to the core anticipated his coming, saving until his arrival the data that they wished preserved. He was always a welcome visitor. Seated at the center table, he brought the Bible records up to date and gossiped a bit about family histories, for his profession of fractur writer to the neighborhood necessarily acquainted him with its family affairs. In his favorite color, red, he carefully lettered and illuminated the *Taufscheine* his clients ordered. A visit to the local pastor furnished him with the names of the newly baptized and the recently confirmed. Forearmed with this information, he called on their families to acquire new customers. . . .

The farm landscape in eastern Pennsylvania is a colorful one. On the warm red of the soil, the diverse crop plantings impose a varicolored pattern of vegetation, a pattern bordered with an edging of distant bright blue hills and accented here and there with the red of barns. And as if this were not enough, the folk who dwell in these regions resort to cans of paint in diverse colors to add their own suggestions for heightening an already brightly pigmented scene.

Both men and women are passionately good housekeepers. The neatness of the farm buildings, the care of the fences and hedgerows, the love of fresh paint noted everywhere, are but extentions of the housekeeping instinct which finds its outlet in constant improvement of every section of the property, whether it be expended all over a farm or confined to the limited space around a village house. In addition to being kept beautifully tidy, a property will be made as colorful as its owner's ingenuity can devise, for the love of strong color is still a dominant passion in the Pennsylvania Germans. Though the aesthetic value of the results, as demonstrated by examples one sees everywhere, may well be disputed, there is no gainsaying this love of color. It stems from a long folk tradition behind these people, a rustic tradition in which bright hues furnished their forebears a cheap and satisfying substitute for bourgeois elegancies in matters of surface and texture. In their use of color there is no restraint or repression.

The eye of a Pennsylvania German would be starved by the white, black, and green of New England, and the grey and white of the lovely stone houses of the English settlers in the State were as little to his taste. When a farmhouse of this type came into his possession, he enlivened its Quaker coloring by any means at hand, for in its original state he thought it cold and repellent.

Perhaps it was this very greyness of the local stone which led the Pennsylvania Germans into such a lavish use of red in flowers and paint, for of all colors it is their favorite. . . .

Venetian red, a red oxide of iron (the pigment known as barn red), was painted on everything that would take it—a gaudy practice which set the Pennsylvania Germans apart from their neighbors, who evidently left their furniture in the browns of nature. . . .

There was a great variety of pattern in the geometrically divided circles [used on the great barns], a variety which seems to be limited only by the decorator's patience and by his ingenuity in wielding the large wooden compass with which he chalks out the designs on the wooden wall. When freshly painted, the colors used are apt to be brilliant yellows, blues, reds, and greens, which, together with white, are defined with vigor against the red ground. Time softens them to a pleasant unity with their background.

The number of the circular decorations used on the barn varies: on the main face there may be only two or as many as seven, for their number is governed by the number of blank spaces available between the openings, a number which changes with each barn, there being no exact pattern for the placement of doors and windows. When they are painted as a pair, the same device is used. When more than two symbols are used, they may vary, and do, both in pattern and size, the central one being the largest. The gable ends of barns are equally well decorated, sometimes with the same devices that are used on the face, often with different ones. The structural lines of the barns are usually bordered with broad white bands, a treatment also used to define the door and window trims. In addition, supplementary false arches are painted over the doors and windows, occasionally interlacing in a Moorish manner. These bands create an additional space-filling feature.

In certain districts the lower edge of the barn face, instead of being defined with the straight white band, has the upper rim of this band carefully marked out in scallops, which stand out against the red background like an old-fashioned white cambric petticoat ruffle against one of red flannel. In addition to painted lines defining non-existent arches, the four corners of the face are sometimes filled with quarter circles, subdivided into fan-like segments, which further enliven the general effect.

In horse-and-buggy days the decorator of barns seems to have limited his output to an area which he could reach conveniently in his leisurely vehicle, for in any given neighborhood there will be found a great similarity in the motifs. Neither the country painter or his client strove for originality. After the decorator, a practical man, planned a pattern, he used it on the barns of all his clients, introducing variations only when the spaces on the barn compelled it. Drive on a few miles beyond the periphery of a certain decorator's art and your eye will be caught by another demonstration of what can be done with a geometrically divided circle. The device most frequently met is based on six divisions, for obviously that is the easiest to make with a compass. Symbols planned with four and eight segments are next in frequency. In certain sections the barns will be taken over by someone who was adept at working on a basis of sixteen divisions. Within these fine subdivisions the decorator created patterns which in their intricacy sometimes roughly suggest rose windows. . . .

At first glance it might seem surprising that the most generally used motif, the tulip, is never in evidence on the barns. But as these designs were painted on the barns at a considerable height from the ground, it is obvious that a free-hand design could never be tackled with any assurance that it would turn out as planned; whereas a rigid, unemotional tool like the compass could be depended upon absolutely to produce the same satisfactory result each time. Even the device of the heart, frequently seen, is constructed geometrically on a base of tangent circles.

These symbols are generally believed to be "hex signs," a term disliked by present-day rural Pennsylvanians.* *Their purpose supposedly was to protect the barn from lightning, and the livestock from harm resulting from the machinations of witches.* Though there is probably reason to think that some such superstition once accounted for the practice, it is evident that it is no longer the controlling motive. The lightning rod salesman has been far more persuasive than the belief in ancient magic, for most of the decorated barns, though dazzling with motifs, are equally well equipped with lightning rods. At the present day, when a farmer renews the decorations on his barn every time the barn is repainted, it is probable that he does it because it appeals to his sense of decoration and enhances the appearance of the farm.

---

* It is suggested that this selection be read in relation to the comments on symbolism made by John Joseph Stoudt in another selection. (REW)

# VI

# POEMS, TALES, AND LEGENDS

I have long been interested in tales and legends. I should have loved to have been a storyteller, had I not been seduced by the securities of scholarship in a modern university. Stories are teaching media. They offer a much fuller representation of what we must know as human beings than do all the critical devices of technical reason. It takes a wise, gifted, and intelligent person to answer a question with a story rather than a discourse. Discourse is the illusory communication of an informational society.

It has been assumed that stories belong to a former nonliterate, less informational, time. Yet we continue to rely upon storytelling in order to communicate the fullest and most meaningful sense of things. Reporters tell their stories of what happened, revealing the perception of the world in which they live and move and have their being. Husbands and wives rely upon story to provide meaningful reference to what they have done and what they hope to do. Story is inescapable in a human society because humanity is indeterminate and story is an indeterminate form of thought and communication. Former societies may have consciously used storytelling more than our own. Yet storytelling persists, and whenever we hear or read a good story we know we have encountered profundity. Even the humorous tale, the joke, tells us many things about our perception of the world. We know that the Sufi tales of the Mulla Nasrudin are frequently very humorous. They are told by the uninitiated as jokes, pure and simple. But their real use is known only through the work of a gifted teacher of spiritual realities. They are often channels of surprise, breaking through the preconceptions of the ordinary mind.

The folk have always told stories to entertain and to educate. And entertainment is no less significant than education. The entertaining tale reminds us who we really are, conveys important values, and sets our world in order by demonstrating the precarious and superficial character of what we assume to be important. The humorous tale may be God's way of reminding us of the mystery of existence, telling us whose world it really is. But that is often the importance of the more serious tale as well.

Some stories preserve culture and relate us to our ancestry. Human identity is a matter of storytelling. It is important in the quest for personal identity to remember to tell of our parentage, the places of our birth and sojourning, the other stories we have learned (religions) that are crucial to our perception of the world. Navel gazing and the discernment of some inner selfhood are insufficient unto themselves. The inner self is not absolutely separable from the self which is involved in the dramas of story.

The Pennsylvania Dutch have been master storytellers. Henry Harbaugh, whom we have met before, was a poet, preacher, and storyteller (perhaps the three roles are inseparable). He was the progenitor of a series of pastors who became the preservers of the culture. Today the storytelling is done by others, as well as pastors. In parts of eastern Pennsylvania there are *versamlings* (gatherings), reunions, liars contests, and church festivals which are occasions for telling the stories of the folk in their old dialect. A dialect tale has its own unique flavor that cannot be produced in translation. However, in this chapter, we shall share stories and poems in translation. Some have been translated by me, others by folklorists such as Thomas R. Brendle and William Troxell. Still others bear the mark of translation by those who originally wrote in the dialect. Here we can discover the rich and earthly character of a folk spirituality that reveals the ancient traditions of magic and legend as well as the values of contemporary Pennsylvania.

# THE LEGENDS OF MOUNTAIN MARY

*(The legend of Mountain Mary continues to be important to the Pennsylvania Dutch. She is the paradigm of forebearance and service to humankind. This version is translated by me from pp. 125–27 of Ludwig A. Wollenweber's* Gemalde aus dem Pennsylvanischen Volksleben, *Philadelphia and Teipzig: Verlag von Schafer and Koradi, 1869.)*

### Mountain Mary

Some years ago in Pike Township, Berks County, there lived an amazing woman whose name was Maria Young. For over thirty years she lived alone in a simple cottage near Moss Mill. During the length of her days she never begged nor harmed anyone, but did much good by means of her understanding of the use of herbs and medicine to heal the sick.

It is said that her records showed she was born in Zweibrücken in the Rhineland and came to this country in 1769 with a young man, of whom her father did not approve. After she was in the country for awhile, her lover left her in Philadelphia. She searched for him for a long time, and when she realized her efforts were for nothing, she sought the solitude of the mountains and lived a forlorn life until the end of her days.

She died in the year 1819, and a friend who knew of the virtues of this poor, rejected human being, and had often travelled with people who wanted to see Mountain Mary, composed the following verses about her.

Here beneath these stones
Softly rest the bones
of devout Maria;
Her heart and entire life
Were surrendered to her God,
As her way of living testified.

Thirty years she passed the time
Entirely without rancor
Living in her solitude.

Her countenance drawn,
Lost the Joy
That once God had given.

255

Afterwards she was different,
One could see the sweet peace
In her countenance;
It was full of love and bliss,
as it reflected the radiance
of the sun of grace.

Now she has been taken away;
God has called her to himself
From out this vale of tears:
Where on the plains of Heaven
She may look at Jesus
With his chosen number.

# THE TALE OF REGINA HARTMAN

*(Another story that is part of the lore of the Dutch.)*

## Regina Hartman

The Hartman family lived in the Tulpehocken region of Berks County, Pennsylvania. Some people will recognize that as Indian territory. It was the land of the Delawares. But it was also Pennsylvania German country. Now, there are "church" Germans and "plain" Germans. The former are, in the main, members of the Reformed and Lutheran traditions. The latter are the so-called sectarians—Mennonites, Amish, Brethren. The Hartmans were of pious Lutheran stock. They read the Bible, sang, and prayed regularly. They had a favorite hymn, "Allein und doch nicht ganz alleine."

On October 16, 1755, Mrs. Hartman and the younger of her two sons had gone to the mill, to take some grain for grinding. While they were gone, a band of Indians, provoked by the tensions that became known as the French and Indian War, descended on the Hartman homestead. The father and the older of the two boys were left dead among the ruins. However, the two daughters were carried away into the mountains of the West, into the vicinity of Delaware suzerainty near Muskingum, Ohio. The two girls were separated, and nothing again was ever heard from the older daughter, Barbara, aged twelve.

Regina was ten years old at the time of the raid and was given over to the care of an Indian squaw. There she spent close to ten years, learning the ways of an Indian maiden. She spoke their language and worked as an Indian woman was taught to do. During those years, she lost all hope of ever seeing any of her family again. And gradually, she forgot faces and voices. She thought and felt as an Indian maiden, and her memory of early life faded almost into oblivion.

Then came the end of the War and the time of peace. The Indians were required to give up all the white children who had been kidnapped during the conflict. These poor, lost souls were taken to Fort Duquesne, where now the city of Pittsburgh stands. They stood forlorn and half-naked in the December cold. Arrangements were finally made to transport them to Carlisle, and all parents who were known to have had children taken from them were invited to make the trip to Cumberland County to identify them. Mrs. Hartman was filled with hope and anticipation as her wagon rumbled along the road to Carlisle. As she thought of what was about to happen, she became anxious and frightened. She wanted to see her two daughters again, but how would she recognize them. Her fears turned into prayers and renewed hope.

When Mother Hartman saw the rows of boys and girls, young men and women, she burst into tears. Nowhere were her daughters to be seen among this band of strange-looking Indians. The colonel in charge tried to console her. Were there any identifying marks? he inquired. There were none. Then perhaps there was something she might do, some action she could take, that would awaken a faded memory. Slowly the disheartened mother stepped forward, and with tears in her eyes, began to sing:

> "Allein und doch nicht ganz alleine
>   Bin ich in meiner Einsamkeit;
> Denn wenn ich ganz verlassen scheine,
>   Vertreibt mir Jesus selbst die Zeit;
> Ich bin bei Ihm und Er bei mir,
> So kommt mir gar nichts einsam für."

Barely two lines were sung when Regina sprang from her place in the row of former captives, embraced her mother, and joined in singing the hymn to its closing verses. Mother Hartman was overcome with joy, hindered in its fullness only when she learned that no one knew anything of Barbara. Regina returned with her mother to their home along the Tulpehocken. Not too much is known of her story after that.

But the memory of Regina Hartman is beloved among Pennsylvania German folks. The famous Lutheran patriarch, Henry Melchior Muhlenberg, was her pastor. He often told of the piety of the Hartman family. It was the faith nurtured by reading the Bible that sustained Regina during her years of captivity, he said. When she returned to her home she asked her mother, "Where is that book you used to read from, the one that had such beautiful thoughts of peace and healing?" The old family Bible had been burned in the Indian raid, but Dr. Muhlenberg gave them a new one. Regina Hartman was buried next to her mother in the graveyard of Christ Lutheran Church, near Stouchsburg, Pennsylvania.

# Poems of Henry Harbaugh

*(The poetry of the Pennsylvania Dutch is difficult to use because much of it is untranslated and not easy to give appropriate form to in English translation. A sample is here provided from the poetry of Henry Harbaugh, translated by him. His poems "Heemweh" and "Das Alt Schulhaus an der Krick" are classics of the dialect and provide interesting insight into the spirit of the people. The material is taken from Linn Harbaugh's* Life of the Rev. Henry Harbaugh, D.D. *and from* Harbaugh's Harfe, *edited B. Bausman, Philadelphia: Board of Christian Education of the Reformed Church in the United States, 1870.)*

HYMNS AND POEMS.

BY HENRY HARBAUGH.

JESUS, I live to Thee,
The loveliest and best;
My life in Thee, Thy life in me,
In Thy blest love I rest.

Jesus, I die to Thee,
Whenever death shall come;
To die in Thee is life to me,
In my eternal home.

Whether to live or die,
I know not which is best;
To live in Thee is bliss to me,
To die is endless rest.

Living or dying, Lord,
I ask but to be Thine;
My life in Thee, Thy life in me,
Makes heav'n forever mine.*

---

\* This hymn remains to this day the official hymn of the Mercersburg Academy, daughter of the Reformed institutions of higher learning at Mercersburg. It is much more representative of Harbaugh's folk spirituality than of his Reformed Catholicity.

\* \* \*

JESUS, my Shepherd, let me share
Thy guiding hand, Thy tender care;
And let me ever find in Thee,
A refuge and a rest for me.

Oh, lead me ever by Thy side,
Where fields are green, and waters glide;
And be Thou still, where'er I be,
A refuge and a rest for me.

While I this barren desert tread,
Feed thou my soul on heavenly bread;
'Mid foes and fears Thee may I see,
A refuge and a rest for me.

Anoint me with Thy gladdening grace,
To cheer me in the heavenly race;
Cause all my gloomy doubts to flee,
And make my spirit rest in Thee.

When death shall end this mortal strife,
Bring me through death to endless life;
Then, face to face, beholding Thee,
My refuge and my rest shall be.

\* \* \*

JESUS, to Thy cross I hasten,
In all weariness my home;
Let Thy dying love come o'er me—
Light and covert in the gloom:
Saviour, hide me,
Till the hour of gloom is o'er.

Where life's tempests dark are rolling
Fearful shadows o'er my way;
Let firm faith in Thee sustain me,
Every rising fear allay:

Hide, oh! hide me,
Hide me till the storm is o'er.

When stern death at last shall lead me
Through the dark and lonely vale;
Let Thy hope uphold and cheer me,
Though my flesh and heart should fail.
Safely hide me
With Thyself forevermore.


THE MYSTIC WEAVER.


At his loom the weaver sitting
Throws his shuttle to and fro;
Foot and treadle,
Hands and pedal,
Upward, downward,
Hither, thither,
How the weaver makes them go!
As the weaver wills they go.
Up and down the warp is plying,
And across the woof is flying;
What a rattling,
What a battling,
What a shuffling,
What a scuffling,
As the weaver makes his shuttle,
Hither, thither, scud and scuttle.
Threads in single,
Threads in double;
How they mingle,
What a trouble!
Every color—
What profusion!
Every motion—
What confusion!
Whilst the warp and woof are mingling,
Signal bells above are jingling,
Telling how each figure ranges,
Telling when the color changes,
As the weaver makes his shuttle
Hither, thither, scud and scuttle.

II.

At his loom the weaver sitting,
Throws his shuttle to and fro;
'Mid the noise and wild confusion,
Well the weaver seems to know,
As he makes his shuttle go,
What each motion—
And commotion,
What each fusion—
And confusion,
In the grand result will show:
Weaving daily,
Singing gaily,
As he makes his busy shuttle,
Hither, thither, scud and scuttle.

III.

At his loom the weaver sitting
Throws his shuttle to and fro;
See you not how shape and order
From the wild confusion grow,
As he makes his shuttle go?
As the warp and woof diminish,
Grows behind the beauteous finish:
Tufted plaidings,
Shapes and shadings;
All the mystery
Now in history;
And we see the reason subtle
Why the weaver makes his shuttle,
Hither, thither, scud and scuttle.

IV.

See the Mystic Weaver sitting
High in heaven—His loom below.
Up and down the treadles go:
Takes for warp the world's long ages,

Takes for woof its kings and sages,
Takes the nobles and their pages,
Takes all stations and all stages.
Thrones are bobbins in his shuttle;
Armies make them scud and scuttle.
Woof into the warp must flow;
Up and down the nations go;
As the Weaver wills they go.
Men are sparring,
Powers are jarring,
Upward, downward,
Hither, thither,
See how strange the nations go,
Just like puppets in a show.
Up and down the warp is plying,
And across the woof is flying,
What a rattling,
What a battling,
What a shuffling,
What a scuffing,
As the weaver makes His shuttle,
Hither, thither, scud and scuttle.


V.


Calmly see the Mystic Weaver
Throw His shuttle to and fro;
'Mid the noise and wild confusion,
Well the Weaver seems to know
What each motion—
And commotion,
What each fusion—
And confusion,
In the grand result will show,
As the nations,
Kings and stations,
Upward, downward,
Hither, thither,
As in mystic dances, go
In the present all is mystery;
In the Past 'tis beauteous History

O'er the mixing and the mingling,
How the signal bells are jingling!
See you not the Weaver leaving
Finished work behind in weaving?
See you not the reason subtle—
As the warp and woof diminish,
Changing into beauteous finish—
Why the Weaver makes His shuttle,
Hither, thither, scud and scuttle?


VI.


Glorious wonder! What a weaving!
To the dull beyond believing!
Such no fable ages know.
Only faith can see the mystery,
How, along the aisle of History
Where the feet of sages go,
Loveliest to the purest eyes,
Grand the mystic tapet lies!
Soft and smooth and even-spreading,
As if made for angels' treading;
Tufted circles touching ever,
Inwrought beauties fading never;
Ever figure has its plaidings,
Brighter form and softer shadings;
Each illumined—what a riddle!—
From a Cross that gems the middle.
'Tis a saying—some reject it—
That its light is all reflected;
That the tapet's hues are given
By a Sun that shines in Heaven!
'Tis believed, by all believing,
That great God Himself is weaving!
Bringing out the world's dark mystery
In the light of faith and History;
And as warp and woof diminish
Comes the grand and glorious finish—
When begin the golden ages,
Long foretold by seers and sages.

HOME-SICKNESS.

I know not what the reason is:
 Where'er I dwell or roam,
I make a pilgrimage each year,
 To my old childhood home.
Have nothing there to give or get—
 No legacy, no gold—
Yet by some home-attracting power
 I'm evermore controlled:
This is the way the home-sick do,
 I often have been told.

As nearer to the spot I come
 More sweetly am I drawn;
And something in my heart begins
 To urge me faster on.
Ere quite I've reached the last hill-top—
 You'll smile at me, I ween!—
I stretch myself high as I can,
 To catch the view serene—
The dear old stone house through the trees
 With shutters painted green!
See! how the kitchen chimney smokes!
 That ofttimes gave me joy;
When, from the fields, that curling cloud
 I witnessed as a boy!
And see! the purple window panes,
 They seem as red as blood.
I often wondered what did that,
 But guess it, never could.
Ah! many a thing a child knows not.
 Did it, it were not good!

How do I love those poplar trees;
 What tall and stately things!
See! on the top of one just now
 A starling sits and sings.
He'll fall!—the twig bends with his weight!
 He likes that danger best.
I see the red upon his wings,—
 Dark shining is the rest.

I ween his little wife has built
On that same tree her nest.

O, I remember very well
When those three poplar trees
Not thicker than my finger were,
And could be bent with ease.

My mother was at grandpa's house,
And trees like these had he;
She brought three scions home, and said,
"Boys, plant them there for me."
Can you believe—they grew so tall
And made the trees you see!

See! really I am near the house;
How short the distance seems!
There is no sense of time when one
Goes musing in his dreams.
There is the shop—the corn-crib, too—
The cider-press—just see!
The barn—the spring with drinking cup
Hung up against the tree.
The yard-fence—and the little gate
Just where it used to be.

All, all is still! They know not yet
That there's a stranger near;
I guess old Watch, the dog, is dead,
Or barking, he'd appear.
What fearful bellowings he made
Whene'er he heard the gate;
The travellers always feared him sore,
He bounced at such a rate;
But though the bark was woful loud,
The bite was never great!
All, all is still! The door is shut.
I muse with beating heart;
Hark! there's a little rattling now
Back in the kitchen part.
I'll not go in! I cannot yet;
I'm overcome, I fear!

The same old bench here on the porch,
I'll rest a little here.
Behind this grape-vine I can hide
The falling of a tear!

Two spots on this old friendly porch
I love, nor can forget,
Till dimly in the night of death
My life's last sun shall set!
When first I left my father's house,
One summer morning bright,
My mother at *that* railing wept
Till I was out of sight!
Now like a holy star that spot
Shines in this world's dull night.

Still, still I see her at that spot,
With handkerchief in hand;
Her cheeks are red—her eyes are wet—
There, there I see her stand!
'Twas there I gave her my good-bye,
There, did her blessing crave,
And oh, with what a mother's heart
She that sought blessing gave.
It was the last—ere I returned
She rested in her grave!

When now I call her form to mind,
Wherever I may be,
She still is standing at that rail
And weeping on for me!
She is in no familiar spot,
As oft in former years;
And never to my fancy she
As in her grave appears;
I see her only at that rail,
Bedewed with holy tears.

What draws my eye to yonder spot—
That bench against the wall?
What holy mem'ries cluster there,
My heart still knows them all!

How often sat my father there
    On summer afternoon;
Hands meekly crossed upon his lap,
    He looked so lost and lone,
As if he saw an empty world,
    And hoped to leave it soon.
Doth a return of childhood's joys
    Across his spirit gleam?
Or is his fancy busy now
    With some loved youthful dream?
He raises now his eyes and looks
    On yon hill's sacred crest;
Perhaps he sees the graveyard there
    Where mother's sleep is blest,
And longs to slumber by her side,
    In death's last peaceful rest.

All, all is still! I hesitate—
    I fain would pass the door,
But fear the pain of missing all
    This home contained of yore.
For, ah, it is not what it was
    Though its inmates are kind;
What with our parents once we lose
    We nevermore shall find;
Death goes before and reaps the sheaves;
    We can but glean behind.

Such is the fate of earthly loves
    Where all things die or change.
Yes, even in the homestead here,
    I feel alone and strange.
O were it not for yon bright heaven,
    With its unchanging rest,
How heavy would our burdens be,
    Our life how sore distressed;
But hope illumes our pathway to
    The regions of the blest.

That is a lovely Fatherland:
    There I shall never roam;
No mother there with tearful eyes,

Shall see me leave that home.
No father there shall seek the grave
Where his beloved lies;
That is no vale of woes like this,
Where all we cherish dies;
The beautiful is permanent
In those unchanging skies.

There we shall find what here we lose,
And keep it evermore;
There we shall join our sainted dead,
Who are but gone before.
I'm fain, in lonely hours, to lift
The veil that let them through,
And wish it were God's holy will
To let me pass it too;
Yet patience! till my hour shall come,
To bid the world, Adieu!


## THE OLD SCHOOL-HOUSE AT THE CREEK.

To-day it is just twenty years,
Since I began to roam:
Now, safely back, I stand once more,
Before the quaint old school-house door,
Close by my father's home.

I've been in many houses since,
Of marble built, and brick;
Though grander far, their aim they miss,
To lure my heart's old love from this
Old school-house at the creek.

Let those who dream of happier scenes,
Go forth those scenes to find;
They'll learn what thousands have confessed,
That with our home our heart's true rest
Is ever left behind.

I've travelled long and travelled far,
Till weary, worn, and sick;
How joyless all that I have found,

Compared with scenes that lie around
 This school-house at the creek.

How home-like is this spot to me!
 I stand, and think, and gaze!
The buried past unlocks its graves,
While memory o'er my spirit waves
 The wand of other days.

The little creek still idles by,
 With bright and playful flow;
And little fish still sport and glide,
Where yon low elder shades the tide,
 As they did long ago.

The white-oak stands before the door,
 And shades the roof at noon;
The grape-vine, too, is fresh and green;
The robin's nest!—Ah, hark!—I ween
 That is the same old tune!

The swallows skip across the mead—
 The foremost one is best!
And, look ye at the gable there,
A house of stubble, mud, and hair—
 That is the swallow's nest!

The young are very still just now—
 They all are sleeping sound;
Wait till the old with worms appear,
Then you the hungry cry shall hear
 From mouths that lie around!

These scenes are as they were of yore,
 Though void of former glee;
But I have changed!—From yonder brook
 The boy's reflected rosy look,
 No more smiles out on me!

I stand, like Ossian in his vale,
 And watch the shadowy train!
Now joy, now sadness me beguile,

And tears will course o'er every smile,
And bring their pleasing pain!

'Twas here I first attended school,
When I was very small:
There was the Master on his stool,
There was his whip and there his rule—
I seem to see it all.

The long desks ranged along the walls,
With books and inkstands crowned;
Here on this side the large girls sat,
And there the tricky boys on that—
See! how they peep around!

The Master eyes them closely now,
They'd better have a care;
The one that writes a billet-doux—
The one that plays his antics, too—
And that chap laughing there!

For all the scholars, large and small,
Are under equal rule;
Which is quite right—whoever breaks
The Master's rules, a whipping takes,
Or leaves at once the school.

Around the cosy stove, in rows,
The little tribe appears;
What hummings make those busy bees—
They better like their A, B, C's,
Than boxing at their ears!

Those benches are by far too high—
Their feet don't reach the floor!
Fully many a weary back gets sick,
In that old school-house at the creek,
And feels most woful sore!

Poor innocents! behold them sit,
In miseries and woes!
It is no wonder, I declare,

If they should learn but little there,
On benches such as those!

With all these drawbacks, that was still
A well conducted school;
For Master such, in vain you look,
Who cyphers through the Ainsworth book,
And never skips a rule!

That he was cross, I must confess;
He whipped us through and through;
But still most wholesome rules observed;
Who felt the rod, the rod deserved—
According to his view!

This duty he with zest performed,
Though charmless to us all!
'Tis strange, our nature never could
Delight in what is for our good—
'Tis owing to the Fall!

When a new Master took the school,
Around the question ran:
"Oh, is he Irish? Is he cross?"
How much our gain, how much our loss,
Depended on that man!

Then when the autumn school began,
We eyed the Master shy!
His rules, his whip, told very quick,
That he to former rules would stick,
And ancient methods ply.

Still was there little of complaint;
We had our pleasures too;
This world does not just always dish
Our fare as sweet as we could wish,
Yet sweeter than is due!

At noon-day, when the school let out,
We had of sport our fill;
Some play the race, some houses wall,

Some love a stirring game of ball,
Some choose the soldier drill.

The large girls sweep; the larger boys—
What mischief they are at!
They tease, they laugh, they hang about,
Until the Master turns them out—
The rules were strict in that!

The little girls, of "ring" most fond,
Their giggling circle drew;
When larger girls joined in the ring—
Now is it not a curious thing?—
The large boys did it too!

The large ones always tagged the large—
The small ones always missed!
Then for the prize began the race;
The one that's caught, has now to face
The music, and be kissed!

Old Christmas brought a glorious time—
Its mem'ry still is sweet!
We barred the Master firmly out,
With bolts, and nails, and timbers stout—
The blockade was complete!

Then came the struggle fierce and long!
The fun was very fine!
And whilst he thumped and pried about,
We thrust the terms of treaty out,
Demanding him to sign!

The treaty signed—the conflict o'er,
Once Master now were we!
Then chestnuts, apples, and such store,
Were spread our joyous eyes before—
We share the feast with glee!

Oh, where are now the school-mates, who
Here studied long ago?
Some scattered o'er the world's wide waste!

By fortune hither, thither chased!
Some, in the church-yard low!

My muse has struck a tender vein!
And asks a soothing flow;
O Time! what changes thou hast made,
Since I around this school-house played,
Just twenty years ago!

Good bye! Old school-house! Echo sad,
"Good bye! Good bye!" replies;
I leave you yet a friendly tear!
Fond mem'ry bids me drop it here,
'Mid scenes that gave it rise!

Ye, who shall live when I am dead—
Write down my wishes quick—
Protect it, love it, let it stand,
A way-mark in this changing land—
That school-house at the creek.


THROUGH DEATH TO LIFE.

Have you heard the tale of the Aloe plant,
Away in the sunny clime?
By humble growth of an hundred years
It reaches its blooming time;
And then a wonderous bud at its crown
Breaks out into thousand flowers:
This floral queen, in its blooming seen,
Is the pride of the tropical bowers.
But the plant to the flower is a sacrifice,
For it blooms but once, and in blooming dies.

Have you further heard of this Aloe plant,
That grows in the sunny clime,
How every one of its thousand flowers,
As they drop in the blooming time,
Is an infant plant that fastens its roots
In the place where it falls on the ground;
And fast as they drop from the dying stem,

Grow lively and lovely around?
By dying it liveth a thousand-fold
In the young that spring from the death of the old.

Have you heard the tale of the Pelican,
The Arabs' Gimel el Bahr?
That lives in the African solitudes
Where the birds that live lonely are?
Have you heard how it loves its tender young,
And cares and toils for their good?

It brings them water from fountains afar,
And fishes the seas for their food.
In famine it feeds them—what love can devise!—
The blood of its bosom, and feeding them, dies!

Have you heard the tale they tell of the swan,
The snow-white bird of the lake?
It noiselessly floats on the silvery wave,
It silently sits in the brake;
For it saves its song until the end of life,
And then in the soft, still even,
'Mid the golden light of the setting sun,
It sings as it soars into heaven!
And the blessed notes fall back from the skies—
'Tis its only song, for in singing it dies.

Have you heard these tales—Shall I tell you one,
A greater and better than all?
Have you heard of Him whom the heavens adore,
Before whom the hosts of them fall?
How He left the choirs and anthems above,
For the earth in its wailings and woes,
To suffer the shame and the pain of the Cross,
And die for the life of His foes?
O Prince of the noble! O Sufferer divine!
What sorrow and sacrifice equal to Thine!

Have you heard this tale—the best of them all—
The tale of the Holy and True?
He dies, but His life, in untold souls,
Lives on in the world anew.

His seed prevails and is filling the earth
As the stars fill the skies above;
He taught us to yield up the love of life,
For the sake of the life of love.
His death is our life, His loss is our gain,
The joy for the tear, the peace for the pain.

Now hear these tales, ye weary and worn,
Who for others do give up your all;
Our Saviour hath told you the seed that would grow,
Into earth's dark bosom must fall—
Must pass from the view and die away,
And then will the fruit appear:
The grain that seems lost in the earth below,
Will return many fold in the ear.
By death comes life, by loss comes gain,
The joy for the tear, the peace for the pain.

# THE PENNSYLVANIA GERMAN POETESS

*(From Vol. III, "Rachel Bahn. Pennsylvania German Poetess," by Preston A. Barba, The Pennsylvania German Society: Breinigsville, Pa., 1970. This poem, written in 1899 by Rachel Bahn, is typical of her work. It is presented here less for its poetic value than for what it reveals of the sentimentality of the spirituality of the folk in the late nineteenth century.)*

A HALF CENTURY

A half a century ago,
Upon a couch of pain,
The Lord saw fit to lay me low,
On which I still remain;

Remain to suffer and to wait
Until my time shall come
To be released from mis'ry great,
And enter that sweet home.

Yes, fifty years, a lifetime most,
It long, O long appears,
Have taken been through murky streams;
Remember, fifty years.

Distress'd and lonely oft have been,
When thinking of the loss
I have sustain'd, have trials seen,
And heavy was the cross.

My friends, who had surrounded me
When first I took my bed,
Are resting in the silent tomb
Where not a tear is shed.

And I am left to linger here—
I often wonder why;
Why 'tis the Lord afflicts me thus;
On Him I e'er rely.

All is intended for my good;
Shall utter no complaint.
I many lessons have been taught,
Though often have been faint.

The seventyeth milestone of my life
I recently have pass'd—
Of them have fifty spent in bed,
Yet time sped onward fast.

It onward sped, though pain I had,
My suff'rings were intense;
Life was at times a blank to me,
And I lived in suspense.

Still in the midst of trouble walk
I often, weary feel—
In dread and fear am wand'ring on;
The Lord alone can heal.

He will not cast forever off;
He will compassion show;
He doth not willingly afflict
His children here below.

He often lifts His chast'ning hand
To ease my burden some.
My heart is weak, is weak indeed;
His will be ever done.

"He maketh sore, and bindeth up,"
He woundeth and makes whole.
O precious blood, shed on the tree,
My spirit still control!

At times I happy feel, it's true—
My friends do visit me;

The Lord inspires their hearts with love;
Me often come to see.

Their presence cheers me truly so,
They ev'ry kindness show;
They come from far, they come from near,
And favors do bestow.

And those who daily wait on me
Great sympathy impart;
They treat me kindly, kindly treat,
Which fills with joy my heart.

The end is drawing nigh, my friends,
When I shall bid farewell;
Shall bid my last farewell to you—
Its nearness none can tell.

May I be ready then to go
When the last summons come,
To glorify God's Holy Name,
With him forever roam.

In endless bliss I hope to meet,
To meet you 'round God's Throne,
And evermore adoring Him
For loving kindness shown.

Oh, what rejoicing there will be
To be released from pain,
And wearing robes of snowy white—
What an eternal gain!

# PENNSYLVANIA GERMAN FOLK TALES

*(The following tales and legends are taken from* Pennsylvania German Folk Tales, Legends, Once-Upon-A-Time Stories, Maxims, and Sayings, *by Thomas R. Brendle and William S. Troxell, Morristown, Pa.: Pennsylvania German Society, 1944.)*

### THE ENCHANTED SISTERS

Long ago, there was a woman who always wept as she rocked her little son to sleep. One day he asked her why she wept. She, with tears and sobs, answered, "You have three sisters and they are all enchanted."

"When I am grown, I will free them," said the boy.

"You cannot free them, and do not try," answered the mother.

"I can, and I will," said the boy.

Now, the names of the three sisters were Hilldegadd, Gaddelheid, and Beaddrees.*

When the boy was grown, he took a tomahawk and a horse, and rode away into the black forest. The forest was thickly grown with underbrush, and often the boy had to cut a way through with the tomahawk. When he could no longer cut a path for his horse, he tied him to a tree, and then forced his way through the undergrowth until he came to a very tall hollow tree.

He called, "Hilldegadd, Hilldegadd." There was no answer. He called again, "Hilldegadd, Hilldegadd." Then came a voice, "What do you want?"

He answered, "I am your brother, and I am come to set you free."

"Go away! Go away!" said his sister. "Here lives an eagle, and the other day he bored the eyes out of a little boy. Go away, before he returns home."

The boy would not leave, and his sister, thereupon, let down a silken ladder, and the boy climbed up into the hollow tree, where she hid him away.

"My husband," said his sister, "is an eagle for one whole week, and then a man for the next week, and when he is an eagle, he is very cruel and merciless."

280

The eagle came flying home. He sensed that something was not as it should be, and restlessly peered around in the hollow tree. His wife, however, quieted him and got him to lie down and sleep. When he awoke, he was a man. Then the boy came out of his hiding place and was received with great kindness. He spent a very happy time with his sister and her husband. When the week was almost over, the man told him to depart, saying, "I shall soon become an eagle, and then I will harm you."

But before the brother left, he gave him three eagle feathers, saying, "When you are in danger rub these feathers in your hands, until they are warm, and then you will receive help."

The boy left the hollow tree and travelled on until he came to a huge cliff, in which there was a bear cave. He called. "Gaddelheid, Gaddelheid."

She answered, "Go away! Go away! Here lives a fierce bear. The other day he came home with his nose covered with blood."

The boy pleaded with her, and finally she took him into the cave and hid him. "My husband," said his sister, "is a bear for two weeks, and then a man for two weeks. At this time he is a bear, and very, very fierce."

After a little the bear returned, sniffed the air, and growled, "I smell human flesh."

"No! No! You do not. Lie down and sleep," said his wife. He did so, and upon awaking was a man.

The boy came out of his hiding place and was kindly received. There he stayed two weeks, and they were happy ones, even happier than the week he spent with Hilldegadd and her husband. When the two weeks were almost up, the man came to the boy and said, "I shall soon become a bear, and then I will harm you. Go away."

But before the boy left, he gave him three bear hairs and told him, "When you are in danger rub these hairs in your hands until they are warm, and then you will receive help."

The boy journeyed on until he came to a large body of water. Far out in the water he saw a smoking chimney. He swam out, looked down the chimney, and saw a glass house. He called, "Beaddrees, Beaddrees." No answer. He called again.

"What do you want," came the answer.

"I am your brother, and I have come to free you," said the brother.

"Go away! Go away! The whale will soon come home and kill you," cried his sister. He, however, went down the chimney into the house.

The whale returned and saw that his wife was ill at ease and troubled, and though he spoke to her, she would not answer. So he went out and swam around the house, lashing the water in his rage until it became murky. Then he came in. His wife, feeling that the murky water concealed the presence of her brother, spoke to the whale and told him to lie down and sleep. When he awoke, he was a man. For three weeks he was a whale and for three weeks a man.

The boy spent a happy time with them in the glass house under the water, even happier than with the other two sisters. Towards the end of three weeks the man told him that he was to go away. "Soon," said he, "I shall again become a whale and then I will harm you."

He gave him three fish scales, telling him, when in danger, to rub them in his hands until warm and help would appear.

The boy left and went back through the forest until he came to the tree where he had tied his horse. He found the horse torn to pieces. This had been done by the bear.

So he went on through the forest until he came to a beautiful piece of ground in the midst of which stood a beautiful small house. He saw nothing living about the place except a large bull that was grazing on the green grass before the house.

The boy bravely walked toward the house, but he had not gotten very near before the bull rushed on him. The boy quickly rubbed the three bear hairs, and immediately the bear appeared and tore the bull into pieces.

Then out of the body of the bull a goose arose and flew away. Seeing this, the boy rubbed the eagle feathers, and the eagle came swiftly through the air and killed the goose.

A golden egg from the body of the goose down through the sky into the water; and the boy rubbed the fish scales, and the whale came and brought the golden egg.

The boy took the golden egg, broke it open and found a golden key. Thereupon, the enchantment was broken, and his three sisters and their husbands appeared at his side.

Together they went to the beautiful house, which they found locked. The boy took the golden key and unlocked the door. Within they found a beautiful girl who had been enchanted. She had been asleep, but when the door was unlocked, the enchantment was broken and she became free from all her bonds.

The boy took the girl for his wife, and together they all went home to the mother who cried for joy when she beheld them.

—*Mrs. Kate Moyer, Egypt, Pa.*

* We have retained the names of the three sisters as they were given by the narrator.

### FROM GOOD TO BAD

Once upon a time there was a hired man who had served his master long and well. One day he came to his master and asked leave to go home to his parents who lived far away. The master was willing and gave him as a reward for his faithful services a lump of pure gold.

The servant set out on his journey. As he travelled on, the gold became heavier and heavier. He saw a man on horseback coming towards him, and thought, "If I only had a horse and could ride instead of walk; this gold is so heavy and makes me so tired. I'll swap with him. My gold for his horse!" So he swapped his gold for the horse, and rode away.

After a while he came upon a man milking a cow in the shade of a tree. "How good," thought the servant, "to have a cow which one can ride, and which one can milk when one is thirsty." So he swapped the horse for a cow, and rode away.

Becoming thirsty, he rode the cow under a tree and got down to milk her. He took his hat as a pail and milked away. The cow, however, kicked him over and would not let herself be milked. About this time a man came along with a goose; and the servant swapped his cow for the goose, thinking of the good dinner that he would have when he got home.

As he went on, the goose became more and more of a burden and he became more and more tired. Nevertheless, he kept plodding along. There came a man towards him, who, when he was nearby, stooped down and picked up an object lying in the road.

"What is that?" asked the servant.

"That is a luck stone," said the man, "and he who carries it in his pocket will have great luck in the future."

"I'll swap my goose for that stone," said the servant.

The swap was made and the servant went on. He had put the luck stone in his pocket, and he found after a while that the stone was rubbing him sore. Thereupon he took the stone out of his pocket and carried it in his hand.

He came to a deep spring, and being very thirsty, lay down to drink, but in doing so, the luck stone dropped out of his hand into the deep water of the spring.

Whereupon he cried out, "God be praised! That trouble is at an end."

*—Richard Peters, Allentown, Pa.*

THE GREAT NEED

Years ago there lived out in the back country a couple that was very saving. The man would often say to his wife, "We must save for the time when the great need comes." *

One day the man went to work and his wife was left alone. There was a knock at the door. She opened the door, and, not knowing the one who knocked, asked, "Who are you?"

"I am Mr. Need," came the answer.

"Are you he whom the people call the "Great Need?" asked the woman.

"Yes, I am he," was the answer.

"Oh! My husband has been waiting a long time for you, and now I shall give you all the money that we have saved for you," said the woman.

She got all the money that they had saved and gave it to him. When her husband came home, she said, "Mr. Great Need was here and I gave him all that we had saved for him."

After the husband had recovered from his surprise, he said, "You are so stupid that I do not care to live with you. I am going away, and I shall never come back unless I find a person more stupid than you."

So he went away and travelled on until he came to a big barn where some men were busily at work.

"What are you doing?" he inquired.

"We are putting the white horse up on the hay loft for a nest egg," ** they replied.

"They are very stupid but not as stupid as my wife," said the man as he continued on his way.

He came to a high hill, and went down into the valley. There a little hut stood, with its windows open, and a little old woman sitting inside. He entered the hut.

When the woman saw him she said, "From where do you come?"

"Down from above," *** he answered.

"I am glad to see you. Tell me, how is my son Michael getting along up there?" she said.

"Not so well," answered the man. "He is very poor. He has no money, no clothes and no food."

"Oh," said the woman as she rose from her chair, "I am so happy that somebody has come with whom I can send things to my Michael."

She gathered food and clothes and all the money she had and told him to take them along for her Michael.

The man concluded that he had now met someone who was more

stupid than his wife, and he went home and lived with his wife happily ever after.

—*Hattie Lerch, Allentown, Pa.*

* "Die gross Nod." An old dialectal expression for famine. The woman took it to be the name of a person.
** "En Neschtoi." When eggs were lifted out of a nest, one was always left in the nest as a nest egg. This was supposed to induce the hen to keep on laying. The white horse was put on the loft as a nest egg to induce some imaginary animal to lay a colt.
*** "Vun owwe runner." This expression means "to come down from a hill into a valley," "to come down from the uplands," and also "to come down from Heaven." The woman took the last meaning.

### THE ENDLESS STORY

A man sentenced to death was promised his life if he would tell a story that had no end. He agreed, and this is the story that he told.

"There was a large room full of wheat. There was no opening in the room except a small hole through which only a cockroach* could crawl. And a cockroach came, crawled in through the hole and carried away a grain of wheat; soon thereafter another came, crawled in through the hole and carried away another grain of wheat; then a third came, crawled in through the hole, and—"

"But there is no end to this," cried his executioners.

"Then give me my life," cried the man.

He was freed.

—*Mrs. Emma Diehl, Freeburg, Pa.*

* The same story is heard at Alburtis, in Lehigh County, with this difference, a "weevil" carried away the wheat instead of a cockroach.

### LOUSEWORT

This plant is known to us by the names "Widderkumm" (Come-again Plant), and "Lewesgraut" (Herb of Life).

Its virtues are said to have been discovered in this wise. One day a tramp came to a farmhouse and begged for food. It was given to him, with a cup of coffee. He took the platter and the cup of coffee, and sat down on the steps of the porch to eat.

The man of the house had been an invalid for a long time. He had recovered from his illness, but had been unable to recover his strength. As the tramp ate his meal, he talked with the sick man who was sitting on the porch in a rocking chair. When he had finished his meal, he said, "You have been good to me, and now I shall bring you a plant that will restore your strength." He went down into the meadow and brought back the lousewort.

"This," said he "is the Come-again Plant. Use it and it will bring back your health and strength."

—*Bucks County.*

### THE PLANTS WITH THE BLOOD SPOTS

When Christ was crucified, drops of his blood fell down upon a plant that stood at the foot of the cross. Ever since the leaves of that plant are marked with blood spots.

This legend is heard of different plants:

The spotted Knot-weed, Polygonum Persicaria L, whose lanceolate leaves are usually marked with a dark lunate or triangular spot near the middle.

The Mildew, Chenopodium album L, whose leaves are sometimes spotted dark purple. It is then called "Himmelsgraut" (Herb of Heaven).

St. John's Wort, Hypericum perforatum L. One of our dialectal names for this plant is "Gottesblut" (Blood of God). The crushed plant yields a reddish juice. All these plants have been naturalized from Europe.

—*Lehigh and Montgomery Counties.*

### SPEEDWELL

Our name for the Speedwell is "Ehr un Preis," which may be translated as a command, "Honor and Praise." The meaning is that men should honor and praise this plant.

The plant is native to Europe and one may assume that our immigrant ancestors were familiar with the lore that has grown up around it.

Our legend tells how a shepherd in taking his sheep to pasture, noted that, before grazing, they always went to a certain plant and ate of the leaves. He became curious, examined the plant closely, and then chewed some of its leaves. This he did for several days, and found his health and strength improved. He told of the plant to others, who in turn found that the plant had wonderful strengthening and curative powers, and all agreed that this was a plant to be honored and praised.

*—Montgomery and Lebanon Counties.*

### A CRY FROM THE GROUND

Years ago there lived a very wicked man in one of the little valleys across the Blue Mountain. One night he stole a horse, and in fleeing from his pursuers fell from the horse to his death.

Now, in those days suicides and murderers were not buried within the bounds of a church graveyard but on the outside of the wall which usually enclosed the burial grounds. So this wicked man whose death was looked upon as a suicide—for was he not the cause of his own death?—was buried along the wall on the outside of the graveyard.

In course of time a plant grew up on his grave, and on the leaves were the words:

"Ah! Can repentance not be found
Between a stiff back and the ground." *

*—Henry Schaeffer, Egypt, Pa.*

* "Ei, kann dar Mensch sich nett bereie.
Vum schteiffen Buckel bis uff dar Grund."

The story implies that he repented while falling to the ground, and that a repentant sinner was buried outside the wall.

### THE HIDDEN TREASURE

(Stories of hidden or buried treasure were frequently heard up to the beginning of the present century. Since then they have become infrequent, and the creative spirit of such stories has apparently died out.

(We have given a large number of these stories, because they embody many old beliefs which today are forgotten, and are only met in stories that come down from former generations.)

Years ago, it is said, men searched for a hidden treasure in the hills north of Brickersville, not far from the old Stiegel furnace.

They were successful in their silent search, and found the chest after little digging. Impatient to see what it contained, they immediately broke open the lid, and to their joy found that the chest was full of gold pieces. Thereupon, one of them, unable to restrain his joy, cried out, "Now, we'll be rich," and immediately the chest was gone.

If they had touched the gold with their hands before speaking, the treasure would have been theirs.

—*Henry Landis, Landis Valley, Pa.*

\*   \*   \*

Not far from the village of N, in Snyder County, along the highway, was a spot that was perennially green. Though other ground was dry as dust, here it was moist, and though other vegetation was dried up and shrivelled, here it was green and thrifty.

People speaking of this remarkable circumstance came to believe that a treasure was buried there, for older people had often said that where treasure was buried the ground was always moist.

Thereupon certain men of the village banded together to dig for the buried wealth, and that their venture might have favor, promised to give to the church and the school, half of what they found.

They went to digging, and after they had gotten down to some depth they sensed that they were getting close to the chest.

Thus far all had been done in silence, but then one of them thought out aloud, saying, "We'll give away only as much as we choose."

Thereupon water began to seep into the hole, and further digging was impossible.

To this day the hole is shown, always partly filled with water and with moisture constantly exuding from its sides.

—*Mrs. Emma Diehl, Freeburg, Pa.*

\*   \*   \*

There lived in the South Mountain, in the southern part of Lebanon County, some years after the War of the Revolution, a notorious robber. He would bury his plunder deep in the woods at night, and that he might find the place in the darkness he stretched a string from the cache to a tree along an old path. One day the string was broken, and the treasure was lost. The robber himself could not find it.

After his death certain men who knew of the lost treasure planned to search for it. They consulted an old woman who had a magical mirror.\* She directed them to a certain spot where they were to draw a magical circle. They were to dig within the circle, and as they dug they were not to throw any ground outside the circle.

The men drew the circle, and started to dig. They had gotten down to the depth of their shoulders when one of the diggers came upon the chest. He was on the verge of crying out, "I have it," when he felt hot breath coming upon his shoulders. He looked back and saw a large black dog with jaws open and teeth bared ready to leap on him. Instinctively he brought his shovel around and struck at the dog, and in so doing threw a little ground outside the circle.

Immediately the dog vanished, and also the chest.

—*Lebanon County.*

* "Erdschpiggel."

\* \* \*

N.N. heard that a treasure was buried at the Sand Bank, not far from Hellertown. He and several others went to a braucher who told them to draw a ring around the spot where the treasure was supposed to be, and then, in absolute silence, they were to dig within the ring.

Soon after they began digging, a flock of blackbirds flew on a tree nearby. The birds whistled and sang, but the men kept on digging.

Then a hen with a flock of chicks came to the ring, but the men paid no attention to her, and kept on digging.

Then came an ugly ferocious looking boar up to the ring, and one of the men became scared and cried out, "Huss!" *

The boar immediately vanished. The men ceased digging for they knew that it would be impossible for them to find the treasure after one had broken the injunction of silence.

—*John Algard, Laurys, Pa.*

* Exclamatory word used in driving pigs.

\* \* \*

A man buried gold beneath the threshing floor of his barn under an agreement with the devil, that after his death the money could only be gotten with the help of seven brothers.

A tramp, lying among the hay, overheard the covenant and also saw where the treasure was hidden.

The farmer died. Several years passed and the tramp, on his rounds, again came that way. He asked for food, and it was given him. While eating, he inquired whether they had found the money which the dead farmer had hidden. They answered that they knew he had hidden money and that they had searched long and in vain for it.

"I know where the money is hidden," said the tramp, "but it can only be gotten with the help of seven brothers."

They overcame what apparently was a great difficulty by taking seven suckling pigs on to the threshing floor, and when they raised the planks, the treasure was there.

—*Lehigh County.*

\* \* \*

A farmer's family had trouble to keep their maid servants any length of time. They would stay only a short while and then leave.

One day a new maid came. It was the day of butchering, and on such a day there is a late supper and many dishes to wash.

When the supper was over, the maid started in on the work of washing the dishes and so forth. The farmer's wife came to her and told her to leave them for the next day.

"Why?" asked the maid in surprise.

"I suppose," said the farmer's wife, "it is best for me to tell you, now, the reason why the maids who were here before you only stayed a short while . . . Well, every evening at 8 o'clock the fire will go out and an old man will come and sit beside the stove."

"That's all right," said the maid. "I'll tell him to go away."

She kept on working. At 8 o'clock the fire went out, and an old man came and sat beside the stove. The maid said to him, "Please, go away. I want to rebuild the fire."

The old man answered, "I have waited a long time for someone to speak to me. Now come with me into the cellar."

They went down into the cellar, and he told her to dig in one of the corners. This she did, and found a box full of money, most of which was gold.

The man said, "All this is yours, and now I shall have rest."

With those words he disappeared.

—*William Coffin, Treichlers, Pa.*

\* \* \*

The man servant on the N.N. farm heard at night all kinds of noises. Several times he heard the rattling of pans, and he arose because he thought breakfast was being prepared. When he got downstairs he found that it was only 2 o'clock in the morning.

"I am not afraid of ghosts," said the servant to his master, "but, when I am sleeping, I don't want to be disturbed by anybody, especially not by ghosts. I am leaving this place."

Several days later a traveler came along who asked for overnight lodging. The farmer told him that only one room was vacant, and in that room his servant had slept and had heard such frightful noises that he would not remain in his employ.

"That is the very room for me," replied the traveler.

The next morning he came downstairs, and asked for a pick and a shovel, and then, telling the farmer to follow, he went into the cellar.

"Dig there," he said to the farmer, pointing to a spot near the cellar wall. The farmer dug, and uncovered an iron kettle filled with money. They divided the money equally, and the traveler went on his way.

No more strange noises were heard in the house.

WHERE TO HUNT FOR THE HIDDEN TREASURE

The great question in treasure hunting was to find the exact spot where it lay hidden. It was said that treasure was buried where ground was continually moist even though all the ground round about was dry; or in bare barren spots in fertile fields; or places where a motionless light shone at night.

To be sure of the place one could consult a person versed in necromancy. Years ago in Carbon County there lived a notorious sorcerer. To him people would bring ground that they thought might contain gold or silver ore, or in which treasure was buried.

He would spread the ground on a table in his room, and then intone an incantation. A fierce storm would arise, and golden colored and silver colored caterpillars would appear upon the table and crawl around upon the ground. They would disappear and the sorcerer would declare that it was useless to seek for silver or gold in the spot from which the ground was taken. Though several persons took ground to him, he always told them that neither gold nor silver was to be found in it.

Another way was to take a black hen or a black cat at night and tie it to a stake that was driven in at the supposed spot. If in the morning the fowl or cat was found torn to pieces, then treasure was there, otherwise not.

—*Montgomery County.*

THE TREASURE GUARDED BY THE DEVIL

One dark night, a tramp sought shelter in an old deserted house that stood alongside the road. He lit a fire in the open hearth, and lay down to sleep. At 10 o'clock he was awakened by a noise, and looking up, he saw a leg falling down through the stove pipe hole. He picked up the leg, saying, "Fine, now I have part of a man."

Soon another leg came down through the chimney, and the tramp as he put the two legs together said, "Two legs! Fine! Now I have a quarter man."

Then the body came down. "Better and better! Now I have half a man," said he as he joined the body to the legs.

Two arms came down through the hole. "All the time, better! Now I have three-quarters of a man," said the tramp, as he joined the arms to the body.

Finally the head came down with a bang, "Best of all! Now I have a whole man," said he.

After he had joined the head to the body, he looked at the skeleton and said, "Well, what do you want?"

The skeleton answered that gold was buried in the cellar of the house, and until that had been dug up, he would have no rest. However, he who hunted for the treasure would be confronted by the devil, the walls would appear to collapse, and the house would seem to tumble down, and there would be fearful noises and rumblings.

The tramp, being a brave man, decided to try for the treasure. He got a block of wood, a wedge, and a mallet. The next night, he went into the cellar. He had not been there long before the walls seemed to collapse, and the house seemed to be tumbling down upon him, and he saw large snakes with fiery eyes and hissing tongues crawl around him, and a lion with open jaws poised as if to spring upon him.

He stood his ground, took the wedge which he had brought along and drove it part way into the block of wood . . . There was a flash of light, a peal of thunder, and the devil stood before him. "What do you want of me?" said the devil.

"I want you to help me pull this block apart," answered the tramp.

The devil laid hold of the log, put his hands into the split, and pulled. As he was pulling, the tramp deftly pulled out the wedge, and the devil's hands were clamped.

"Now," said the tramp, "you are caught, and I shall not free you until you promise not to molest me as I dig for the treasure, and never hereafter."

"I promise," said the devil.

"What you promise you must keep," said the man.

"My promises I keep," said the devil.

The devil was freed, and left. Thereupon the tramp went ahead and found the gold, and lived in plenty ever after.

—*Ray Meissner, Lehighton, Pa.*

### THE HIDDEN TREASURE GUARDED BY A SKELETON

One day a tramp came to a farmhouse, and asked permission to sleep over night in the barn.

"No," said the farmer, "I do not permit anyone to sleep in my barn over night. There are those who will smoke while lying on the hay, and there are others who will strike matches to see in the darkness—No! No one may sleep in my barn. I do not want my barn burned down. However, down there in the meadow is a little log house where you may spend the night, and in it you will find a fireplace where you can build a fire if the night becomes chilly."

The tramp, thanking the farmer for his kindness, turned to go down to the log house. The farmer, thereupon, raised his hand as in warning, and continued, "One thing I must tell you, before you go. The log house is haunted and no one ever spent a whole night in it."

The tramp laughed and said, "Ghosts! They never frighten me." He continued, "I have not eaten for several days, would you not kindly give me some flour, lard, salt and milk. With these things I can bake pancakes on the hearth, and I shall have a good meal."

The farmer gave him all that he desired, and in addition some sugar and butter, and wished him a good night's rest.

The tramp went down into the log house, built a fire, and began to bake his pancakes on the hearth. Before the cakes were half baked, a bone fell down the chimney upon the cakes. He grabbed the bone and threw it aside. Soon another bone, and another, and more bones came down the chimney. As they fell the tramp picked them up one by one and cast them aside.

The cakes having been baked, the tramp took them, and, since there was no furniture in the house, sat on the floor in the middle of the room, and began to eat ravenously. As he sat thus, there was a noise at the door, and looking up he saw a skeleton which beckoned to him. The tramp would not be disturbed in his eating, and between gulps told the skeleton to come and take a pancake or two, adding, "You are so thin that your bones rattle."

The skeleton wouldn't move but continued to beckon with its index finger. The tramp, eyeing the skeleton between bites, said, "All right! Odd Fellow. I'll be with you when I have eaten."

Having satisfied his hunger, he arose and went over towards the skeleton. As he approached, the skeleton moved towards an open door that led into the cellar, all the while looking back over his shoulder at the tramp, and beckoning him to follow.

When they had gotten down into the cellar, the skeleton pointed to a large stone. "All this fuss so that I should lift this stone for you," exclaimed the tramp. The skeleton nodded assent, and kept pointing to the stone with its bony hand.

The tramp laid hold of the stone, and to his surprise it came up light as a feather, and underneath were three large pots of gold. Now the skeleton spoke for the first time, "One pot is for the church, another for the poor, and the third is for you because you have freed me and brought me rest."

The tramp faithfully carried out the injunction of the skeleton, gave one pot of gold to the church, another to the poor, and kept the third for himself, and in it there was so much gold that he was wealthy the remainder of his life.

—*Gertrude Frantz, Mountainville, Pa.*


MYSTERIOUS TALES

*The Legend of Tambour Yokel*

Tell the story with bated breath—
A story of horror, and gloom, and death.

A little church on a lonely hill;
A churchyard near it, calm and still;

Fair in the morning's early light;
Dark and gloomy it seems at night.

There it is said, in the olden time,
Happened a nameless deed of crime;

And stalwart men, with swiftest pace,
Haste when they pass that dreadful place.

Home, with the troop, from the war had come
Tambour Yokel, who beat the drum.

A worthless wretch who, on his way;
Had learned but the arts of a bird of prey;

Who had sold, it was said, in the dreadful strife,
His soul to Satan to save his life.

"Now where," he cried, "is my ancient foe?
I have come from the battle to lay him low."

"Peace! Peace!" they answered. "Your boast is vain;
The man will never fight again;

The foe you hated and sought to kill,
Now rests in the churchyard on the hill."

"Ho! What of that?" the drummer cried,
"Perhaps it was well the coward died;

But I know a way, as you'll see tonight,
To bring this man from his grave to fight!"

Then a dreadful oath the ruffian swore,
He would call him forth to fight once more.

In their cups that night, at the tavern near,
His comrades met him with mock and jeer;

"Ho, wizard!" they cried. "Why don't you go
To the churchyard now to meet your foe?"

Then Tambour Yokel cursed and swore,
And sallied forth from the tavern door.

"Come forth!" he cried through the startled night,
"Come forth, thou fiend, from the grave and fight!"

He reached the churchyard gate, and then
The fearful challenge was heard again.

But soon a cry that was wild and shrill
Was heard from the churchyard on the hill.

"Help! Help!" he cried, but none drew near,
His comrades trembled, aghast with fear.

In silence waiting—that godless crew—
While the cries still fainter and fainter grew.

Next morning, they came, with silent tread
Seeking their comrade among the dead.

There mid the graves, the man they found,
Naked and cold on the trodden ground;

Scattered his garments, far and wide;
Bloody the soil where the wretch had died.

And this was all; but who can tell
Who wounded the victim and how he fell?

Did a panther, perchance, of the forest tear
The limbs of the wretched boaster there?

Or, was it the fiend, as the neighbors say,
That bore his godless soul away?

Ah! none could tell—nor cared to know—
But a mighty hand had laid him low.

Yet with a shudder men still relate
The tale of Tambour Yokel's fate;

And none forgets the legend grim—
How a fearful judgment was sent to him.

This is a poetic version of a story still told in Lehigh County. It was written by Professor Dr. Dubbs and appeared in "The Guardian," a religious magazine, in the year 1884. Prof. Dr. Dubbs states that, at the time of his writing, the legend was over a hundred years old, that the story was generally credited, and always told with due solemnity.

The scene is the graveyard of the Salisbury church in lower Lehigh County.

\*    \*    \*

A man, A— by name, was spoken of as having dealings with the devil. He was known to possess a book by which he was able to do all kinds of evil. One night as A— lay in bed there was a noise of a chain being dragged across the roof.

A— arose and said, "I must go outside."

His wife begged him, "Don't go! Oh, don't go!"

However, he went out of the house, and that was the last time he was ever seen.

The son found his father's book and read in it. He read so much that he came under the power of the devil. He lost his peace of mind; he could not eat by day, nor sleep at night. Finally he took sick with a high fever; and at night his room was all fiery.

Then a man came along and read him free from the devil. The book which had caused all the trouble was taken and put in a log in the pig stable.\*

*—Albert Schuler, Orefield, Pa.*

\* By reading an "evil book" one can summon the devil voluntarily or involuntarily.

Suppose one should come across an "evil book," as the "Seventh Book of Moses," and, merely out of curiosity, start to read in it. Were one to read on and on, one would finally come to a point beyond which one could not continue; one would "lose himself" among the words and become confused and puzzled like a fly entangled in a spider's web. This is spoken of as reading "until one is fast," "sich fascht lese."

Then, if still able, one should retrace his steps by reading backwards, and in this way retreat out of the maze over the same road by which one entered. If this is not done, the devil will appear, and seek to lay hold of the reader.

The only way to escape from the devil is to have someone read a formula which will compel the devil to relinquish his hold. This is "reading one free," and can be done by a braucher.

## MAKING A COVENANT WITH THE DEVIL

"I have been told that I could sell myself to the devil for twenty years. On Christmas night, between the hours of midnight and one, I was to go to a cemetery with a live young cock that had been raised wholly apart from hens. It was to call the devil to come, saying, 'Come devil! Come!' Then I was to tear the cock apart.

"The devil would appear and I could then make a bargain with him. He would give me riches and power for twenty years; if I should die within that time I would belong to him body and soul, but if I should live beyond twenty years I would be free."

So said a resident of Montgomery County.

### THE SPEAKING HORSES

The month of December, called in the dialect, "Grischdmunet," is the month of spirits. Then, as at no other time, the spirits are abroad, and he who has been born in this month can see, hear, and speak with them. The activity of the spirits reaches its height on Christmas Eve, at midnight, when all living nature is moved and becomes articulate;* bees in their hives buzz a language which then and only then can be understood by the hearers. They may even leave the hive, fly around and speak; horses and cattle speak, and tell of things that shall come to pass.

There was a farmer of rough speech, and of harsh ways towards his horses. He had heard of the mysterious happenings at midnight on Christmas Eve, but would not believe that they were true, and persisted in this attitude despite the asseverations of his friends that they themselves had heard horses and cattle speak at that hour. He would "see for himself" and only after he had seen with his own eyes and heard with his own ears would he believe.

So, one Christmas Eve, several hours before midnight, he stole into the horse stable and hid in a pile of straw that was used for bedding for the horses. At midnight he heard one horse say to the other, "We have a very cruel master and this night we shall kick him to death."

The farmer rose up from the pile of straw, and in groping his way to the stable door was kicked to death by the horses.

*—Lebanon County.*

* In the dialect, "Alles bewegt sich."

\* \* \*

The aged Rev. Mr. Helfrich was a widely known and much beloved pastor in the northern part of Lehigh County. In driving home from a pastoral visitation on Ascension Day, his horse lost a shoe. The pastor drove up to the nearest smithy and asked the smith to shoe the horse.

"Yes," said the smith, "this I would gladly do, but pastor, today is Ascension Day."

"Don't think of that," said Helfrich.

Now it was thought that when work had to be done, or food bought on Sunday or a religious holiday as Ascension Day, no payment was to be asked or made that day, that could be done on the following day, but rather not at all than on a holy day.

After the shoeing was done, the pastor asked, "What are the costs?"

The smith replied, "Nothing!"

As the pastor was leaving, he said, "While I was standing around here, I dropped a dollar. Should you find it when you clean up, as I suppose you will, keep it."

The smith returned to this shop and found the dollar lying on the floor.

*—Lehigh County.*

### A LOST DAY

There is a certain day in the year, upon which one should cut off thistles, weeds, and thorns, for everything cut off on that day will die. The old people called the day "Abdannsdag," and it had that name in the calendar.

There is a day in our calendars that has the name Abdon, but it is not the real day. The real "Abdannsdag" is not marked any more, on account of the evil that was committed on that day.

One could easily bring about the death of one's enemy on that day. One took a sharp knife and thrust it into a tree to which had been given the name of the enemy; and said, "I thrust this knife into the heart of N.N."

Such things were done on "Abdannsdag," and the calendar makers became alarmed and gave a different name to the day.

There was a certain man who determined to discover the real day. He cut off a small patch of weeds every day during the month of July, which is the month in which the real "Abdannsdag" occurs, and, then, he found that every patch grew again save one. Thus he discovered the real day. However, he would not tell anyone which the real day was, because he was afraid that it might be used to work evil, and he took his knowledge with him to the grave.

*—Lehigh, Montgomery, and Lebanon Counties.*

\* \* \*

There was a farmer who found that his horses would not enter the stable when he brought them in from the fields, after a day's hard work. They refused to cross the door sill, and, though he took off their harnesses, they only entered after he had used the whip upon them.

He consulted a braucher, and was advised, that should they again refuse to cross the door sill of the stable, he was to take a sixteen or twenty penny nail and slowly pound it into the sill.

A short time thereafter it again happened that the horses balked against entering the stable. Thereupon, he took a nail and hammered it into the sill, to one-third or one-half its length. He had scarcely done this before an old woman came along and told him to draw out the nail or she would die.

Thereafter the horses never balked.

—*Lehigh County.*

\* \* \*

"My uncle's horse ran away, and went out to the S\*— place. I ran after, and caught him in the barnyard. But when I tried to lead him home, I lost the way out, and kept on going around and around in the barnyard. I walked around and around in a circle. Then came S—, "What's the matter?" he asked.

"I can't find the place to get out," said I.

"Right in front of you is the place," said S—. And so it was.

"S—, every evening, took holy water, and squirted a ring around his buildings. This he called his golden ring, and whoever trod into that ring was bound and could not leave without his permission.

"I was not the only one who got into that ring. Two men drove on the road past the S— place one night, and came upon a blown down willow tree that blocked the way. They decided to drive through the S— barnyard, and then back to the road. They drove into the barnyard, and there they were held immovable all through the night. When daylight appeared in the east, S— raised the window of his bedroom, and called down, 'Now, you can go.' "

—*As told by a resident of Egypt.*

\* S— was a noted braucher whose cure was holy water, which was nothing more than water from snow that fell in the month of March.

THE ETERNAL HUNTER

On cold still winter nights the Eternal Hunter is abroad and can be heard as he urges his pack of dogs on to the chase. Woe to that person who is out on the hills and is met by the Hunter and his dogs. He will be torn to pieces, or will be carried away.

It was not so long ago that people would say, "Tonight the Hunter is out. Tonight one had better stay at home."

One night a group of hunters was out in the South Mountain for raccoons. They had ascended on a high ridge to listen for the yelping of their dogs. To their alarm they heard from the other side of a deep valley the Eternal Hunter calling to his pack.

Soon their own dogs came running back to them and were so scared that they would not return to the hunt but hung around the legs of their masters. The hunters started for home, and the dogs, instead of going ahead, kept close behind.

This was strange to the hunters until by the light of their lanterns they saw a small black animal in the path ahead of them. Then they knew that the Eternal Hunter was near by and that only the light of the lanterns protected them from his attack.

*—Lebanon County.*

\* \* \*

A man while hunting in the Blue Mountain had wounded a deer. He followed the bloody trail, at times sighting the deer but never able to get in the killing shot, until towards evening. Then he met a man with dark clothes who inquired what he was doing.

"I have wounded a deer and I am on its trail," said the hunter.

"The hour is late and soon darkness will fall. It is best for you to give up the chase and return home," said the stranger.

"I won't go home until I have gotten the deer," replied the hunter as he took up the chase anew.

And now, in the Blue Mountains, the hunter is eternally pursuing a wounded deer.\*

*—Lehigh County.*

\* (Note provided by the compilers, Brendle and Troxell.)

Two distinct traditions are represented by these stories. The first has to do with a spirit of the air, the second with the maker of an unfulfilled vow.

Prof. Dr. Herbert Beck in his article on "The Pennsylvania German Names of Birds," *The Auk,* April, 1924, writes of the Canada Goose: "As the result of its clanging note, which in the mass and in the night suggests a pack in full cry, it is called Awicher Yager (Ger. Ewiges Jaejer), to connect it with the story, still current in South Germany, of the restless soul of some riotous huntsman doomed to follow the hounds through eternity.

\* \* \*

N.N. bought a farm. He had not occupied in the place any length of time before he became aware that a spirit walked at night along one of his boundary lines. He suspected that something was amiss and sought advice from one who was versed in such matters. He was told to go at night and stand three paces away from the stake that marked the corner and at the same time he was to carry a silken handkerchief in his right hand.

He did as he was directed and he had not taken his station very long before the spirit appeared. It came up to the stake and moaned, "Where shall I put it? Where shall I put it?"

The man answered, "At the very spot where you got it."

The spirit sighed deeply and said, "Now I shall find rest," and stooped down and drew out the stake. It took the stake in its left hand and extended its right as if to thank the farmer for what he had spoken.

Instead of taking the hand of the spirit, the farmer held out the silken handkerchief and that part which the spirit touched immediately turned to ashes. The spirit disappeared.

The next day the farmer and his wife found the stake moved to a new spot, which they, from that time on, took to be the original corner.

The spirit was not seen thereafter.

*—Lehigh County.*

\* \* \*

A drunken man met at night a ghost that sighed, "Where shall I put it? Where shall I put it?"

The drunken fellow exasperated at the sighing said, "If you don't know where to put it go and put it where you got it."

The man answered, "For many years I have waited for those words. When I was living I quarreled with my neighbor about a boundary line and I pulled out a corner stone; and all these years I have been wandering about seeking rest. Now I have found it."

*—Montgomery County.*

## BRAUCHE AND HEXE

There are two words in the Pennsylvania Dutch dialect which lend themselves to a misunderstanding of our beliefs. These two words are *brauche* and *hexe*. The first is generally translated powwowing, and thus conjures up the image of an Indian medicine man and his way of healing.

*Brauche* is a way of healing which has its roots in ancient and Christian folk beliefs, and employs prayers, blessings, and conjurations. It had its greatest vogue among us around the middle of the last century. It has declined rapidly since the beginning of this century and will soon be a thing of the past.

This is very evident to one who endeavors to collect stories on *brauching.* Forty years ago it would have been a simple matter to collect a large number; today one hears comparatively few. This holds true also of *hex* and ghost stories.

*—Brendle and Troxell*

* * *

An old woman came along the road and met a neighbor's child. The woman was carrying a basket of apples, and she took one and gave it to the child.

Soon thereafter the child became violently ill and vomited tacks, pins and nails.

The father went to a *braucher* and told his story, and also that he suspected the old woman of working evil.

"You are right," said the *braucher*, "that old woman worked this evil, but I'll compel her to take her hands off your child."

He gave the father a small peg, and directed him to take an augur, upon returning home, and bore a hole in a tree in the yard near the house. He was to drive in the peg with three light strokes. These strokes would cause such discomfort to the woman that she would soon appear and beg for relief, promising to cease annoying the child.

"Don't strike heavily on the peg so as to drive it in all the way," warned the *braucher*. "If you do that you will kill the woman."

The man bored the hole and set the peg. Then a wave of anger swept over him and he drove in the peg with one mighty blow. Immediately he ran to the home of the suspected woman.

Just when he got there, she drew her last breath.

—*O.P. Leh, Egypt, Pa.*

* * *

Two men had gotten hold of the Seventh Book of Moses and decided to call upon a rich and avaricious old miller with the expectation of getting money from him.

When they got close to his mill they found him at his cider press. One of them went up to him while the other stealthily stole into the building and concealed himself in a dark corner.

Said the first one to the miller, "I have here the Seventh Book of Moses and I can raise the 'Old One' and he will make you very rich. What say you? Shall I go ahead?"

"Go ahead," answered the miller.

"Lock the door, and then I shall read."

The door of the room was locked and the man opened his book and read. After a little while he paused and said, "We are now coming to a more difficult part."

He read on, and after a little pause, again looked at the miller and said, "From here on it will become even more difficult."

He read on a little, paused again, looked up at the miller and said, "Now comes the most difficult part—and then the devil will appear—and then the whole matter is up to you."

He read on, and his companion, who was waiting, at a given signal came forth from his dark corner blowing a flame out of his mouth. Seeing which the miller dashed headlong through the window, breaking glass and taking sash and frame with him.

In relating the experience one of the two men said, "If the old devil hadn't broken away from us we would have gotten five hundred dollars out of him."

—*Sydney Wotring, Ballietsville, Pa.*

\* \* \*

Witches would hold gatherings in fields, and the places of such gatherings were circular spots where nothing grew. Such spots were called "witch rings."

There was a servant in the home of a witch. One night he saw that she greased her feet with lard, and then she went to the fireplace and said, "Up the chimney I go and touch no part of it." She immediately was wafted up through the chimney.

The servant also greased his feet and going to the chimney said, "Up the chimney I go and touch everything." He was whisked up through the chimney, bumping from side to side all the way up.

Through the air he was taken until he came to the place where the witches were assembling, and there he partook of a most wonderful meal.

At four o'clock the cocks crowed and everything disappeared. The servant was left alone with nothing around but some old bones.

He didn't know where he was, but he started to walk away in the hope that he would meet someone who could tell him where he was. When dawn came, he recognized his surroundings. He was a good day's journey from home.

—*Lehigh County.*

\* \* \*

"A brauch book is no evil book," said old Mr. N—. "There is nothing in such a book but prayers and there are some persons who call it a prayer book. *The Sixth and Seventh Book of Moses,* however, is an evil book. With that book one can do all kinds of evil, if one renounces God and swears allegiance to the devil.

"They say that book is printed in black and red, black pages with

white letters and white pages with red letters. I never saw a copy. The D—
family of the D— valley got possession of such a book and swore allegiance to the devil. An old dragon—a dragon is a devil with a big fiery
head and a long tail—lived in the Blue Mountain not far from the
D— home.

"One night the dragon came down from his den and passed close by
the D— home. The D—s ran out and yelled, 'Dragon, dragon, we need
money. Give us money. We need money.'

"The dragon turned around, and rumbling and hissing, came upon
them. They fled indoors and had barely time to close and bar the door
against him. Thereafter, whenever they went out of doors at night, something unseen would lay hold of them and cast them to the ground.

"I would not like to touch the *Sixth and Seventh Book of Moses*.
There was a maid who read in her master's copy in his absence. She read
until the devil appeared and took her into his power, and made her do his
will; she took the chaff out of the chaff bags and burned it; she pulled up
the newly planted onions and reset them with their heads up and stalks
down; and then the devil took a crock, knocked out the bottom and
directed her to pump it full of water; and this she was doing when her
master came home and released her by reading backwards.

"There was a famous hunter who had such a book which he used in
hunting. He told his boys that they could never shoot a deer.

"The boys went out hunting and came upon a giant buck deer. They
shot at him, and missed; they shot again, and missed. Despite all the
shooting the buck stood still and looked at them. Then one of the boys
cried out, 'By Judas, that must be our father.' I don't know but that he
was right."

\* \* \*

On the hot afternoons of summer, a mother was accustomed to give
her child of two years or so, a bowl of bread and milk out in the yard under
a great oak tree. Then, leaving the child, she would return indoors to
her work.

One day, she felt an impulse to look after the child, and went out into
the yard. To her awe and fright she saw a big blacksnake with its head
upraised, lying near the child. Her fright was so great that she was unable
to move. Then to her still greater fright, she saw the child bring its spoon
down on the head of the snake, saying, "Eat crumbs too, not only milk."

The story is heard, throughout our Pennsylvania Dutch region, and
even down in the Valley of Virginia. Occasionally one comes across a
person who insists that he was the baby, and that the snake lived in a hole

in the wall of the springhouse, or under the roots of a large tree near his home.

*  *  *

There was a very rich woman who had everything that she wanted. Near her lived a very poor woman who had hardly any bread to eat. The poor woman fell sick from hunger.

A neighbor came in and finding no food in the house went to the rich woman and requested food for the sick woman. The request was refused.

She went a second time and requested food. Again her request was refused.

"Kindly give some food, or the poor woman will die," said the friend.

"No!" said the rich woman, firmly closing the door upon her.

The poor woman died, her desire for food unfulfilled. The rich woman lived on, proud in the belief that her wealth could purchase anything. But she too fell ill and as she lay on her bed one day, a desire arose in her for a bite out of a cloud. For this she begged day after day. "I want a piece of cloud. I must have a piece of a cloud. I must have a piece of a cloud," she continually cried. And with these words on her lips she died.

—*Mrs. John Algard, Jr., Laurys, Pa.*

*  *  *

Old Lady Mumbauer reasoned that if she gave her horse a little less food day after day she would have him so that he would need no food. She, thereupon, gave him a little less corn day after day. It finally came to this that she gave him only one grain. Then her horse died.

She told her neighbors, "If he had borne up one day longer I would have succeeded.

The story is widely told, and almost always without mentioning by name the person who made the attempt. We have heard it told of the "stupid Swabians," and of Eilenschpijjel.

The last ration is a handful of oats, one fourth ear of corn, or as above a grain of corn.

—*Heard in many counties.*
*Above heard in Lehigh County.*

*  *  *

One night a man was going across a field to his home when he came upon a heap of glowing coals. He picked up one of the fiery coals and put it into his pipe which had gone out.

In the morning when he took his pipe he found a piece of gold in it. He had come across what the old people called a Devil's Fire.

\* \* \*

In the record book of the Egypt Reformed Church is this note, "A singular phenomenon happened on the 13th of November 1833; the stars fell from Heaven as the saying was."

On that day people were greatly disturbed, especially in the rural sections. Some of them looked for the end of the world.

Those living in the vicinity of Wesnersville turned to Reuben Grimm the community miller and also the most learned man in the community. They found him in his mill cutting furrows in his millstones. They asked him whether he was not afraid to keep on working when the world was coming to an end.

Grimm, without pausing in his work, replied, "Letting stars fall— that is God's work; cutting millstones is my work. And I shall work as long as I have strength."

*—William Christ, Allentown, Pa.*

### EILESCHPIJJEL

(The Pennsylvania Dutch developed their own version of the Til Eulenspiegel tales. In Pennsylvania he was Eileschpijjel, but he was the same kind of trickster figure as in Germany.)

Eileschpijjel and the devil both boasted about their ability to swim long distances. To settle matters they agreed to have a contest, on a certain day, in a great river.

They met at the river bank on the appointed day. The devil was ready for the contest, but not so Eileschpijjel.

"Before we start, a calf must be butchered," said he.

"Why?" asked the devil.

"I am not going to swim fourteen days without eating," answered Eileschpijjel.

The devil fled.

*—Wind Gap, Pa.*

\* \* \*

Eileschpijjel and the devil disputed as to which one could stand most heat. To settle the matter they constructed an oven, and built a roaring fire in its fireplace. Then they crawled into the oven.

The heat was so great that Eileschpijjel could no longer bear it. He crawled towards the door.

The devil in a tone of triumph asked, "What are you doing?"

Eileschpijjel answered, "I want to add more wood to the fire; I feel chilly."

Said the devil, "I must get out of this. I am almost burned up."

*—Very widely heard.*

\* \* \*

The devil and Eileschpijjel farmed on shares. The first year they agreed that the devil should have that part of the crop which grew above ground, and Eileschpijjel that part of the crop which grew under the ground. Turnips were planted and when the division of the crops was made, Eileschpijjel got the roots and the devil the foliage.

The second year, the devil said that he wanted what grew under the ground and Eileschpijjel should have what grew above the ground. Wheat was planted and the devil got the roots and Eileschpijjel the grain.

The third year, the devil, hoping to get the better of Eileschpijjel, said that he wanted both the tops and the roots of the crop, and Eileschpijjel should have the middle parts. Corn was planted, and Eileschpijjel got the ears.\*

*—Lehigh County.*

\* This story is very widely heard. The first part of the story is sometimes given as an explanation of the proverb, "Ausmache wie dar Deiwel an di Riewe." "To make out like the devil with the turnips."

\* \* \*

Eileschpijjel was sent by his master to pick peas in a field that lay a goodly distance away.

"After you have picked the peas," said the farmer, "hull them on the field and then you will be able to carry them all home at one time."

Eileschpijjel obeyed his master. He picked the peas and hulled them on the field. Then he put them in a bag and set out for home.

There was a small hole in the bottom of the bag and as Eileschpijjel was going down hill he saw some peas which had fallen through the hole roll down in front of him.

"If you prefer to go that way," said he, "that way you shall go." Thereupon he emptied out the bag on the hillside, and went on home.

"Where are the peas?" asked the master.

"They are coming after," answered Eileschpijjel, "a little slowly, but they are coming."

*—Heard in different versions.*

\* \* \*

Eileschpijjel came across a pumpkin and did not know what it was. As he was looking it over, a man came along and asked, "Do you know what that is?"

Answered Eileschpijjel, "I do not. I never saw anything like it."

The man said, "That is a mule's egg and if you sit on it for three weeks there will be a young mule."

Eileschpijjel reflected upon the matter and decided that it would be worthwhile to sit on the mule egg for three weeks. He proceeded to sit on the pumpkin.

Becoming tired in a short time, he arose and rolled the pumpkin down the hill. The pumpkin rolled on until it hit a boulder and flew into pieces. At that very moment a rabbit that had been nesting at the boulder scurried away.

Seeing the rabbit, Eileschpijjel cried,

"Hee-haw little colt

Here is your mammy." \*

\* This story is widely heard, though only occasionally associated with Eileschpijjel.

\* \* \*

Eileschpijjel had made himself obnoxious to his neighbors and they planned to drown him, so that they would be rid of him once for all. They put him in a cask, and started out for the sea. On their way they came to a tavern, and leaving the cask outside, went in to drink to the success of their undertaking.

Meanwhile a drover came along with a large drove of cattle. Now when Eileschpijjel heard that someone was approaching, he began to moan, "I can't do it, and I won't do it. I can't do it, and I won't do it."

The drover hearing the moaning stopped and listened. Eileschpijjel again moaned, "I can't do it, and I won't do it."

"What can't you do?" asked the drover.

"They want me to marry the king's daughter, and I won't do it. And they are taking me to the king to compel me to marry his daughter," answered Eileschpijjel. "I can't do it, and I won't do it."

"Let me take your place," said the drover, "I'll marry the king's daughter."

The drover took Eileschpijjel's place in the cask and Eileschpijjel took the cattle and drove them to his home.

The neighbors came out of the tavern, took the cask to the sea and sank it. Then with the feeling that they had finally got rid of Eileschpijjel, they went home with great spirits.

Their astonishment was great when they saw Eileschpijjel, and even greater when they saw the cattle which he had gotten.

Said Eileschpijjel, "Down on the bottom of the sea are many such cattle. These I drove up the bank and out on the shore, and brought them home."

All the neighbors, eager to get cattle, rushed to the sea and jumped in. All of them were drowned.

—*Mrs. Jennie M. Kline, Bernville, Pa.*

\* \* \*

When Eileschpijjel's end drew near, he filled a box with worthless things and nailed it up tightly. Then taking the box he went to his pastor. He asked the pastor to preach a good sermon over his remains.\*

"As a reward for your services you will receive this box which I have filled with things for you," said Eileschpijjel.

The pastor conducted the funeral with an eye to the reward that was coming to him. After the burial he was given the box that Eileschpijjel had made ready. He hastened home and eagerly opened the box, and found in it nothing but rubbish.

—*Mrs. Emma Faustner, Bath, Pa.*

\* These sermons typically say very little that is critical of the deceased.

PARRE SCHTOY

HENRY WILLIAM STOY

Henry William Stoy came to Pennsylvania in the year 1752 as a minister and took up the pastorate of the Tulpehocken Reformed Church. The greater part of his ministry was spent among the churches in the northern parts of Berks and Lebanon counties.

In the later years of his life he turned to the practice of medicine, and herein he gained his greatest fame. He died in Lebanon in 1801.

He is remembered even to this day for his cure for the bite of a mad dog. Recently we were told, "There was a man named Stoy who was the only person that was ever able to cure madness. Persons bound with chains and ropes were brought to him from as far away as a hundred miles, and he cured them. When Stoy died, his cure was lost, and now there is no help for mad persons. If one could find that cure one could not only help many people but also make very much money."

Stoy is taken to be the one referred to in the entry which appears in Gen. Washington's account book:

"Oct. 18, 1797. Gave my servant Christopher, to bear expenses to a person at Lebanon in Pennsylvania celebrated for curing persons bit by wild animals, $25.00."

On his visits to outlying churches, Stoy carried a gun to protect himself from attack and also to shoot such game as might appear along his path. One day he had an appointment to preach. When he got to the church he found only women present. He sat down and waited impatiently for a while. Then looking over the group of women, he muttered aloud, "Why preach to a few old women who have no understanding of things? I'll go grouse hunting." Thereupon taking his gun he stalked out of the church and went hunting.

The reason for Stoy's reluctance to preach to the women lay in his style of preaching. In the diary of the Moravian pastor at Hebron, near Lebanon, is this entry:

"1790, Feb. 3. I visited Dr. Stoy in town. We had a very pleasant conversation. He is likewise a Reformed preacher and has still charge of two congregations in the country. He is well versed in natural sciences. In his sermons he is philosophical, deep and expatiating, which obscures and taints the evangelical doctrines which he at times propounds."

Stoy was a man of great physical prowess. In his day, as through the next century, there were men who took great pride in their reputation for strength and could not brook having another spoken of as being strong and powerful. Such a one went forth on horseback to seek out Stoy and to make a test of his strength.

When he had come near to Stoy's home, he met Stoy upon the road. He did not know Stoy, and asked to be directed to his home. When told that he was speaking to Stoy, he dismounted and, advancing upon Stoy, challenged him to fight. Stoy not reluctant for the combat, grabbed the man, and with little effort lifted him bodily from the ground and cast him over the roadside fence into a field. The man slowly picking himself up called to Stoy, "Kindly throw my horse over here to me."

Stoy was famous not only for his cure for the bite of a mad dog but also for a salve which he had compounded for the itch. This salve was known as "Stoy's Itch Salve."

One day a man came to Stoy for some of the salve. Stoy, however, had none on hand, and told his visitor that he would prepare some salve for him and bring it along on Sunday to church where he could get it.

When Stoy came to church, he ascended the pulpit, and announced that he had brought along Itch Salve for the man who had been to his house, and that that man should now come forward and get it.

No one came forward.

Stoy's activities as a pastor have been well treated in histories of the early colonial churches of the Reformed Church. His activities as a doctor are described in "Some Doctors of the Olden Time," a paper read before the Lebanon County Historical Society by J.M. Redsecker, and appearing in Vol. I of the publications of that society.

\* \* \*

We never heard who the preacher was that had the experience which we shall relate. In Lebanon County they say it was a preacher who lived near the Blue Mountain; in Lehigh County, a preacher of the Pine Swamp Region; in Montgomery County, a preacher upcountry. Often he is merely an "old preacher." Here is the story:

There was a preacher in the Pine Swamp who wore buckskin trousers during the winter. In summer he would change to linsey-woolsey, and hang his buckskins in the attic until cold weather set in.

One cold Sunday in autumn he fetched his buckskins down from the attic and donned them. Then he went to church.

Unknown to him the wasps had built a nest in the trousers. They had become dormant from the cold, but the heat of his body revived them and they began to crawl to and fro. Finally, one of them stung. Down came the preacher's hand with a resounding whack. Another sting and another whack. Then sting after sting, and whack after whack in rapid succession. Preaching was forgotten, and the preacher devoted all his attention to the enemy in the rear. And then becoming aware of the amazement which had spread over the faces of the hearers, the preacher exclaimed, "The Word of God is in my mouth, but the devil is in my trousers."

# BIBLIOGRAPHICAL NOTE

The study of folk religion is a relatively new facet of scholarship in American religion and culture. To the extent that it has been done it has been an enterprise all to itself, abandoned to the provocations of folklorists or presentation societies. Little has been done to integrate interest in folk religiousness into the concerns of the conventions of the academic study of American religion. We have not yet examined what an understanding of folk religiousness contributes to our knowledge of religion in America; and we are far from revising our definitions of Christianity in the light of the discovery of the complementarity of folk religiousness in the lives of American Christians. The spirituality of the American people is a virtually untouched field of study.

I have found Hori Ichiro's *Folk Religion in Japan: Continuity and Change* (Chicago and London: University of Chicago, 1968, 1974) to provide a helpful model. Japanese religion and culture are obviously quite different from our own. Yet Hori's careful study of the role of folk elements in the lives of the people and in the formation of the definitive traditions serves as an example of the importance of this kind of study. Folk traditions, he tells us, have not faced the dilemma of secularization experienced by Buddhism and Christianity, because the latter traditions are enmeshed in the *super*structures, while folk traditions are substructural. This is not exactly so, of course; however, the complementary and substructural character of folk traditions make them important for understanding the power of human religiousness in a society of "invisible religion" (Thomas Luckmann).

I first called attention to these issues in "The American Character and the American Revolution: A Pennsylvania German Sampler," *Journal of the American Academy of Religion* XLIV, 1 (March, 1976), "The Lily and the Turtledove: The Spirituality of the Pennsylvania Dutch,"

*Religion in Life* (Summer 1977), and "The Use of Folklore in the Study of American Religion," *Bulletin of the Council for the Study of Religion* 13, 5 (December 1982).

The work of preservation of Pennsylvania German folk materials goes on under the direction of several societies, library collections, and folklorists. At the forefront of this work are the Pennsylvania German Society and the Pennsylvania Folklore Society. The former organization, with its predecessors, has published annual volumes all during this century. Most of the material bears little interpretation or commentary and is the work primarily of collectors and translators, seeking to preserve the substance of a dying culture. Works by William Parsons and Frederic Klees, cited in the introductory chapters, are excellent introductions to the Pennsylvania Dutch. I cannot recommend too highly the works of John Joseph Stoudt, also cited throughout this volume. Particularly helpful are Stoudt's *Pennsylvania Folk-Art: An Interpretation* (Allentown: 1948), *Pennsylvania German Poetry, 1685–1830,* Pennsylvania German Folklore Society, vol. XX (1955), and *Consider the Lilies How They Grow,* Pennsylvania German Folklore Society, vol. II (1937). In addition Julius Sachse's *The German Pietists of Provincial Pennsylvania, 1694–1708* (Philadelphia: 1895; AMS Press, 1970) and F. Ernest Staeffler's *Mysticism in the German Devotional Literature of Colonial Pennsylvania,* Pennsylvania German Folklore Society, vol. XIV (1949).

When I think of spirituality I think of Friedrich Heiler's *Prayer* (Oxford University Press, 1932, 1958) and of Rufus M. Jones' work in the study of mysticism: *The Flowering of Mysticism* (New York: Macmillan Company, 1939) and *Spiritual Reformers in the 16th and 17th Centuries* (London: Macmillan & Co., Ltd., 1914). Of course, anyone pursuing an interest in the themes of this series will be familiar with the contemporary literature of spirituality, which probably begins with the writings of Thomas Merton and includes numerous anthologies and the Paulist Press collection, Classics of Western Spirituality. I call special attention to Martin Thornton's *English Spirituality* (London: SPCK, 1963), *The Way of a Pilgrim,* translated by R.M. French (New York: Harper and Brothers, 1952), Louis Bouyer, et al., *A History of Christian Spirituality,* Volumes I, II, III (New York: Seabury Press, 1969, 1982), and *Soul Friend* by Kenneth Leech (New York: Harper and Row, 1977).

# INDEX

## Other Volumes in This Series

Walter Rauschenbusch: Selected Writings
William Ellery Channing: Selected Writings
Devotion to the Holy Spirit in American Catholicism
Horace Bushnell: Sermons
Alaskan Missionary Spirituality
Elizabeth Seton: Selected Writings
Eastern Spirituality in America
Henry Alline: Selected Writings
Charles Hodge: The Way of Life
William Porcher DuBose: Selected Writings
American Jesuit Spirituality:
   The Maryland Tradition 1634–1900
Isaac T. Hecker: The Diary
Josiah Royce: Selected Writings
Phoebe Palmer: Selected Writings
Early New England Meditative Poetry:
   Anne Bradstreet and Edward Taylor
Felix Varela: Letters to Elpidio
Marie of the Incarnation: Selected Writings
Joseph Smith: Selected Sermons and Writings
Orestes A. Brownson: Selected Writings
Bartolomé de las Casas: The Only Way
Sisters of Mercy: Spirituality in America 1843–1900